Ibn al-ʿArabī and the Sufis

Also available from Anqa Publishing

The Seven Days of the Heart: Awrād al-Usbūʿ (Wird)
by Ibn ʿArabī
Translated by Pablo Beneito and Stephen Hirtenstein

Contemplation of the Holy Mysteries: Mashāhid al-Asrār
by Ibn ʿArabī
Translated by Cecilia Twinch and Pablo Beneito

The Universal Tree and the Four Birds: al-Ittiḥād al-Kawnī
by Ibn ʿArabī
Translated by Angela Jaffray

A Prayer for Spiritual Elevation and Protection: al-Dawr al-aʿlā
by Ibn ʿArabī
Study, translation, transliteration and Arabic text
by Suha Taji-Farouki

The Four Pillars of Spiritual Transformation: Ḥilyat al-Abdāl
by Ibn ʿArabī
Translated by Stephen Hirtenstein

The Unlimited Mercifier: The Spiritual Life and Thought of Ibn ʿArabī
Stephen Hirtenstein

Ibn ʿArabi and Modern Thought: The History of Taking Metaphysics Seriously
Peter Coates

The Nightingale in the Garden of Love: the Poems of Üftade
by Paul Ballanfat
Translated from French by Angela Culme-Seymour

Beshara and Ibn ʿArabi: A Movement of Sufi Spirituality in the Modern World
Suha Taji-Farouki

The Lamp of Mysteries: A Commentary on the Light Verse of the Quran
Translated and edited by Bilal Kuşpınar

The Teachings of a Perfect Master: An Islamic Saint for the Third Millennium
Henry Bayman

Ibn al-ʿArabī and the Sufis

Binyamin Abrahamov

ANQA PUBLISHING • OXFORD

Published by Anqa Publishing
PO Box 1178
Oxford OX2 8YS, UK
www.anqa.co.uk

British Library Cataloguing in Publication Data.
A catalogue record for this book is available from the British Library.

ISBN: 978 1 905937 52 3

Cover design: meadencreative.com

Printed and bound in the UK by
4edge Ltd, Hockley, SS5 4AD

Preface

The present work followed two articles I wrote on two important Sufi figures that influenced Ibn al-ʿArabī: 'Ibn al-ʿArabī's Attitude toward al-Ghazālī', and 'Ibn al-ʿArabī and Abū Yazīd al-Bisṭāmī'. I owe thanks to Brepols Publishing for giving me permission to publish the first article in the present volume. My thanks are also extended to the journal *al-Qanṭara* for allowing me to incorporate the second article in my work.

I am extremely grateful to Stephen Hirtenstein of Anqa Publishing, whose comments and suggestions undoubtedly improved the discussions in *Ibn al-ʿArabī and the Sufis*. Thanks also to my students in the course of *Fuṣūṣ al-ḥikam*, at Bar Ilan University. They enriched my insights of the Greatest Master. Michael Tiernan prepared the text for copyediting and Anne Clark successfully performed the copyediting. Both deserve my gratitude for their exact work. Thanks are also extended to Judy Kearns for her meticulous proofreading. I thank David Brauner, who became fascinated by Ibn al-ʿArabī's thought, for skilfully correcting my English.

I hope this modest volume will contribute to our understanding of the thought of one of the greatest thinkers of humanity, who bestowed on us an original and penetrating perception of the cosmos.

Contents

Preface v
Reference abbreviations viii
Introduction 1

THE EARLIER SUFIS

Al-Muḥāsibī 13
Dhū al-Nūn al-Misrī 19
Abū Yazīd al-Bisṭāmī 35
Sahl al-Tustarī 53
Abū Sa'īd al-Kharrāz 63
Al-Junayd 69
Al-Ḥakīm al-Tirmidhī 85
Al-Ḥusayn ibn Manṣūr al-Ḥallāj 91
Ibn Masarra 97
Abū Bakr al-Shiblī 103
Abū Ṭālib al-Makkī 111

THE LATER SUFIS

Al-Ghazālī 117
Ibn Barrajān 135
Ibn al-'Arīf al-Ṣanhājī 139
Ibn Qasī 145
'Abd al-Qādir al-Jīlānī 151
Abū Madyan 157
Abū al-'Abbās al-'Uraybī 165

Conclusion 171
Bibliography 181
Index 189

Reference abbreviations

The following are commonly cited in the notes. Full details are given in the Bibliography.

Bezels	*The Bezels of Wisdom*, trans. R.W.J. Austin
Dimensions	*Mystical Dimensions of Islam*, A. Schimmel
EI	*Encyclopaedia of Islam Online*
FM	*Al-Futūḥāt al-Makkiyya*, Dār Sādir
Fut.	*Al-Futūḥāt al-Makkiyya*, Dār al-Kutub al-Ilmiyya
JMIAS	*Journal of the Muhyiddin Ibn ʿArabi Society*
MP	*The Mystical Philosophy of Muhyid Dīn-Ibnul ʿArabī*, A.E. Affifi
Quest	*Quest for the Red Sulphur*, C. Addas
SDG	*The Self-Disclosure of God*, W.C. Chittick
Seal	*Seal of the Saints*, M. Chodkiewicz
SPK	*The Sufi Path of Knowledge*, W.C. Chittick
Sufis	*Sufis of Andalusia*, trans. R.W.J. Austin

Introduction

Every scholar of Ibn al-ʿArabī's thought has been impressed by the wealth of his mystical and philosophical ideas, parables and poems. From the earliest research on Ibn al-ʿArabī's thought, scholars have tried to trace his sources and to evaluate his originality.[1] This is an extremely difficult task not only due to the huge quantity of his writings,[2] but also with regards to the complexity of his theories. An analysis of the Greatest Master's attitude toward the Sufis, both his predecessors and contemporaries, has not yet been accomplished, except for William Chittick's discussion of three mystics.[3] Such a work is needed to enhance our knowledge of the foundations of his thought and answer, at least as an initial step, the question of the measure of his originality.

The present volume examines Ibn al-ʿArabī's attitude toward the Sufis and assesses the extent of their influence on him. A crucial point is Ibn al-ʿArabī's general acceptance or rejection of the Sufis' views and practices. We do not pretend to be exhaustive, because the basis of our research is mainly *al-Futūḥāt al-Makkiyya*, *Fuṣūṣ al-ḥikam* and some of the author's epistles. We believe that these writings are representative of his thought and hence appropriate to serve as the basis of our investigation.

1. *MP*, pp.174–94.

2. Osman Yahia counts 700 books, treatises and collections of poetry, but only some 95 are extant. For details see J. Clark and S. Hirtenstein, 'Establishing Ibn ʿArabī's Heritage', *JMIAS*, 52 (2012), pp.1–32.

3. *SDG*, pp.371–86. Affifi's treatment of the Sufis in Ibn al-ʿArabī's writings is rather brief and does not teach us much about the latter's attitude toward them. Also his examination of Ibn Masarra's role in the development of the Greatest Master's thought should be revised in the light of Addas' research, which will be referred to in the present work. C.W. Ernst's article, 'The man without attributes: Ibn Arabī's interpretation of Abu Yazid al-Bistami', *JMIAS*, 13 (1993), pp.1–18, examines a number of Ibn al-ʿArabī's interpretations of the sayings of Abu Yazid but lacks an overall view of Abu Yazid's impact on Ibn al-ʿArabī. See the section on Abū Yazīd al-Bisṭāmī below.

We assume that the recurring mention of a name in Ibn al-ʿArabī's texts testifies to the importance the author ascribes to the individual, whether the author learns from this individual or criticizes him.[4] However, the possibility of a Sufi or other thinker influencing Ibn al-ʿArabī without the author explicitly referring to him must not be excluded.[5] A note should be made on Ibn al-ʿArabī's criticism of individuals and groups. On the one hand, he does not hesitate to censure individuals and groups regarding their approaches, while, on the other, we discern a mild attitude toward opposing views. For example, he opposes the Ashʿarite theory according to which the attributes are added to God's essence. However, he says that his way is not to refute this opposing view, but to clarify it and its sources, and to ask whether the view has any effect on the success of the Ashʿarite school of thought. The reason for this approach is the vastness of the Divine (*al-ittisāʿ al-ilāhī*), or God's infinite manifestations, among which the Ashʿarite position concerning the attributes is included.[6]

One should bear in mind that throughout his life Ibn al-ʿArabī met many hundreds of people, both in the West and the East. He learned from many of them, especially from the Sufi way of life.[7] However, he had contacts not only with Sufis, but also with scholars from other fields of thought, such as theologians,[8] philosophers, grammarians and poets.[9] For the present study I concentrate on those Sufis who seem to me to have had the greatest influence on him.

4. Ibn al-ʿArabī's self-confidence was so great that he did not hesitate to criticize even his outstanding teachers. *Sufis*, p.3.

5. See the case of al-Ghazālī.

6. *Fut.*I:309f.; *FM*.I:204, ll.16–27; *SPK*, p.96.

7. Ibn al-ʿArabī held that there is no fault in learning from many teachers. He acknowledged that he had three hundred teachers. *Quest*, p.67.

8. B. Abrahamov, 'Ibn al-ʿArabī on divine love', in S. Klein-Braslavy, B. Abrahamov and J. Sadan (eds.), *Tribute to Michael*, pp.7–36.

9. *Quest*, pp.93–103.

It is impossible to include a detailed discussion of every Sufi who appears in this work. Hence, I confine my examination to the broad lines of their teachings, in order to show how their ideas expressed the principal perceptions of Sufism. In other words, the Sufis of the ninth and tenth centuries, often mentioned in Ibn al-ʿArabī's writings, introduced the foundations of Sufism. We can generally point to each individual's specific contribution to Sufi thought and practice.

Dhū al-Nūn al-Miṣrī (d.860) established the scholarly nature of Sufism. His piety also served as a model of conduct for many Sufis. He was the first to formulate the theory of gnosis (*maʿrifa*), that is, knowledge which comes to the Sufi from the divine source, and differentiated this kind of knowledge from knowledge (*ʿilm*) acquired by the human being through his own efforts. He also taught the Sufis the doctrines of annihilation (*fanāʾ*) and perdurance (*baqāʾ*) in God and the unique attributes of God's beauty (*jamāl*) and God's majesty (*jalāl*), which are among the attributes of God's self-manifestation.[10]

The Sufis used the theme of Muhammad's ascension to heaven (*miʿrāj*) as a motif of the Sufi gradually coming close to God. Thus, **al-Bisṭāmī** (d.874) discusses the *miʿrāj* in mystical terms. He also talks about the destruction of human selfishness with the ultimate aim of becoming united with God. He was so overwhelmed by God's presence that once he fainted after uttering the call for prayer and at other times expressed ecstatic phrases (*shaṭaḥāt*), such as 'Praise be to Me, how great is My Majesty', and paradoxical sayings. No doubt he may be considered a sound representative of intoxicated Sufism.[11]

The Sufi who, to the best of our knowledge, discussed psychological matters as part of spiritual training is **al-Muḥāsibī** (d.857). He was so nicknamed because he analysed the nature of the human

10. *Dimensions*, pp.42–4; A. Knysh, *Islamic Mysticism*, pp.40f.
11. *Dimensions*, pp.47–9.

soul and the ways to achieve one's purity. Opposing extreme asceticism, such as complete reliance on God (*tawakkul*) to the point of refusing to earn a livelihood, he preferred inward piety. In addition, his writings delved into the essence of the intellect and he was acquainted with Muʿtazilite doctrines and terms. His doctrines influenced al-Ghazālī.[12]

It is very interesting that three Sufis – **Abū Saʿīd al-Kharrāz** (d.899), **Sahl al-Tustarī** (d.896), and **al-Ḥakīm al-Tirmidhī** (d. between 905 and 910) – wrote about the phenomenon of the *walāya* (friendship of or proximity to God, or sainthood) during more or less the same period. Annemarie Schimmel explains this as a wish to systematize mystical thought.[13] However, it seems to me that this approach owes its existence to the Sufis' awareness that prophethood should be explained in spiritual terms which are relevant to the Sufi way, and to their growing conviction that they share certain traits with the prophets.

Sahl al-Tustarī wrote a commentary on the Quran which explains each verse according to a fourfold meaning. He is also characterized by his emphasis on the importance of repentance (*tawba*) and the function of letters in the Sufi way, which supposedly influenced **Ibn Masarra** (d.931).[14] Sahl's disciple, Ibn Sālim (d.909), is the eponym of the Sālimiyya school to which **Abū Ṭālib al-Makkī** (d.996), a mystic and theologian who composed a comprehensive manual of Sufism, belonged.[15] Sahl was a faithful representative of the Baṣra school of Sufism. This school was characterized by conservatism and asceticism, while the Baghdad school of Sufism was more speculative. Sahl believed that recollection of God (*dhikr Allāh*) enables the Sufi to relive the experience of the primordial covenant with God mentioned in Quran 7:172. According to his

12. Ibid. pp.54f.; Knysh, *Mysticism*, pp.43–6.
13. *Dimensions*, p.55; Knysh, *Mysticism*, p.58.
14. Michael Ebstein and Sara Sviri question the authenticity of *Risālat al-Ḥurūf* which is attributed to Sahl.
15. *Dimensions*, pp.55f.; Knysh, *Mysticism*, p.84.

belief, God is pure light from which derives the luminous essence of Muhammad, the perfect archetype of the worshipper of God, who existed before creation.[16]

Al-Ḥakīm ('the philosopher') al-Tirmidhī is so called because he introduced Hellenistic philosophical ideas into Islamic mysticism. Like Sahl, he also wrote a commentary on the Quran, in which he tried to find the esoteric meaning of the Sacred Text. But his fame, no doubt, derives from his doctrine of sainthood as is developed in his book *Sīrat al-awliyā'* (*The Way of the Saints*). Also, he described God as the only true entity; however, he believed that the human being can attain God through a gradual mystical process of ascension which corresponds to the Sufi stations.[17]

Schimmel writes the following appraisal of **al-Junayd** (d.910): 'The undisputed master of the Sufis of Baghdad was Abū'l-Qāsim al-Junayd, who is considered the pivot in the history of early Sufism. The representatives of divergent mystical schools and modes of thought could refer to him as their master, so that the initiation chains of later Sufi orders almost invariably go back to him.'[18] Al-Junayd represents sober Sufism, contrary to the intoxicated Sufism of al-Bisṭāmī, **al-Ḥallāj** (d.922) and others.[19] He held al-Muḥāsibī's psychological perceptions in high esteem and regarded Sufism as a way leading to purity and mental struggle. He elaborated on the primordial covenant mentioned by Sahl: according to him, the aim of the Sufi's way is to find the origin of humanity in God, that is, to attain the state of the primordial covenant of human beings with God, as attested in Quran 7:172 in which all human beings witnessed the existence of their God before they were created. This state embodies the highest perception of God's oneness, which means the separation of the eternal from what is created in time.[20]

16. Ibid. p.86.

17. *Dimensions*, pp.56f.; Knysh, *Mysticism*, pp.105–8. B. Radtke, *Drei Schriften des Theosophen von Tirmidh*.

18. *Dimensions*, p.57.

19. Ibid. p.58; Knysh, *Mysticism*, p.53.

20. *Dimensions*, p.58; Knysh, *Mysticism*, p.55.

One of the most debated issues in Sufism was how to express Sufi mysteries and experiences. In al-Junayd's view, the best way was by speaking through allusions (*ishārāt*), so that people who were not qualified to deal with esoteric matters would not discuss them and cause damage to the Sufis by distorting their teachings. This approach coincides with al-Junayd's sober Sufism and contradicts the intoxicated Sufism of figures such as al-Ḥallāj, which sometimes expressed itself by manifest and bold sayings.[21] Had al-Ḥallāj, who was al-Junayd's disciple, not divulged his views and mystical experiences, he very probably would not have been executed. Al-Ḥallāj's central theme in his sermons and prayers was the love for God. He claimed to have reached perfect union with God. Instead of performing the Pilgrimage, he advocated the performance of other commandments, such as feeding orphans and poor people. Such teachings, in addition to his involvement in politics, contributed to his alienation from Islamic orthodox circles.[22]

Another important Sufi of the ninth and tenth centuries is **Abū Bakr al-Shiblī** (d.946), al-Ḥallāj's friend, who was a high-ranking government official before his conversion to Sufism. Al-Junayd admired him, while other Sufis claimed that he did not properly interpret the notion of God's oneness, which was one of his favourite themes along with love for God. His ideas were frequently expressed in paradoxes.[23]

Like al-Sarrāj (d.988), author of *Kitāb al-Lumaʿ fī'l-taṣawwuf* (*The Book of the Essentials of Sufism*) and al-Kalābādhī (d.990), author of *Kitāb al-Taʿarruf li-madhhab ahl al-taṣawwuf* (*The Book of Acquaintance with the Sufis' School*), Abū Ṭālib al-Makkī wrote a manual on Sufism entitled *Qūt al-qulūb* (*The Nourishment of the Hearts*).[24] This book can be characterized as a blend of Islamic

21. *Dimensions*, p.59; Knysh, *Mysticism*, pp.53f.
22. *Dimensions*, pp.62–74; Knysh, *Mysticism*, pp.72–82.
23. *Dimensions*, pp.77–80.
24. Ibid. pp.84f.

law and mysticism. Abū Ṭālib claims that Sufi teachings and ethics represent the ideas and customs of Muhammad and his Companions, which were transmitted by al-Ḥasan al-Baṣrī (d.728) and preserved by the Sufis. In this respect, we can safely say that al-Makkī is the link between the earlier Sufis and **al-Ghazālī** (d.1111), who also contributed much to the synthesis between Islamic law and mysticism.[25] Al-Makkī also influenced **'Abd al-Qādir al-Jīlānī** (d.1166), the author of *Kitāb al-Ghunya li-ṭālibī ṭarīq al-ḥaqq* (*That Which is Sufficient for the Seekers of the True Path*), who became the most popular saint in the Islamic world.[26]

However, the difference between al-Ghazālī and the earlier Sufis, including al-Makkī, is the former's philosophical mysticism, which, for example, discusses love for God in terms of intellectual reasoning[27] and states that syllogism is the basis of all the mystical tenets.[28] Al-Ghazālī exerted some influence on **Ibn Barrajān** (d.1141), who was nicknamed 'the al-Ghazālī of al-Andalus'.

This short survey of the earlier Sufis dealt with in the present work, along with mentions of some later Sufis, introduce the central features of Sufism. These characteristics can be described by sets of opposing approaches: intoxication and sobriety, manifestation and concealment, conservatism and revolutionism, practice (ethics) and thought, extremism (for example in asceticism) and moderation,[29] seclusion and involvement in society.[30] Having been acquainted with all these Sufis, Ibn al-ʿArabī was well aware of these traits, embracing some and rejecting others.

25. Knysh, *Mysticism*, pp.120f.

26. Ibid. pp.180–2.

27. Abrahamov, 'Divine Love', Chap. II.

28. Al-Ghazālī, *Iḥyā' ʿulūm al-dīn*, al-Maktaba al-Tijāriyya al-Kubrā, Vol. IV, *Kitāb al-tafakkur*.

29. The border between moderate and extreme Sufism is not always clear. Knysh, *Mysticism*, p.311, n.156; p.313, n.173.

30. This last set of contraries can also be examples of extreme and moderate asceticism.

The question of Ibn al-ʿArabī's originality seems at first glance very simple and easy to answer. Many scholars who know his writings would immediately state that he was undoubtedly an original thinker whose thought exceeds the boundaries not only of orthodox Islam but also of Sufism.[31] However, my point of departure is different and I do not take his originality for granted. I will examine his approach in each of the essential foundations of his thought in order to evaluate his originality and its extent.

Regarding the question of Ibn al-ʿArabī's originality, Affifi makes the following observation:

> It is practically impossible to say that any particular philosophy or mysticism is the source of Ibnul ʿArabī's whole system. Ibnul ʿArabī had a foot in every camp, so to speak, and derived his material from every conceivable source. His system is eclectic in the highest degree, but we can easily find the germs from which many parts of this system seem to have developed, in the writings of older philosophies, Ṣūfīs, and scholastic theologians. He borrowed ideas from Islamic as well as non-Islamic sources, orthodox as well as heterodox.[32]

The question of originality is not only about whether similar ideas are found in earlier and later sources, but also concerns the structure, arrangement and development of these ideas. M. Chodkiewicz uncovers an instance of pure originality in his proof that there is a connection in terms of content between the waystations (*manāzil*) and the arrangement of the *sūra*s in the Quran; each waystation represents the beginning of a *sūra*, and the Sufi disciple (*murīd*) goes through 114 (the number of the *sūra*s in the Quran) waystations from the last *sūra* to the first.[33] The arrangement of the waystations in such a way is unprecedented in earlier Sufism.

31. T. Izutsu, *Sufism and Taoism*, pp. 2f.
32. *MP*, p. 174.
33. M. Chodkiewicz, 'The *Futūḥāt Makkiyya* and its commentators: some unresolved enigmas', in L. Lewisohn (ed.), *The Heritage of Sufism*, Vol. II, pp. 226–8.

We shall see that Ibn al-ʿArabī has various ways of tackling his predecessors' views. Sometimes he puts forward an earlier notion as corroboration of his own thought; at other times he polemicizes against scholars, before finally accepting their view with some modifications.[34] Also, he does not hesitate to reject ideas introduced by famous Sufis. In my discussion, I show not only the influences exerted on Ibn al-ʿArabī, but also his attitude toward earlier authorities.

The present work is divided into two main parts:

1. Earlier scholars, finishing with al-Ghazālī.
2. Later scholars beginning with al-Ghazālī and ending with Ibn al-ʿArabī's contemporaries, some of whom were his followers and colleagues.

In general his contemporaries are mentioned in his writings mainly in the context of Sufi ethics and practice, whereas the earlier scholars appear as those who express mystical and philosophical ideas.[35] I have focused my attention on Sufis who appear in Ibn al-ʿArabī's writings several times, and those recognized as eminent Sufis. After analysing the material in this order, I conclude with the question of whether Ibn al-ʿArabī was an original thinker. To the extent that the evidence points to an affirmative answer, I shall try to assess the measure of his originality and the issues in which he distinguished himself as an exceptional Sufi figure.

The present work will not enter into the influence of great streams of thought such as Neoplatonism on Ibn al-ʿArabī, or the influence of particular philosophers,[36] for these issues have been

34. See the chapter on Sahl al-Tustarī below.

35. See, for example, Abū al-ʿAbbās al-Sabtī (d.1205) who appears as a preacher of charity, and Rābiʿa al-ʿAdawiyya (d.801) who regards devotion to God as an element which overwhelms any other principle of religion. *SDG*, pp.371–6. M. Takeshita rightly concludes that the Greatest Master owes much to the early Sufis. M. Takeshita, *Ibn ʿArabī's Theory of the Perfect Man and its Place in the History of Islamic Thought*, p.170.

36. Among the philosophers he only admires Ibn Rushd (*SPK*, p.384, n.13) and the divine Plato (*Aflāṭūn al-ilāhī*) who, according to Ibn al-ʿArabī, experienced revelation. Our author says that philosophy (*ḥikma*) is truly the science of prophecy, and the philosophers are really those who know God (*al-ḥukamāʾ hum ʿalā al-ḥaqīqa al-ʿulamāʾ*

discussed by Affifi, who finds that Ibn al-ʿArabī's Neoplatonism goes back to the Epistles of the Brethren of Purity (*Rasāʾil Ikhwān al-Ṣafāʾ*), and by other scholars.[37]

bi-Allāh). However, the philosophers and all the people of speculation erred, because they learned their metaphysics not from God, but from their intellect. *Fut.*IV:227f.

37. Affifi points out some similarities between the Ikhwān and Ibn al-ʿArabī. *MP*, pp. 185–8. For Ibn al-ʿArabī's citation of some phrases in the *Rasāʾil Ikhwān al-Ṣafāʾ* (Vol. III:306), see his *al-Mawʿiza al-ḥasana*, in *Majmūʿat rasāʾil Ibn al-ʿArabī*, Vol. I:87. Possibly, Ibn al-ʿArabī also learns the notion that the philosophical sciences originate in divine inspiration from the *Rasāʾil Ikhwān al-Ṣafāʾ* (Vol. III:291). This notion was prevalent in the Middle Ages. It appears in the writings of the Karaite Yefet ibn Eli (*fl.* second half of the tenth century). H. Ben-Shammai, 'On a polemical element in Saadya's theory of prophecy', (in Hebrew) in *Jerusalem Studies in Jewish Thought*, Vol. VII:142.

There are some points of similarity between Ibn al-ʿArabī and the Brethren of Purity regarding the Perfect Man (*al-insān al-kāmil*). Takeshita, *Perfect Man*, pp. 82f.; *Quest*, pp. 58ff.

Some of our author's philosophical notions show Ibn Sīnā's influence. For example, like Ibn Sīnā, Ibn al-ʿArabī states that God's knowledge of the particulars derives from His knowledge of the universals, whereas the human being's knowledge works from the particulars to the universals. Ibid. pp. 55f. See also S. Bashier, 'An excursion into mysticism: Plato and Ibn al-ʿArabī on the knowledge of the relationship between the sensible forms and the intelligible forms', *American Catholic Philosophical Quarterly*, 77 (2003), pp. 499–533; Bashier, 'The standpoint of Plato and Ibn ʿArabī on skepticism', *JMIAS*, 30 (2001), pp. 19–34. Addas' evaluation that Ibn al-ʿArabī's knowledge of philosophy was 'very superficial' (*Quest*, p. 107) should be carefully examined in the light of all his ideas which derive from philosophy. This is not the place to do this; however, my impression is that he was familiar with a fair number of philosophical tenets and interwove them into his doctrines.

THE EARLIER SUFIS

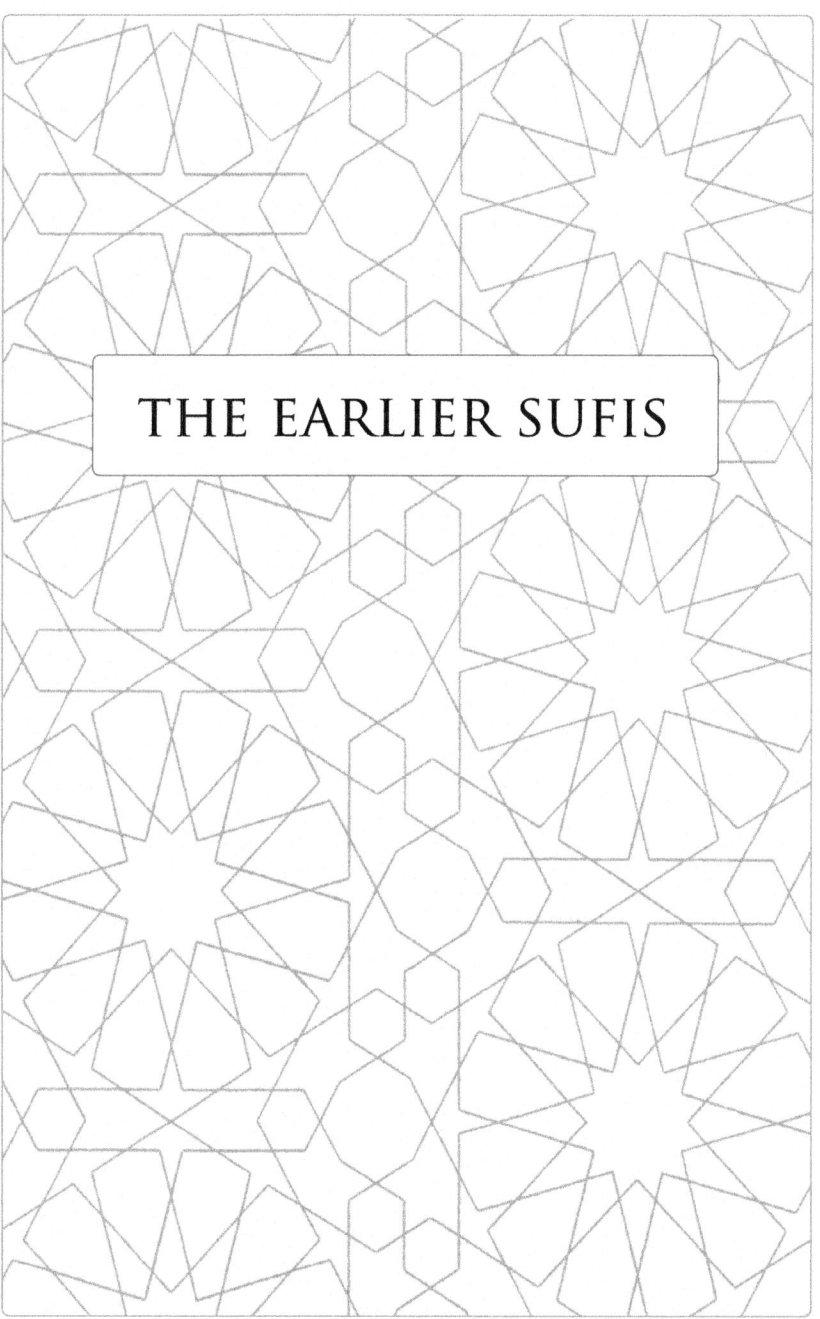

Al-Muḥāsibī

781–857

Al-Ḥārith ibn Asad al-Muḥāsibī's main concern was mystical psychology, as attested by his principal work *Kitāb al-Riʿāya li-ḥuqūq Allāh* (*The Book of Observance of the Rights of God*), which concerns what one is obliged to do for the sake of God. In this book he teaches the mystic how he can gain control over his carnal soul and its traits such as hypocrisy (*riyāʾ*), arrogance (*kibr*), envy (*ḥasad*) and self-conceit (*ʿujb*). A special emphasis is given to piety (*taqwā*) and repentance (*tawba*).[1] He also wrote a treatise on the intellect entitled *Kitāb Māʾiyat al-ʿaql wa-maʿnāhu wa-ikhtilāf al-nās fīhi* (*The Book on the Essence of the Intellect and its Meaning and the Dispute of the People on it*)[2] and other works, such as *Kitāb al-Tawahhum* (*The Book of Vision [of the World to Come]*).[3]

We begin by examining Ibn al-ʿArabī's attitude toward this early mystic of Baghdad; firstly, by seeing how Ibn al-ʿArabī surveys the content of al-Muḥāsibī's teachings. According to Ibn al-ʿArabī, al-Muḥāsibī focuses on four issues which constitute the fundamentals of knowledge:

1. Passion (*al-hawā*).
2. The soul (*al-nafs*).
3. This world (*al-dunyā*).
4. The devil (*al-shayṭān*).[4]

1. Al-Muḥāsibī, *Kitāb al-Riʿāya li-ḥuqūq Allāh*, ed. ʿAbd al-Qādir Aḥmad ʿAṭāʾ. M. Smith, *An Early Mystic of Baghdad*. Smith's edition of *Kitāb al-Riʿāya* was not available to me. J. van Ess, *Die Gedankenwelt des Ḥārith al-Muḥāsibī*.
2. Ed. Ḥusayn al-Quwwatilī.
3. A.J. Arberry (ed.), *Kitāb al-Tawahhum*, trans. A. Roman. R. Arnaldez, in *EI*.
4. *Fut.*III:81; *FM*.II:53, l.11.

Their common denominator is that they are concerned with the improvement of one's morals. Elsewhere,[5] instead of the knowledge of passion (1), al-Muḥāsibī is reported as saying that the first object of knowledge is the knowledge of God. However, Ibn al-ʿArabī is not satisfied with al-Muḥāsibī's enumeration of the objects of knowledge and puts forward his own seven subjects of knowledge:

1. Knowledge of God's names.
2. Knowledge that God manifests Himself in things.
3. Knowledge that God addresses the people through the laws He gives them.
4. Knowledge of perfection and imperfection in existence.
5. Knowledge of one's soul, that is, the essence of the human personality.
6. Knowledge of imagination (*khayāl*), both the knowledge of the world of continuous imagination (*khayāl muttaṣil*) and the knowledge of the world of discontinuous imagination (*khayāl munfaṣil*).[6]
7. Knowledge of diseases and remedies.

The four points mentioned by al-Muḥāsibī and others are included in these seven points, Ibn al-ʿArabī says.[7]

In an article published in the *JMIAS*[8] I summarized Ibn al-ʿArabī's approach to the stations thus:

> in his philosophical mysticism, the Greatest Master puts forward fixed and stable *vis-à-vis* unfixed and unstable values. In the first class we encounter the following items: God is the only real existent and hence the only real agent, God's transcendence and immanence, God's infinity, God's revelation and orders, the multiplicity of God's names, the unity of all the world's

5. *Fut.*III:449; *FM.*II:298, l.29.

6. By the first term Ibn al-ʿArabī means the personal imagination, which is connected to one's soul, and by the second, the world of imagination, which is disconnected from the human view and has independent status. *SPK*, p.117.

7. *Fut.*III:450ff.; *FM.*II:299ff. From this page onward Ibn al-ʿArabī explicates the seven points, but this is not our concern here.

8. B. Abrahamov, 'Abandoning the Station (*tark al-maqām*), as reflecting Ibn al-ʿArabī's principle of relativity', *JMIAS*, 47 (2010), pp.23–46.

phenomena, the human inability to perceive God's essence and the Quran as a criterion of knowledge. All the stations are included in the second class. The relative standing of the stations is established through the impact of the permanent values. There is no absolute station. The greater influence of the stable values over the unstable values is the paradox that the perfect station means abandoning the station (see, for example, the case of *futuwwa*). In addition, the circumstances of the mystic play a role in the fulfillment of the station. Sometimes abandoning indicates the objective state of affairs and not an action or avoidance of action to be taken (see the case of *ṣuḥba*). At other times, abandoning becomes an epistemological principle; the individual knows that from a certain point of view he abandons the station (see, for example, the station of the *mujāhada*).[9]

It seems to me that Ibn al-ʿArabī's attitude toward the stations informs his attitude toward al-Muḥāsibī and other Sufis whose principal aim was the fight against the carnal soul and seeking to create a person devoid of blameworthy traits. The Shaykh does not disregard the stations, but places them on a lower plane.

In this regard, his approach is very similar to al-Tirmidhī's doctrine according to which coming close to God is preferable to the fight against the carnal soul. Al-Tirmidhī believes that when one is absolutely devoted to God, blameworthy behaviour will disappear. The believer should go out from the servitude of the soul to the servitude of God.[10]

A proof of this approach is given in Chapter 309 of the *Futūḥāt* in which our author divides God's people (*rijāl Allāh*) into three categories:

1. People of renunciation and devotion to God (*zuhd*, *tabattul*) who perform only praiseworthy and virtuous acts. However, these people do not know the states and the stations and divine revelations and secrets. They are afraid of self-conceit and hypocrisy. If one of them engages in reading, the books

9. Ibid. p.45.
10. See p.89 (section on al-Tirmidhī), below.

appropriate for him are al-Muḥāsibī's *al-Riʿāya* and its like. They are called *al-ʿubbād* (worshippers).

2. The second kind of people are like the first concerning their personality, but they also regard all acts as deriving from God. They aspire to gain states and stations, divine revelations and secrets and miracles. If they gain some of these things, they show them publicly. They are called Sufis (*al-ṣūfiyya*), and in relation to the third group they are frivolous and possessors of egos. They also manifest leadership over the people of God.
3. The third group are designated the People of Blame (*al-malāmiyya*);[11] they are the most sublime people in their ethics and behaviour. However, contrary to the Sufis they conceal themselves from people, because their master, God, is concealed from people.[12]

Ibn al-ʿArabī regards al-Muḥāsibī as belonging to the first group because of his book *al-Riʿāya*, which serves the people of this group. Besides, he considers the subjugation of the carnal soul the first step in the perfection of human beings, while revelations and divine mysteries are at a higher level. This approach coincides with Ibn al-ʿArabī's idea about abandoning the stations, since proximity to God is a higher level than the fight against one's lusts. Moreover, the Greatest Master makes a distinction between the common people of this path (*ʿāmmat ahl hādha al-ṭarīq*), among whom he counts al-Muḥāsibī and al-Ghazālī, and the elite (*al-khāṣṣa*). Even in the discussion of the station of abstinence (*waraʿ*), al-Muḥāsibī is ranked among the common people, whereas Abū Yazīd al-Bisṭāmī and Ibn al-ʿArabī's master Abū Madyān belong to the elite. Our author characterizes these last two individuals as special because they abstain from applying names designating God or His messenger to others. For example, a ruler is not called a king (*malik*), since *malik* is God's name; instead he is called *sulṭān*.

11. Very probably they are not the historical group named *al-Malāmiyya*.
12. *Fut.*V:50–2; *FM*.II:33f.; *SPK*, pp. 373–5.

This means that their abstinence goes beyond what is usually understood as abstinence: that is, abstaining from what resembles something forbidden, or what is suspected as forbidden.[13]

To sum up, al-Muḥāsibī did not influence Ibn al-ʿArabī, who classifies the former's teachings as being at a lower level. Al-Muḥāsibī is seen as representative of a kind of mystic whose theories help humans lay the foundations for the attainment of higher spiritual levels.

13. *Fut.*I:370–1; *FM.*I:244–5.

Dhū al-Nūn al-Miṣrī

796–859

Abū al-Fayḍ Thawabān ibn Ibrāhīm, nicknamed Dhū al-Nūn al-Miṣrī, was called 'the head of the Sufis'. His mystical ideas are known only through the writings of later Sufis,[1] and he was the first Sufi to introduce the Sufi doctrines of states (*aḥwāl*) and stations (*maqāmāt*) in a systematic way. He also proposed the true nature of gnosis (*ma'rifa*).

Ibn al-'Arabī, however, does not mention him in this context: the term gnosis is absent from the passages in *al-Futūḥāt al-Makkiyya* in which Dhū al-Nūn appears. Ibn al-'Arabī speaks about two major issues with regards to Dhū al-Nūn: firstly, his power, piety, miracles and moral behaviour; and, secondly, his philosophical ideas.

Ibn al-'Arabī devotes an entire book to Dhū al-Nūn al-Miṣrī entitled *Al-Kawkab al-durrī fī manāqib Dhī al-Nūn al-Miṣrī* (*The Illuminating Star Regarding the Virtues of Dhū al-Nūn al-Miṣrī*), composed because Dhū al-Nūn travelled so widely and met so many saints and pious people: in writing about him, says Ibn al-'Arabī, we mention many Sufis, who, we hope, may bless us.[2] Ibn al-'Arabī also apparently appreciated the fact that Dhū al-Nūn learned lessons from the people he met,[3] lessons that might benefit all Sufis.

1. *EI*; *Dimensions*, pp.42–7.
2. Ibn al-'Arabī, *Al-Kawkab al-durrī fī manāqib Dhī al-Nūn al-Miṣrī*, in *Rasā'il Ibn 'Arabī*, Vol. III, ed. S. 'Abd al-Fattāḥ, pp.56, 61. In the book's introduction Ibn al-'Arabī quotes a tradition that justifies mentioning pious people: 'When God's righteous servants (*al-ṣāliḥūn*) are mentioned, compassion descends.' Ibid. p.53. C. Twinch, 'Created for compassion: Ibn 'Arabī's work on Dhū-l-Nūn the Egyptian', *JMIAS*, 47 (2010), p.110.
3. *Al-Kawkab al-durrī*, pp.238, 249.

This is not the place to survey all the information Ibn al-ʿArabī introduced about Dhū al-Nūn, a project worthy of exhaustive treatment, but rather to point out the principal views of this earlier and important Sufi.

Apart from seeking knowledge and moral traits in saints and pious people, Ibn al-ʿArabī points out, Dhū al-Nūn was gifted with an extraordinary personality, which combined scrupulousness (*waraʿ*) with loyalty, gentleness and exaltation toward the people of knowledge; he also paid homage to God, and possessed integrity, purity, the ability to enter states of ecstasy (*wajd*) and gnosis, and to perform miracles (*karāmāt*).[4]

One of the constant themes of Dhū al-Nūn's life was his devotion to God, which derived from his conviction that all things are dominated by God. His way to God stems from God's favours towards him, and all the stations and states are explained in terms of relying on God, knowing God's Providence and being attached to Him.[5] Even God's unity is defined as the knowledge that His power permeates everything and that He is the cause of everything. Similarly, the perfect gnostic is he who is exclusively connected to God in all his states without ever paying attention to things other than God.[6] Since God dominates everything, the Sufi should turn to Him in everything, for the Sufi should not adhere to the means, but adhere to God who gives all means.[7] An exception is the intellect, the device characterized as the best adornment God bestows on humankind, which helps people to perceive God, because through the intellect one can perceive everything.[8]

One characteristic of Dhū al-Nūn's teachings is the delineation of signs (*ʿalāmāt*) referring to persons, stations and states. For example, asked what is the sign of the one to whom God comes

4. Ibid. pp.61–84.
5. Ibid. pp.89–92, 108, 112, 123, 148.
6. Ibid. p.151.
7. Ibid. p.162.
8. Ibid. pp.113, 165.

close, he says that being patient (*ṣābir*), thankful (*shākir*) and recollecting God's name (*dhākir*) are the signs of this in a person.[9] In like manner, all stations and states are treated.[10]

Dhū al-Nūn's notion that whoever knows God best is the most perplexed about God was developed by Ibn al-ʿArabī and did not remain a mere statement. The knower's perplexity derives from the impossibility of attaining an absolute knowledge of God and from the idea that the human being, like God, encompasses within himself contradictory attributes.[11]

Ibn al-ʿArabī's aim in *Al-Kawkab al-durrī* is to introduce Dhū al-Nūn's mystical personality and teachings. Thus, he hardly makes any comments on Dhū al-Nūn's text, although two exceptions to this behaviour are given below. Asked when it is correct to go into seclusion from people, Dhū al-Nūn answered: 'When you are capable of isolating yourself from the lower soul.' Ibn al-ʿArabī comments on this recommendation, saying: 'If he had isolated himself from his lower soul, he would have attained that which he sought without being in want of seclusion from people.' For corroboration he cites al-Bisṭāmī, who asked God how one should reach Him and heard the following reply: 'Leave your lower soul and come.' The Shaykh responds to the effect that whoever isolates himself from his lower soul isolates himself from everything except God.[12]

As we shall see, Dhū al-Nūn was distinguished as a saint who performed miracles, including revivification of the dead. Ibn al-ʿArabī states that his prowess here was the inheritance of ʿĪsā (Jesus), because the latter also conducted such miracles. To prove his statement Ibn al-ʿArabī relates that bats resided in his bier, because they were the animals that ʿĪsā created and resuscitated.[13]

9. Ibid. p.121.
10. Ibid. pp.122–4, 134 and passim.
11. Ibid. p.149; *SPK*, pp.114, 211, 380.
12. *Al-Kawkab al-durrī*, p.127.
13. Twinch, 'Dhū al-Nūn', pp.118–20.

Chapter 8 of the *Futūḥāt* is entitled 'On the true knowledge of the earth that was created from the leftover ferment of Adam's clay, which is named the earth of the reality, and on the mention of some of the marvels and wonders within it.' Ibn al-ʿArabī refers to this earth as a place of wonders that contradicts the perception of the rational mind.[14] One of the gnostics who visited this earth told Ibn al-ʿArabī about its wonders and referred to Dhū al-Nūn as a witness of it. According to this gnostic, Dhū al-Nūn himself related that in this earth one can turn a big thing into a small thing without the former becoming small or the latter big.

This world in which rules of logic do not work is the world to come (*al-dār al-ākhira*). In it one can be in different places at the same time, contrary to reason. Likewise, every person will be revealed to another in the form loved by the former, and each individual can appear in different places in different forms at the same time. Ibn al-ʿArabī points out that he was not aware of anyone referring to this station except in the reported instance of Abū Bakr al-Ṣiddīq who entered Paradise through its eight gates at the same time.[15] Relevant to our discussion is the second and last example of this phenomenon that Ibn al-ʿArabī mentions, recalling Dhū al-Nūn al-Miṣrī's *Famous Issues* (*Masāʾil mashhūra*). Here, Dhū al-Nūn says that a man sees before him a dead person in a motionless state, while another man sees him alive at the same time. In this example there is no mention of the next world.[16]

Elsewhere, the notion of illogical phenomena that take place in the higher world is repeated. Ibn al-ʿArabī speaks of a vision he experienced in which he saw the Throne (*al-ʿarsh*).[17] Asked how it can be that the angels encircle the Throne while there is

14. *SDG*, pp.357f.

15. This account takes for granted the pre-existence of Paradise, an issue much debated in Islamic theology. B. Abrahamov, 'The creation and duration of Paradise and Hell in Islamic theology', *Der Islam*, 79 (2002), pp.87–102.

16. *Fut.*II:294; *FM.*I:578, ll.2–3.

17. Quran 39:75: 'And you see the angels encircling about the Throne expressing the praise of your Lord, and they (the people) are judged justly.'

no space for them, because the Throne occupies the whole space (*wa'l-'arsh qad 'amara al-khalā'*), our author rejoins by adducing several principles. First, he states that that which does not occupy a place (*taḥayyaza*) neither has contact with another nor is separate from another. In other words, one cannot judge this issue from the point of view of a physical relationship. Secondly, the Throne of which we are speaking, Ibn al-'Arabī says, is not the Throne which occupies space, but rather the Throne which God will bring at the Resurrection to judge people. This is proven by the verse quoted in n.17, in which it is said: 'they (the people) are judged justly'. Besides, says Ibn al-'Arabī, pointing to an important principle, on the day of the Resurrection and in the place of the congregation (*al-ḥashr*) of the people for the judgement, the relation of the Throne to this place is like the relation of Paradise to the wideness of Muhammad's wall which shows the direction of Mecca (*qibla*).[18] By this statement he means that a large entity enters a small entity, an illogical statement in ordinary time, but acceptable in the time of the Resurrection. Here again, one of the issues dealt with in Dhū al-Nūn al-Miṣrī's *Famous Issues* comes up, concerning the bringing of the wide entity into the narrow one, without the wide entity becoming narrow or the narrow entity becoming wide. Ibn al-'Arabī adds that for whoever knows that there are different spheres (*mawāṭin*) in existence, it is easy to hear such notions.[19] By a sphere our author means both places, such as this world and the world to come, and devices of perception such as reason and imagination.[20]

It is worth noting that, just as God conjoins contraries – that is, 'He is the First and the Last, the Manifest and the Hidden' (Quran

18. I have not found any explanation of why Ibn al-'Arabī mentions the prayer of eclipse (*ṣalāt al-kusūf*) in this context.

19. *Fut.*IV:98f., 211; *FM.*II:436, ll.18–35, 512, ll.16–21.

20. *SDG*, p.46. Chittick renders *mawṭin* as 'homestead' which, in my view, does not include perception; therefore I prefer the word 'sphere' which covers both place and action. *Mawṭin* also means 'abode', namely, a waystation (*manzil*) in which one dwells without passing to another waystation. *SPK*, p.281.

57:3) – the world also combines motion and rest (*ḥaraka wa-sukūn*) and combination and separation (*ijtimāʿ wa-iftirāq*). Thus, things do not only act in an illogical way in the world to come, but also in this world.[21] Dhū al-Nūn's notion corroborates Ibn al-ʿArabī's idea in all spheres.

Another theological issue raised by Ibn al-ʿArabī is human knowledge and its relationship to God's knowledge. He expresses a revolutionary idea in this context, according to which human knowledge and God's knowledge of all things are infinite, thus drawing an equivalence between human and divine knowledge: 'The fact that what does not end, meaning the objects of knowledge (*mā lā yatanāhā min al-maʿlūmāt*), enters human existence, just as it enters divine knowledge, is the most wonderful of God's secrets.'[22] However, the difference between human knowledge and God's is that God knows the objects of knowledge in a particular and detailed manner (*taʿyīnan wa-tafṣīlan*), whereas the human being knows them only in a general way (*mujmalan*). This notion of the likeness between God's knowledge and human knowledge on the one hand, and the difference between the two on the other, is reminiscent of the Muʿtazilite idea of human knowledge of the moral values. According to the Muʿtazilites, man knows moral values in a general way, while the Revelation supplies him with the details of these values and how to behave in accordance with them.[23] It might be that Ibn al-ʿArabī, who knew Muʿtazilite theology well, adopted the idea of the two ways of knowledge, general and detailed, and incorporated this idea in the context of God's and human knowledge. We shall see that taking an existing idea and interweaving it into another context is a characteristic of the Shaykh's thought.

21. *Fut.*IV:211; *FM.*I:512.

22. *Fut.*IV:470; *FM.*II:686, l.11.

23. R.M. Frank, 'Several fundamental assumptions of the Baṣra school of the Muʿtazila', *Studia Islamica*, 33 (1971), pp. 5–18.

After elucidating the difference between God's knowledge and human knowledge, Ibn al-ʿArabī next explains how one knows. Possibly influenced by the Platonic idea of recollection, he states that just as God made people forget their testimony of His Godship (Quran 7:172), so He made them forget all that they had known. There are some people among us such as Dhū al-Nūn al-Miṣrī, says Ibn al-ʿArabī, who, when being made to remember, know that they had known a certain object of knowledge before and forgot it (*fa-minna man idhā dhukira tadhakkara annahu qad kāna ʿalima dhālika al-maʿlūm wa-nasiyahu*).[24] Thus, these people are aware of the whole process of knowing. Other human beings, notwithstanding their inability to remember this process, believe that this process really takes place, and for them knowledge is a beginning and not a continuance of a process. The first kind of people gain this awareness because of the light God casts on their intellect.

Ibn al-ʿArabī states that this waystation is included in Dhū al-Nūn's *Famous Issues*: the issues include letting one find rational absurdity (*al-muḥāl al-ʿaqlī*) through the divine relationships; knowing the precedence among contrary things from every aspect; and the knowledge that just as each name of God designates all God's names (Quran 17:110), each particle (*jawhar*[25]) in the world contains every reality of the world. Here Ibn al-ʿArabī adds a personal note to the effect that the last knowledge of the particle belongs to him alone, and he does not know whether someone

24. Elsewhere (*Fut.*II:426; *FM.*I:670, l.16), Dhū al-Nūn said that it is as if he is hearing Quran 7:172 (*ka-annahu al-ān fī udhnī*). Ibn al-ʿArabī interprets this statement as meaning Dhū al-Nūn's knowledge of the state of one's acknowledgment of God's existence and unity. The Shaykh al-Akbar cannot decide whether Dhū al-Nūn's state means recollection (*tadhakkur*) or a continuous state of awareness of the covenant between God and humanity mentioned in this verse. *Fut.*III:162; *FM.*I:108, l.30.

25. This word also designates the atom (*al-juzʾ alladhī lā yatajazzʾu*). I do not know whether the author uses it here in its technical meaning. For the Islamic theory of atomism see S. Pines, *Studies in Islamic Atomism*, trans. M. Schwarz and ed. T. Langermann, pp. 4f.

else, among the saints but not among the prophets, found it or if it was revealed to another.[26]

Sometimes the experience of a Sufi reminds Ibn al-ʿArabī of his own. Such is the story of a young man who used to attend Dhū al-Nūn's sessions. Then, after an absence of some time, this young man returned to Dhū al-Nūn with a yellow face, thin body and signs of worship and effort. Asked what he had received from his Lord to cause him to serve Him, he answered that it was not appropriate for a slave, whose Lord had chosen him, given him the keys to His treasures and then revealed to him a mystery (*sirr*[27]), to reveal this mystery. A poem cited by the young man states that one cannot trust a person who reveals mysteries transmitted to him. The young man adds that if one wants to reveal a divine mystery, one should wait for God's order; if God orders him to make the mystery known, he must reveal it. But basically mysteries should remain concealed.

Exploiting this story, Ibn al-ʿArabī relates that God conferred a mystery on him. It was in the city of Fas (Fez) in AH 594. I divulged this mystery, says the Shaykh, without knowing that this mystery is among the mysteries that should not be spread. The Beloved (God) reproved Ibn al-ʿArabī for making this mystery known; so Ibn al-ʿArabī asked Him to remove this mystery from the hearts of the people who heard it, and God did so. Consequently, our author praises God, who did not punish him with alienation as he punished the young man.[28]

In the context of mysteries, another story is put forward about a conversation Dhū al-Nūn had with a slave girl. Circumambulating the Kaʿba, he met this slave girl who was reciting a poem that expressed her hidden love for God, saying that her thin body and low spirit revealed this love. Her words stirred Dhū al-Nūn's

26. *Fut.*IV:471; *FM.*II:686, ll.24–5.

27. This word can be rendered mystery (*SPK*, pp.100, 169, 201, 340, 353) or innermost consciousness (ibid. pp.152, 257).

28. *Fut.*III:522; *FM.*II:349, ll.2–3.

feelings and he cried. The girl continued to speak, now asking God's mercy because of His love for her. However, Dhū al-Nūn, who was impressed by her words, told her that it is sufficient to say 'because of my love for You (*bi-ḥubbī laka*), forgive me', and not 'because of Your love for me (*bi-ḥubbika lī*)'. The slave girl replied: 'Have you not known, Dhū al-Nūn, that there are people whom God loves before they love Him' (Quran 5:54)? To Dhū al-Nūn's question, 'How did you know that I am Dhū al-Nūn?' she replied: 'The hearts wander about the field of mysteries, therefore I knew you.' Then she disappeared without Dhū al-Nūn knowing how.[29]

Apart from the motif of the seemingly simple person who turns out to be mysterious and who teaches a truth to a great Sufi,[30] what is interesting here is the lesson Ibn al-ʿArabī learns from the episode. The Shaykh says that this story resembles the state of Mūsā (Moses) when he saw the mountain disappearing after God was revealed to it (Quran 7:143). He seems to compare the disappearance of this girl to the disappearance of the mountain. However, the slave girl story serves as a point of departure for the notion that God has fields or theatres (*maydān*, pl. *mayādīn*) of love, and each field is named with a description of love, for example, the field of longing (*maydān al-shawq*). Each state in which there is wandering and motion (*jawalān* and *ḥaraka*) has a field.[31] Ibn al-ʿArabī connects the notion of fields with the state of the slave girl in a way that I do not understand.

Ibn al-ʿArabī tells us another story about Dhū al-Nūn, who, again while circumambulating the Kaʿba, saw a person clinging to the Kaʿba curtains, crying and saying that he revealed his secret

29. *Fut.*III:523; *FM.*II:349, ll.11–21. The motif of pious people or slave girls knowing Dhū al-Nūn though they had never met him before recurs several times in *al-Kawkab al-durrī* (pp.235, 238, 258, 270). Each time, Dhū al-Nūn is astonished and asks how they know him. They answer that God bestowed knowledge on them for the purpose of knowing him or by identifying him through his smell.

30. If we accept the meaning of *ummī* as an illiterate person, Muhammad is the first person to experience this phenomenon.

31. *Fut.*III:523; *FM.*II:349, ll.22–8.

only to God and devoted himself only to God, but now was afraid of separation from God. When Dhū al-Nūn came close he saw that this person was a woman.[32]

Dhū al-Nūn reportedly met an anonymous person from Yemen. He asked this person: 'What is the sign of the lover of God?' This person, whom Ibn al-ʿArabī calls a gnostic (*ʿārif*), answers that the rank of love is high, because God splits the lovers' hearts and they see through the light of their hearts God's exaltedness. Their bodies are mundane (*abdānuhum dunyāwiyya*), their spirits are curtains (*arwāḥuhum ḥujubiyya*) and their intellects are divine (*ʿuqūluhum samāwiyya*). Ibn al-ʿArabī immediately notes that these are the only three epithets that exist in Being. An explanation of each epithet follows.

Initially we would think the first epithet refers to the material dimension of the human being; however, for Ibn al-ʿArabī *abdān dunyāwiyya* means God's proximity to humanity, as God is nearer to man than his jugular vein (Quran 50:16), which is a part of one's body. The second epithet, which in the explanation appears as the third, points to the fact that one's essence is a curtain between the human being and God. And, according to our author, *ʿuqūl samāwiyya* means the limitation of humans to a certain place, like the limitation of the angels to a certain place (Quran 37:164).[33]

Here the words of an anonymous person who talked with Dhū al-Nūn serve as a point of departure for Ibn al-ʿArabī to explain his idea of the structure of the world.

Apart from theological, philosophical and mystical notions that his sayings or experiences inspire, Dhū al-Nūn appears as a mystic who has the power to perform miracles. A principle mentioned in Dhū al-Nūn's six 'illogical' issues serves as the basis for performing miracles: whatever imagination (*khayāl*) can conceive may take place in reality. Thus, a certain al-Jawharī saw in his imagination in

32. *Fut.*III:521; *FM.*II:348, ll.12–25.
33. *Fut.*III:523f.; *FM.*II:349, l.30 – 350, l.6.

wakefulness that he was married in Baghdad and had six children, a daydream which came true when this woman and six children came to visit him. God, says Ibn al-ʿArabī, has many powers, which are as different from each other as the difference between the faculties of seeing, hearing, etc. Ibn al-ʿArabī particularizes the saints by the special powers they have to perform extraordinary acts, such as Muhammad's nocturnal journey to Jerusalem from Mecca in a short time.[34] In this case, a principle expressed by Dhū al-Nūn helps Ibn al-ʿArabī to explain the miracles of the saints and the prophets.

Ibn al-ʿArabī mentions Dhū al-Nūn and Abū Yazīd al-Bisṭāmī[35] as two mystics who knew how to perform miracles and did actually perform them. For example, Dhū al-Nūn rescued a child who was swallowed by a crocodile in the Nile and brought him to his mother alive.[36] In this context, Ibn al-ʿArabī ascribes prophets' and saints' abilities to perform miracles to their firm belief, and, in their state of pure and firm belief, their use of God's names for this purpose.[37] Elsewhere[38] he speaks again of the miracles of al-Bisṭāmī, who revived an ant after he had killed it, and of Dhū al-Nūn rescuing the boy from the crocodile, stating two important conditions for performing miracles:

1. Miracles[39] can only be performed when God permits them (*bi-idhni Allāh*).
2. Miracles appear in the domain of the imagination, which gives the seer the impression that something is animate, while in actuality it is inanimate. Ibn al-ʿArabī brings as an example the Egyptian sorcerers who made Moses believe that he saw their ropes running, when in reality they did not run.

34. *Fut.*III:124; *FM.*II:82, ll.24–32.
35. See section on al-Bisṭāmī, below.
36. *Fut.*V:136; *FM.*III:93, ll.5–6. Cf. Ibn al-ʿArabī, *Al-Kawkab al-durrī*, pp. 100f.
37. *Fut.*VI:53; *FM.*III:328, ll.15–18.
38. *Fut.*VII:160; *FM.*IV:108, l.33 – 109, l.8.
39. Here a miracle is called 'the breaking of habit' (*kharq al-ʿāda*).

It is interesting that Ibn al-ʿArabī regards the saints' miracles (*karāmāt*) as the outcome of an act of the imagination.

Dhū al-Nūn is reckoned a model of moral behaviour in the context of the moral teachings which Ibn al-ʿArabī delivered to novices. According to these, when one is reproached for doing something blameworthy, one should not rejoin by blaming another for being a liar, nor acknowledge what was ascribed to one, but adhere to silence. Dhū al-Nūn behaved in this way: when the Caliph al-Mutawakkil (d.861) asked Dhū al-Nūn what he had to say to the accusation of heresy (*zandaqa*) levelled against him, he said, 'If I deny, I shall make the people liars, and if I agree with what they said, I shall make myself a liar.'[40] Here the story of Dhū al-Nūn serves to corroborate Ibn al-ʿArabī's moral guidance. He begins with the piece of advice and then tells the story.

Another literary device is to begin with the story, and then to learn the lesson from it. This happens with the following story about Dhū al-Nūn. A person said to Dhū al-Nūn: 'By God! I do not love you.' Dhū al-Nūn responded: 'It is sufficient for you if you know God, and if you do not know Him, seek out one who does know Him in order that he will guide you to God.' A similar event, says Ibn al-ʿArabī, happened to our follower, one of the great pious people, ʿAbdallāh ibn al-Ustādh al-Mawrūrī,[41] who saw his dead brother in a dream. He said to his brother: 'What has God done to you?' He said: 'God made me enter Paradise to eat, drink and to have sexual relations.' Then Mawrūrī said: 'I am not asking you about these acts, but did you see your Lord?' He said: 'Only whoever knows Him, sees Him.' As a result of this dream, Ibn al-ʿArabī relates, Al-Mawrūrī came to me, told me about his dream, and asked me to make him know God. He accompanied Ibn al-ʿArabī until he knew God to the degree that an interlocutor

40. *Fut.*VIII:296; *FM.*IV:488, ll.29–32.
41. He was one of Ibn al-ʿArabī's close friends and followers. *Sufis*, pp.101–8.

(*muḥaddith*) is able to make one know God through revelation, not through rational arguments.[42]

Another counsel, also linked to Dhū al-Nūn, immediately follows. When leaving Dhū al-Nūn, a certain Yūsuf ibn al-Ḥusayn asked him whom he should accompany. Dhū al-Nūn answered that he should accompany one who will remind him of God and who has moral traits. Such a person preaches to others through his acts and not through his sayings.[43]

It seems that Ibn al-ʿArabī was influenced by Dhū al-Nūn's moral counsels. According to Dhū al-Nūn, three signs of belief reflect how a Muslim should feel and behave toward his coreligionists:

1. One should grieve when disasters befall Muslims.
2. One should counsel them, even if they distrust him.
3. One should guide them to their interests, even if they hate him.

This relationship is strongly connected with the counsel according to which the defects of the people should not distract one from one's own defects, because one is not the people's supervisor.[44] Very probably Ibn al-ʿArabī links these two counsels, for one should help one's coreligionists even if they are not perfect people. Also, the notion, with which Ibn al-ʿArabī agrees, that there is a connection between belief and moral behaviour is very interesting.

A series of counsels dealing with different moral virtues follow. These concern rationally taking heed of the world to come, humbleness, abstaining from anger, abstinence in the right place, being just, thanking God, etc.[45] Ibn al-ʿArabī writes in the

42. *Fut.*VIII:326; *FM.*IV:510, ll.11–17.

43. *Fut.*VIII:327; *FM.*IV:510, ll.25–31.

44. *Fut.*VIII:328, 331; *FM.*IV:511, l.14, 513, ll.11–12. 'Whoever looks at the defects of people, is blind to his own defects.' Cf. Babylonian Talmud, Tractate Qiddushin 70b: 'Whoever disqualifies the defects of people, disqualifies his own defects.' Notwithstanding, one should be careful of some kinds of people such as manumitted slaves. *Fut.*VIII:345; *FM.*IV:524, l.4.

45. *Fut.*VIII:330; *FM.*IV:512, l.35 – 513, l.8.

Futūḥāt[46] that Dhū al-Nūn reportedly gave Ibrāhīm al-Akhmīmī five pieces of good advice and promised him that if he followed them he would be given another five good traits. The first five are to adhere to poverty (*faqr*), to act in patience (*ṣabr*), to hate lusts, to oppose passion (*hawan*)[47] and to take refuge in God in all one's affairs. Consequently, God gives one who keeps these five counsels five stations: thankfulness (*shukr*), contentment (*riḍā*), fear (*khawf*), hope (*rajā'*) and patience,[48] which in turn give rise to five other traits, and so on. Worth mentioning is the series of five things needed in the world, without which all other things are superfluous. These are food, water, clothes, home and knowledge of practical things.[49]

Paragraph 59 in Ibn al-ʿArabī's *Kitāb al-Tajalliyāt*, entitled the Vision of the Permeation of God's Unity, deals with the question of God's transcendence *vis-à-vis* His immanence. Ibn al-ʿArabī saw Dhū al-Nūn in this vision and expressed his astonishment at Dhū al-Nūn's view that the Real is a totally transcendent Being. How can Being, asks the Shaykh, be emptied of God, while God made it exist and while God is the essence of Being? Ibn al-ʿArabī urges Dhū al-Nūn not to make the object of his worship an entity perceived by his speculation, but to adhere to what God said in Quran 42:11: 'There is none like Him, and He is the All-Hearing, the All-Seeing.' The first part of the verse conveys negation of any likeness to Him, that is, transcendence, and the second part affirmation of His immanence expressed in traits He shares with humans (hearing and seeing). Thereupon, Dhū al-Nūn admits that he has not acquired this knowledge, and hears Ibn al-ʿArabī's response that knowledge is not restricted to time, place, realm and state. In other words, one can perceive even after one's death what one has not acquired before, as is the case of Dhū al-Nūn who

46. *Fut.*VIII:338; *FM.*IV:518, l.25 – 519, l.5.
47. I do not understand the difference between the third and the fourth trait.
48. Here he is given that which he has already done.
49. *Fut.*VIII:338; *FM.*IV:518, l.35.

learned from Ibn al-ʿArabī the double perception of God after his death.

Once again we see that Ibn al-ʿArabī, being fully convinced of his teachings, does not hesitate to instruct great Sufis like Dhū al-Nūn in the principles of his thought. He emphasizes that knowledge has no limit and can be taught even in the next world. This is reminiscent of al-Ghazālī's idea that humans do not cease to acquire knowledge even in the world to come. However, according to al-Ghazālī it is one's efforts, and not engaging in conversations with other people, that lead one to gain more knowledge.[50]

This story, which ends with Ibn al-ʿArabī's view that knowledge is not restricted by time and place and that even after death one continues to learn, does not seem to diminish our author's high appreciation of Dhū al-Nūn. He is impressed by Dhū al-Nūn's personality, his righteousness, abstinence and his power to perform miracles, and gives his approval to some of Dhū al-Nūn's ideas: the existence of a domain in which the rules of logic do not work, the consideration of a subject from different angles,[51] and the joining of contraries and the differences in the nature of God's knowledge and human knowledge.

50. B. Abrahamov, *Divine Love in Islamic Mysticism*, pp. 76–8.

51. An example of this is Dhū al-Nūn's consideration of *samāʿ* (literally: listening, i.e. listening to music or dancing that causes ecstasy; *Dimensions*, pp. 178–86). Whether this is permissible or prohibited is much debated in Sufism. Dhū al-Nūn solves the problem by examining the aspects or the causes leading the Sufi to *samāʿ*: if he practises it with the true aim of reaching God, it is permissible, however, if he turns to it to satisfy his lower soul, he becomes an unbeliever (*tazandaqa*). Ibn al-ʿArabī, *Al-Kawkab al-durrī*, p. 135.

Abū Yazīd al-Bisṭāmī[1]

804–?874

A.E. Affifi notes the appearance of Abū Yazīd in Ibn al-ʿArabī's writings, principally in his capacity as an adherent to pantheism.[2] References to Abū Yazīd have also appeared in other studies published in recent decades, such as the detailed analyses carried out by W.C. Chittick.[3] However, the only work which deals exclusively with the subject of Abū Yazīd's contribution to Ibn al-ʿArabī's thought is C.W. Ernst's article,'The man without attributes: Ibn ʿArabī's interpretation of Abū Yazīd al-Bisṭāmī',[4] which examines a number of the Shaykh's interpretations of the sayings of Abū Yazīd in the light of the latter's legacy as it was understood by other Sufis. Although Ernst's article is of great importance to the study of the sources of Ibn al-ʿArabī in general and to the influence of Abū Yazīd on the Shaykh in particular, it lacks an overall vision of Abū Yazīd's impact on Ibn al-ʿArabī. A comprehensive assessment of his contribution to Ibn al-ʿArabī's thought will perhaps only be achieved by examining all references to the former in our author's writings, but my discussion here will be limited to the *Futūḥāt al-Makkiyya*, the *Fuṣūṣ al-ḥikam* and two collections of epistles.[5]

My aim is to introduce Abū Yazīd, his personality and his mystical notions as they appear in Ibn al-ʿArabī's work. It is not my objective to make comparisons between the versions of Abū Yazīd's

1. An earlier version of this section was first published in *al-Qanṭara*, 32 (2011).
2. *MP*, pp.138, 190.
3. *SPK*; *SDG*.
4. *JMIAS*, 13 (1993), pp.1–18.
5. *Rasāʾil Ibn al-ʿArabī*; *Majmūʿat rasāʾil Ibn al-ʿArabī*. Ibn al-ʿArabī wrote a book (not extant) on Abū Yazīd entitled *Miftāḥ aqfāl ilhām al-waḥīd wa-iḍāḥ ashkāl aʿlām al-murīd fī sharḥ aḥwāl Abī Yazīd*. O. Yahia, *Muʾallafāt Ibn ʿArabī taʾrīkhuhā wa-taṣnīfuhā*, p.573, n.851.

sayings in other sources, such as Abu Nasr al-Sarraj's *Kitāb al-Luma' fi'l-taṣawwuf*,[6] and those contained in Ibn al-'Arabī's text. Rather, I will assess these sayings in terms of the place that Ibn al-'Arabī assigns to them and how they might have influenced his thoughts.[7]

It is worth noting again that the study of Ibn al-'Arabī's sources and the very likely possibility that he was influenced by a number of Sufis does not detract from his originality, as expressed both in his major ideas and his minor remarks on the Sufi way.[8] A great deal of work remains to be done in the study of Ibn al-'Arabī's sources, and I would go so far as to say that as long as such research continues our admiration for the achievements of al-Shaykh al-Akbar will not diminish.

The 1999 Beirut edition of the *Futūḥāt* includes a reliable index which demonstrates that Ibn al-'Arabī mentions Abū Yazīd 143 times in the text, more than any other Sufi (al-Ḥallāj appears only 15 times and al-Junayd 34). This suggests that Ibn al-'Arabī ascribes significant importance to his predecessor.

Ibn al-'Arabī refers to Abū Yazīd in relation to several important issues. Of these, I will first address the question of Abū Yazīd's personality as presented in the *Futūḥāt*. There is a clear difference, the Shaykh writes at one point in the text, between physical entities: just as spiritual waystations (*manāzil ruḥaniyya*)[9] transcend one another, so do corporeal waystations (*manāzil jismāniyya*). A pearl is different from a simple stone, and a house built of mud bricks differs from a house built of gold or silver bricks. Subtle hearts are impressed by places, such as mosques, in which pious people once lived and worked. One such place, Ibn al-'Arabī writes, was

6. Abu Nasr al-Sarraj's *Kitāb al-Luma' fi'l-taṣawwuf*, ed. R.A. Nicholson.

7. Al-Sarrāj points out that the materials transmitted in Abū Yazīd's name took different forms owing to the different periods and the various countries in which his sayings were spread. Ibid. p.380. According to this assessment, which seems correct, we are not dealing with the historic Abū Yazīd, or the true Abū Yazīd, but rather with the way he is reflected in Islamic mystical literature.

8. Cf. M.A. Sells (ed.), *Early Islamic Mysticism*, p.358, n.66.

9. *SPK*, p.281, p.407, n.3.

the house of Abū Yazīd, known as the house of the pious (*bayt al-abrār*).[10] Al-Junayd's solitary dwelling place (*zāwiya;* literally: corner) and Ibn Adham's cave are also mentioned in this context. These men had long since died, but their impressions (*athar*) remained in these places and continued to influence visitors' hearts. This proves the great personality of Abū Yazīd who was deemed Pole (*quṭb*)[11] by Ibn al-ʿArabī.[12]

Ibn al-ʿArabī also introduces Abū Yazīd's perception of asceticism (*zuhd*). He characterizes him as having stated that asceticism was an easy matter and that he had been an abstinent for three days. On the first day he renounced this world (*al-dunyā*), on the second the world to come (*al-ākhira*), and on the third everything which was not God.[13] The saying is quoted in full in two additional passages in the text. In one of them, after expressing the idea that in his view abstinence had no value and that he abstained from this world, the next world and all that existed except God, Abū Yazīd was asked what he willed. He answered: 'I will not to will, for I am the object of will (*anā al-murād*) and you (God) are the one who wills (*wa-anta al-murīd*).' The passage ends with Ibn al-ʿArabī's remark that Abū Yazīd had established the principle that renunciation of all things except God is the true meaning of asceticism.[14]

At the beginning of Chapter 93 (*fī'l-zuhd*), the saying occurs again, this time with a reference to it by Ibn al-ʿArabī.[15] Contrary to some Sufis who censured Abū Yazīd's attitude toward *zuhd*, our author does not regard *zuhd* as a notion elaborated by Abū Yazīd, who did not consider *zuhd* a *maqām* or permanent station, but rather a station which must disappear when the cover of the heart's essence is removed by revelation (*kashf*). On the one hand, one cannot renounce that which was created for one's sake, because

10. *Fut.*I:153f.; *FM.*I:99, l.1.
11. *Dimensions*, index.
12. *Fut.*III:11; *FM.*II:6, l.32. *Seal*, pp. 94f.
13. *Fut.*II:137; *FM.*I:469, ll.29–30.
14. *Fut.*III:29; *FM.*II:19, ll.1–3.
15. *Fut.*III:267; *FM.*II:178, ll.6–8.

one cannot free oneself from that which is in one's possession. On the other hand, it is impossible to abstain from that which does not belong to one. In fact, according to the essence of reality or truth (*ʿayn al-ḥaqīqa*) there is no *zuhd*. Besides, writes Ibn al-ʿArabī, God does not renounce His creation, hence, one should follow God in one's actions. Elsewhere, Ibn al-ʿArabī argues against renunciation, saying that it actually means cancelling out the possibility of increasing one's knowledge of God,[16] which is one of the cornerstones of his philosophy. Emphasizing the role of revelation in the life of the Sufi, Ibn al-ʿArabī thus employs Abū Yazīd's evaluation of *zuhd* as a corroboration of his own thesis.

In the *Futūḥāt* Abū Yazīd serves as a model of ethical behaviour. His scrupulousness (*waraʿ*)[17] is best expressed in the following story. One night when Abū Yazīd was in a state of scrupulousness, he felt distressed by loneliness (*waḥsha*)[18] and attributed his distress to a certain lamp. Thereupon, his followers told him that they had borrowed a jar from a greengrocer to bring the oil for this lamp, with the stipulation that this be done only once, but had subsequently, and in violation of their promise, used the jar twice. Abū Yazīd ordered them to inform the greengrocer concerning the matter and to please him. They did so and Abū Yazīd's distress consequently disappeared.[19] Elsewhere Ibn al-ʿArabī relates that Abū Yazīd travelled some miles to return a fruit dropped from a greengrocer on his own fruits.[20]

Likewise, one day when Abū Yazīd entered into a state of disengagement (*tajrid*)[21] and felt the need to absent himself from

16. *Fut.*V:389; *FM.*III:263, l.35; *SPK*, p.157.

17. Sometimes this term is translated as equivalent to *zuhd* (abstinence). *SPK*, pp.279, 282; *Dimensions*, pp.31, 110. L. Kinberg, 'What is meant by *zuhd*?' *Studia Islamica*, 61 (1985), pp.42–4. However, in the story told here it is suitable to translate it as scrupulousness.

18. Cf. *Dimensions*, p.132.

19. *Fut.*II:152; *FM.*I:480, ll.13–15.

20. Ibn al-ʿArabī, *Mawāqiʿ al-nujūm*, in *Majmūʿa*, Vol. III:319.

21. According to Chittick this term means literally 'stripping' the spirit from its attachment to the body. *SDG*, p.274.

the accumulation of material things (*'adam al-iddikhār*), he said to his followers, 'I lost my heart', and instructed them to search the house. They did so and found a bunch of grapes, upon which he said to them: 'Our house has become a house of greengrocers.' His followers gave alms equal to the number of grapes and Abū Yazīd found his heart.[22]

In addition to being a man of scrupulousness or *wara'*, Abū Yazīd is here revealed as a sensitive person who knew when a transgression had been made, a man who knew the causes of his feelings and acted accordingly.

When asked whether the gnostic (*al-'ārif*) disobeyed God, Abū Yazīd answered by quoting Quran 33:38, 'God's commandment is predetermined decree'. Ibn al-'Arabī points out that Abū Yazīd's answer was an example of most correct behaviour (*adab*), for he did not answer either in the affirmative or the negative. According to our author, this correct behaviour stemmed from Abū Yazīd's general perfection of state, knowledge and behaviour. The phrase 'May God be pleased with him and others like him' concludes Ibn al-'Arabī's appreciation of Abū Yazīd's personality.[23]

Ibn al-'Arabī's admiration of Abū Yazīd's conduct is best exemplified by the story he cites about Abū Yazīd honouring his mother. On a cold night his mother asked him to bring her a cup of water. Abū Yazīd got out of bed with some effort and fetched it for her, but found that she had fallen asleep again. He stood beside her until she awoke and then gave her the cup, on whose handle a piece of skin from his finger had stuck because of the freezing temperature, thereby causing her grief.

Ibn al-'Arabī writes about Abū Yazīd's mistaken belief that honouring his mother derived not from an inclination of his soul, but rather from veneration of the Law. Abū Yazīd was frustrated to realize that this act of honouring his mother was accompanied

22. *Fut.*II:152; *FM.*I:480, ll.15–17.
23. *Fut.*II:205; *FM.*I:516, ll.19–21.

by laziness and reluctance to leave his bed. Consequently, he also became fully aware of the fact that all those other acts of honouring his mother which he had carried out with gladness and pleasure were due to an inclination of his soul and not for the sake of God. If they had been for the sake of God, says Abū Yazīd, it would not have been difficult for the soul, since that which the beloved (God) commands, the lover loves. He therefore blamed his soul for deceiving him, for he had thought that that which he had done for seventy years was for the sake of God, whereas in fact it had been a result of the soul's inclination. Thereupon he repented.[24]

There can be no doubt that Abū Yazīd's behaviour serves Ibn al-ʿArabī as a model for the minute analysis of acts of the soul (*muḥāsabat al-nafs*).[25] Likewise Ibn al-ʿArabī reckons him among the People of Blame (*malāmiyya*), the perfect Gnostics[26] and the Verifiers.[27] It is thus hardly surprising that Ibn al-ʿArabī refers to Abū Yazīd as 'the great Abū Yazīd al-Bisṭāmī'.[28]

This reverence for Abū Yazīd might have resulted, *inter alia*, from the story about God saying to him: 'Go out to My creatures with My attributes, so that whoever sees you, will see Me.' Ibn al-ʿArabī interprets these words to mean the appearance of the Lord's attributes in Abū Yazīd. Just as rulers have the power to prescribe, prohibit, rule and judge, and these are God's attributes, so Abū Yazīd also assimilated God's attributes.[29]

It is therefore no surprise that Abū Yazīd, according to the Shaykh, was one of those who inherited the attributes of the angel Israfīl[30] (*kana ʿala qalb Israfīl*; literally: he was upon the heart

24. *Fut.*II:494; *FM.*I:717, ll.17–29.
25. *Dimensions*, p.54.
26. Ibn al-ʿArabī, *Mawāqiʿ al-nujūm*, in *Majmūʿa*, Vol. III:309.
27. *Kitāb al-Isfār ʿan natāʾij al-asfār*, in *Rasāʾil Ibn al-ʿArabī*, Part 2, p.3.
28. *Fut.*II:535, IV:55; *FM.*I:745, l.35, II:408, l.9.
29. *Fut.*II:550; *FM.*I:757, ll.4–5.
30. Israfīl is the name, probably derived from the Hebrew *serafīm*, of an archangel whose mission is to transmit the divine decisions written on the Preserved Tablet to the Archangel who is responsible for the fulfillment of these decrees. A.J. Wensinck, 'Israfīl', in *EI*. In Sufi mythology Israfīl is the angel of the Resurrection. *Dimensions*, p.200.

of).[31] If he possessed God's qualities, it was certainly possible to ascribe angelic qualities to him. I do not know whether Abū Yazīd's adherence to belief in God's predetermination is connected to Israfīl in Ibn al-ʿArabī's view, but our author certainly presents him as answering the question of the possibility of the gnostic's disobedience, twice citing Quran 33:38: 'God's commandment is predetermined decree'.[32] Abū Yazīd seems to suggest that even the gnostic is not exempt from God's decree. On the one hand, Ibn al-ʿArabī cannot deny Abū Yazīd's opinion on God's predetermination and, on the other, he cannot ascribe the transgression of God's laws to a person who experiences His revelation (the gnostic). Consequently, he tries to soften Abū Yazīd's view by stating that God makes the gnostic consider the sin in favourable terms due to an interpretation, also caused by God, which includes a true aspect through which the gnostic feels that he does not violate a prohibition. In fact, when the gnostic commits a sin he does not know that it is a sin, because this fact is revealed to him only after his action. Ibn al-ʿArabī compares the gnostic's situation to that of a legist (*mujtahid*) who errs in his decision, and whose error is revealed to him by proofs only after he has made his decision.[33] In such a way, reminiscent of the solutions put forward to maintain the immunity of prophets from sin (*ʿiṣma*), Ibn al-ʿArabī reconciles God's decree with the elevated position of the gnostic who, like the prophets, cannot be believed to commit sins.

Abū Yazīd belonged to a special group called 'the people of the Quran', and these people were identified, according to a prophetic tradition, with the people of God and His elect. What characterized them was the preservation of the Quran in their memory and through their acts. The Quran was firmly rooted in their memory, not because they learned it, but rather because it was revealed to them by God. It is worth noting that Sahl al-Tustarī (d.896) gained

31. *Fut.*III:18; *FM.*II:11, ll.6–7.
32. *Fut.*III:36; *FM.*II:23, ll.15–16.
33. *Fut.*IV:180; *FM.*II:491, ll.21–30.

this station when he was just six years old; as for Abū Yazīd, Ibn al-ʿArabī states that he did not die until the Quran was rooted in his heart.[34] This indicates the high estimation in which Ibn al-ʿArabī held al-Tustari.

Abū Yazīd and al-Tustarī share still another trait: both were among the saints who had achieved all the waystations (*manzil*, pl. *manāzil*).[35] Ibn al-ʿArabī dedicates a detailed discussion to the number and characteristics of these waystations, although this is not our concern here.

Let us now turn to Abū Yazīd's mystical philosophical notions as they were incorporated into the *Futūḥāt* and other works, and to the impact they had on Ibn al-ʿArabī's mystical philosophy. The notion that Abū Yazīd had no attributes appears several times in Ibn al-ʿArabī's *magnum opus* and is connected to Ibn al-ʿArabī's distinction between the world of phenomena and the divine world. In the context of a discussion concerning bliss (*naʿīm*) and chastisement (*ʿadhāb*), the Shaykh states that both concepts exist in the material world. Those who attain the stage of being aware of the unity of God's essence (*ahl ahadiyyat al-dhāt*) have no feeling of either bliss or chastisement. That is because God's essence has no plurality of attributes. Abū Yazīd said: 'I have been laughing for a while and crying for a while, and now I do not laugh or cry.' Then he was asked: 'How are you in the morning?' And he said: 'I have no morning and no evening. Morning and evening belong to those who are delimited by an attribute and I have no attribute.'[36] Elsewhere our author attempts to explain the meaning of the rather obscure words 'morning' and 'evening'. Morning points to the east where the sun rises, and thus designates manifest things, while evening alludes to sunset and hence to hidden things. The gnostic is the 'olive tree that is neither of the east nor of the west' (Quran

34. *Fut.*III:32; *FM.*II:20, ll.17–20. Ibn al-ʿArabī, *al-Isfār ʿan natāʾij al-asfār*, in *Rasāʾil Ibn al-ʿArabī*, Part II:16; *SDG*, p.394, n.4.

35. *Fut.*III:62; *FM.*II:40, l.17.

36. *Fut.*III:111; *FM.*II:73, ll.30–1; cf. *SPK*, p.376.

24:35). In this station the gnostic shares God's incomparability, as stated in Quran 42:11 and 37:180.[37]

In the *Futūḥāt*,[38] with regard to Abū Yazīd's saying 'I have no attribute', Ibn al-ʿArabī writes that the Sufis differed as to whether or not it was a phrase of ecstasy (*shaṭḥ*). Incidentally, we learn of Ibn al-ʿArabī's unfavourable attitude toward this term through his definition of it: '*Shaṭḥ* is a word with a flavor of frivolity (*ruʿūna*) and false (?) claim (*daʿwā*). It is rarely found among the verifiers, the people of the Revealed Law.'[39]

A different explanation of Abū Yazīd's saying, 'I have no attribute', appears in Chapter 105, 'On the abandonment of sorrow'. Here the aforementioned words, morning and evening, are said to indicate that the mystic has no dominion over time; on the contrary, he is dominated by time, whereas for God time is an attribute. Ibn al-ʿArabī very probably means by God's attribute the power by which He created the morning and the evening and is controlling them. Ibn al-ʿArabī rejects the view of those who claim that by making this statement Abū Yazīd laid claim to divine status (*taʿallaha*). Abū Yazīd, says the Shaykh, was too sublime to ascribe such an interpretation to himself.[40]

In sum, on this issue, Abū Yazīd appears in Ibn al-ʿArabī as a man of two facets. On the one hand he is depicted as one who transcends all states and stations, like God's essence, which is unlimited, whereas on the other the absence of attributes points to his lack of ability in relation to God who, by His attributes, rules the world. The first aspect seems to have caused some to censure Abū Yazīd for claiming divine status for himself, an accusation firmly rejected by Ibn al-ʿArabī.

37. *Fut.*IV:412ff.; *FM.*II:646, ll.29–33; *SPK*, p.376.

38. *Fut.*III:198; *FM.*II:133, ll.20–2.

39. For a discussion of *shaṭḥ* in the *Futūḥāt* see Chap. 195. C.W. Ernst, *Words of Ecstasy in Sufism*, p.22.

40. *Fut.*1999, III:281; *FM.*II:187, ll.13–20.

As we have seen, according to Ibn al-ʿArabī, God spoke to Abū Yazīd, and this fact alone testifies to Abū Yazīd's magnitude in our author's eyes. One of God's sayings to Abū Yazīd, which serves as a point of departure for Ibn al-ʿArabī's notion of the relationship between God and His creatures, reads: 'O Abū Yazīd, come close to Me through that which (the attributes) I do not possess: lowliness and neediness' (*al-dhilla wa'l-iftiqār*). Ibn al-ʿArabī states that there are several kinds of relationship between God and human beings. Acts such as fasting (*ṣawm*)[41] serve to link the attribute of Lordship and the attribute of servanthood, while prayer, although it is common to the servant and God, is divided between the Real (God) and the servant; that is, the servant prays in a certain manner and God in another. In most other cases things belong to God alone. Ibn al-ʿArabī uses two terms to designate these relationships: *qirān* (connection), which denotes any kind of connection between God and human beings; and *infirād* (isolation), which designates an act or an attribute that belongs only to the servant (the human being) or to the Master (God).[42] God's saying to Abū Yazīd is an example of *infirād*, because lowliness and neediness pertain to human beings alone and not to God.

In a slightly different version of the saying, Abū Yazīd asked God, 'Through what may I come near to You?' and God answered, 'Through that which I do not possess, lowliness and neediness.' Connecting this exchange to Quran 51:56 ('I created the Jinn and humankind only to worship Me'), the Shaykh interprets this verse to mean that people were created to be submissive to God. They are submissive, for they come to know that God exists in things, meaning that God is the source of all things. Ibn al-ʿArabī emphasizes that people do not yield to God's manifestations, but rather to God Himself, for their existence is identical with God.[43]

41. *Ṣawm* is the infinitive of *ṣāma ʿan*, meaning, 'he refrained from'. Thus God's abstention, i.e. His refraining from doing something is in principle like the human's.

42. *Fut.*II:455; *FM.*I:689, l.34 – 690, l.5.

43. *Fut.*III:26f., III:322; *FM.*II:16, l.32 – 17, l.1, II:214, ll.7–11.

Here our author makes use of Abū Yazīd's report, together with a verse from Quran, in order to lay out his basic notion of the world as God's manifestation and of the meaning of worshipping God, namely the knowledge that all phenomena are His manifestations. Abū Yazīd's saying serves not as the source of these ideas but merely as their corroboration.

In another formulation of Abū Yazīd's report of his perplexity concerning how he might come close to God, however, God said to him: 'Leave yourself and come' (*utruk nafsaka wa-taʿāla*). Leaving one's self amounts to leaving the category of servitude (*ʿubūdiyya*), which connotes distance from God. However, leaving one's self also means emulation of God's attributes, and through this emulation God and human beings meet. Very probably aware of the paradox involved in the formula 'leave yourself', Ibn al-ʿArabī makes an interesting distinction between servitude and one's knowledge that one is a servant. Whereas servitude requires distance from God, he writes, the knowledge that one is a servant requires nearness to God. Thus the same state, servitude, demands two opposing values, nearness and distance, depending on the aspects to be considered.[44] Ibn al-ʿArabī probably refers to this duality when he states elsewhere, with regard to the saying 'Come close to me', that the essence of nearness is here identical with the essence of distance.[45]

Ibn al-ʿArabī also follows Abū Yazīd's definition of the station of *maʿrifa* (gnosis). According to the Shaykh, the Sufis differed in their opinions concerning the station of *maʿrifa* (gnosis) and *ʿārif* (gnostic) *vis-à-vis* the station of *ʿilm* (knowledge) and *ʿālim* (knower). Elevating the term 'gnosis', some Sufis believed that the station of *maʿrifa* pertained to Lordship, whereas the station of *ʿilm* pertained to Godship. Among the Verifiers (*al-muḥaqqiqun*), says Ibn al-ʿArabī, Sahl al-Tustarī, Abū Yazīd, Ibn al-ʿArīf and

44. *Fut.*IV:285; *FM.*II:561, ll.15–21; *SPK*, p.319.
45. *Fut.*IV:173; *FM.*II:487, ll.8–9.

Abū Madyan held this view and he agrees with them.[46] *Maʿrifa* was probably higher than *ʿilm*, because the divine name 'Lord' (*rabb*) designates the relationship between creation and the Divine Essence, which is the source of all created things.[47] Thus, the lordly station (*maqām rabbānī*) seems to denote a direct relationship between the human being and God's Essence, whereas the divine station (*maqām ilāhī*) seems to convey the notion of an indirect relationship. So the gnostic receives knowledge directly from God, and the knower receives knowledge through mediators, such as God's signs in the world.[48]

One specific phenomenon characteristic of Sufism is the use of ecstatic expressions (*shaṭaḥāt*). According to Ernst's analysis of this phenomenon, the Sufis sometimes express their ideas through boasting (*fakhr*), the origins of which are traced back to ancient Arabic literature. In this context the Sufis communicate their thoughts through audacious sayings.[49] I would add to Ernst's classifications of the forms of *shaṭḥ* the form of exaggeration which, as we shall see, corresponds to the following examples that Ibn al-ʿArabī, notwithstanding his reservations concerning this device, puts forward in the name of Abū Yazīd.

In the context of treating the lover, the Shaykh states that there are acts, such as the lover mentioning the beloved, which cannot be measured. Other things that belong to humans are compared to and surpass those of God: for example, the heart of the lover is wider than God's mercy. Here our author cites Abū Yazīd's saying: 'If the Throne and that which it contains were multiplied a million

46. *Fut.*III:478; *FM.*II:318, ll.30–3; *SPK*, p.149.

47. Ibid. p.310.

48. When Abū Yazīd wanted to emphasize the difference between the formal scholars and the Sufis he said: 'You all took your knowledge like a dead person (receiving it) from another dead person. But we took our knowledge from the Living One who never dies (Quran 25:58).' *Fut.*I:423; *FM.*I:280, ll.25–6; *SPK*, pp.248f. J.W. Morris, 'How to Study the *Futūḥāt*: Ibn ʿArabī's own advice', in S. Hirtenstein and M. Tiernan (eds.), *Muhyiddin Ibn ʿArabī*, p.76, p.85, n.13.

49. Ernst, *Ecstasy*, pp.38–40.

times and put in the corner of the gnostic's heart, he would not feel them, all the more so regarding the state of the lover.'[50]

In another example of *shaṭḥ*, Ibn al-ʿArabī tries to moderate Abū Yazīd's seemingly audacious saying by setting forth a rational argument. When Abū Yazīd heard Quran 85:12, 'Surely, the assault of your Lord is strong' (*inna baṭsha rabbika la-shadīd*), he said: 'My assault is stronger.' Ibn al-ʿArabī interprets these words to mean that one's assault is stronger than God's because, in contrast to God's assault, it is not mixed with mercy. He understands *baṭsh* to mean anger, saying that when one is angry because of one's own interests, one's anger does not contain mercy. However, when one is angry for the sake of God, this anger is considered to be God's, and, hence, it is not exempt from His mercy.[51] Elsewhere he repeats the notion that God's assault when coming from the human being is stronger than when it comes from God, and he adds without explanation that such an assault coming from a natural servant is stronger than that which comes from a divine servant.[52] All in all, the nearer the assault is to God, the weaker it is.

Ibn al-ʿArabī employs yet another rational argument to mitigate Abū Yazīd's daring assertion. God's speech remains His speech even if it is indirectly heard from His messenger. However, owing to the messenger's nearness to human beings because of their common essence, which can be summarized by the word 'many' in contrast to the word 'one', which characterizes God, the messenger's assault is stronger than God's when it reaches their hearing.[53] By implication we learn the importance of the messenger in bringing God's message to human beings; the messenger's speech is, somewhat paradoxically, more effective than God's.

Our author's attitude toward the saints' miracles (*karamāt*), likewise, is heavily influenced by Abū Yazīd's view on this issue.

50. *Fut.*III:540–1; *FM.*II:361, ll.6–7.
51. *Fut.*VI:59; *FM.*III:333, ll.26–33. Cf. Ernst, *Ecstasy*, p.39.
52. *Fut.*VII:128; *FM.*IV:87, ll.1–4.
53. *Fut.*VII:236; *FM.*IV:160, ll.28–31.

When asked about flying through the air (*ikhtirāq al-hawā'*), Abū Yazīd answered: 'The bird passes through the air. However, the believer is better than the bird in God's eyes. So how can this act which is common to the bird and the human being be considered a miracle?' Dividing the saints' miracles into two kinds, physical (literally: sensuous – *ḥissī*) and abstract (*ma'nawī*), Ibn al-'Arabī regards flying as a physical miracle. The common people know only of this type of miracle, while the elite know of the abstract kind, which includes the carrying of precepts and morality to perfection. On the basis of Abū Yazīd's saying, Ibn al-'Arabī considers knowledge of God and the world to come to be the most exalted gift that God can bestow upon humans and thus the greatest miracle. Thus, the Shaykh emphasizes that the true saint is one who is pious and has divine knowledge. Physical miracles, in which deception may be involved, do not play a role in characterizing this category of saints.[54]

Nevertheless, Abū Yazīd appears in the *Futūḥāt* and *Mawāqi' al-nujūm* as a man with the ability to perform miracles. Comparing Abū Yazīd to 'Īsā (Jesus), who had the noble knowledge of how to heal the blind and the leprous and revive the dead,[55] Ibn al-'Arabī tells us that when Abū Yazīd killed an ant inadvertently, he immediately blew upon it and it came back to life.[56] Moreover, Abū Yazīd is said to have possessed God's power to such an extent that he was identified with God: a novice reportedly stated that he had dispensed with seeing God in order to see Abū Yazīd. He said: 'Seeing Abū Yazīd once is better than seeing God a thousand times.' Then Abū Yazīd passed near him and the novice was told that this was Abū Yazīd, and when he saw Abū Yazīd he died. On hearing that the novice had died, Abū Yazīd said: 'He saw that

54. *Fut.*III:553f.; *FM.*II:369, l.34 – 370, l.1. Ibn al-'Arabī, *'Anqā' Mughrib fī khatm al-awliyā' wa-shams al-maghrib*, in *Majmū'a*, Vol. III:19; G.T. Elmore, *Islamic Sainthood in the Fullness of Time*, pp.302f.

55. Quran 5:110.

56. *Fut.*V:136; *FM.*III:93, ll.4–5. *Mawāqi' al-nujūm*, in *Majmū'a*, Vol. III:320; *'Anqā' Mughrib*, in *Majmū'a*, Vol. III:56; Elmore, *Islamic Sainthood*, p.514, n.23.

which he was not capable of seeing, for God was revealed to him through me.' Abū Yazīd compares this situation to the revelation of God on the mountain which caused Mūsā (Moses), who had asked to see God, to fall down senseless (Quran 7:143).[57]

How can one explain Ibn al-ʿArabī's attitude toward the saints' miracles? As we have seen above, he regards physical miracles unfavourably while simultaneously holding abstract miracles in great esteem. However, the last story glorifies the physical aspect, i.e. the physical influence of Abū Yazīd on a Sufi. A possible explanation for this, I suggest, is that, although the last report includes a miracle, it does not involve the saint's actual activity, but rather his presence alone. In such an instance there was no possibility of deception, the subject of warnings by our author, because the saint does nothing at all.

One finds other proofs elsewhere that Abū Yazīd did not act to influence people. When he was told that people touched him in order to be blessed, he said: 'They do not touch me for blessing; rather they touch an ornament with which God has adorned me. Shall I prevent them from touching the ornament, since it is not mine?'[58]

Abū Yazīd appears in Ibn al-ʿArabī's writings as a Sufi model. Ibn al-ʿArabī often mentions an outstanding personality alongside that of Abū Yazīd for the purpose of comparing the two. For example, the Shaykh tells us that he once met a veracious person, a possessor of a state who followed Abū Yazīd's way, and that this person had told Ibn al-ʿArabī that no evil thought had come into his mind for fifty years.[59]

Another person, a Sufi shaykh who belonged to the people of God, is also mentioned by Ibn al-ʿArabī as comparable and, in fact, even stronger than Abū Yazīd with regard to his state (*amkan minhu*). This Sufi told Ibn al-ʿArabī about his state with God, saying

57. *Fut.*V:173f.; V:174 (ll.3–4 are not clear); *FM.*III:117, ll.26–30.
58. *Fut.*V:201; *FM.*III:136, ll.10–11.
59. *Fut.*IV:20; *FM.*II:384, ll.27–30.

that God pointed out to him the greatness of His rule. Thereafter the shaykh said to God: 'O my Lord, my rule is greater than Yours.' And God asked: 'How can you say so, while God knows best?' And the shaykh explained that acts he carried out, such as calling to God who answers and asking God something which He bestows, were not fulfilled by God; God does not call or ask anyone, hence no one has influence over Him, while, through calling and asking, the shaykh has some dominion over God.[60]

In spite of this statement, Abū Yazīd emphasized several times the seeming existence of the human being, a point which, as we know, is central in Ibn al-ʿArabī's mystical philosophy. As we have seen, according to the Shaykh, will (*irāda*) in Abū Yazīd's view means the absence of will, and he expressed this notion by his saying: 'I will not to will' (*urīdu an la urīda*). Abū Yazīd justifies this statement by saying 'I am the object of will (*al-murād*) and You are the one who wills' (*al-murīd*). Since Abū Yazīd knew, says Ibn al-ʿArabī, that the object of the will, as a possible thing, is nonexistent, he referred to himself as nonexistent and ascribed existence, and hence will, only to God.[61]

Ibn al-ʿArabī seems to have agreed with Abū Yazīd on the latter's consideration of God as the real existent. However, in this context Ibn al-ʿArabī contradicts him, in specifying a will that pertains to human beings. This is the intention to know God not through rational arguments but through revelation. Faithful to his idea that all things in the cosmos are God's manifestations, he only wishes to increase his knowledge of the cosmos through God's help. Knowledge about God is an object of will which can be supplied by God Himself, hence such knowledge becomes the object of God's will; if He wills, He bestows this knowledge on humans. In such a way, Ibn al-ʿArabī accepts Abū Yazīd's principle of the real existence, but also leaves a sort of will to the human being. If he

60. *Fut.*IV:58; *FM.*II:410, ll.3–7.
61. *Fut.*IV:225; *FM.*II:521, l.33 – 522, l.1.

had been asked who causes this will in the human being, he would undoubtedly have said that the cause is God.

However, Abū Yazīd elsewhere points to the existence of a will which can be connected to God's absolute rule of the cosmos. In a poem cited several times in *Futūḥāt*, Abū Yazīd said that he wanted God not to give him reward but punishment. He wanted to have pleasure by suffering (*ʿadhāb*). Apart from explaining the etymology of *ʿadhāb* (the root *ʿ.dh.b* in the first form [*ʿadhuba*] denotes 'to be pleasant'),[62] the Shaykh writes that, as he understands it, Abū Yazīd expresses the idea that he wants to have pleasure not by nature, but by miracle, that is, by that which breaks custom, something which is unnatural and made by God.[63]

Ibn al-ʿArabī further elucidates Abū Yazīd's idea of seeking pleasure in suffering as referring to the general idea of God's absolute power. According to him, God can do what contradicts the human intellect or, to put it another way, He can do what the intellect regards as absurd (*muḥāl*). Basing himself on Quran 33:27 ('God is capable of doing everything'), Ibn al-ʿArabī concludes that God's absolute power can produce that which is absurd.[64]

To sum up, Ibn al-ʿArabī admires Abū Yazīd and regards him as a Sufi model in his moral conduct and connection to God. He employs Abū Yazīd's sayings to corroborate and explain his own teachings. When he discerns boldness in Abū Yazīd's sayings, he tries to ameliorate it. He has reservations concerning the phenomenon of *shaṭḥ*, but does not refrain from citing ecstatic sayings. In his attitude toward the saints' physical miracles he seems to rely on Abū Yazīd. One cannot argue, however, that Abū Yazīd's

62. *Fut.*IV:452, VII: 273; *FM.*II:673, l.26, IV:185, ll.22–4.

63. *Fut.*IV:229; *FM.*II:524, ll.18–20. Some mystics regarded affliction as a sign of closeness to God. Ernst, *Ecstasy*, p.97.

64. *Fut.*IV:364f.; *FM.*II:614, ll.14–19. Most Muslim theologians oppose the notion that God can do everything, including absurd things, and state that His power is limited by rational considerations, so that, for example, He cannot create a thing and its opposite in the same time and place. B. Abrahamov, 'Al-Ghazali's theory of causality', *Studia Islamica*, 67 (1988), pp.75–98.

pronouncements serve as the source of Ibn al-ʿArabī's idea of the seeming existence of creation, because this idea was already well established in early Sufism. Moreover, the idea that the relationship of God to the world is expressed through both transcendent and immanent aspects does not appear in the sayings of either Abū Yazīd or other Sufis, but remains original to Ibn al-ʿArabī.

Sahl al-Tustarī

?818–896

Our knowledge of Sahl al-Tustarī's mystical views has increased significantly owing to the thorough research in Gerhard Böwering's *The Mystical Vision of Existence in Classical Islam.*[1] However, Ibn al-'Arabī regards al-Tustarī as one of the saints, along with al-Bisṭāmī, who reached the highest rank,[2] and seems to have been influenced by al-Tustarī's major ideas. For example, in al-Tustarī's view, God revealed Himself to human beings on three occasions:

1. In making the covenant with them before their creation (Quran 7:172).[3]
2. At their creation.
3. At the Resurrection.

The third occasion constitutes an eternal face-to-face encounter with God.[4] This tripartite method of God's revelation, which is a cornerstone of al-Tustarī's teachings, is not found in Ibn al-'Arabī. Nevertheless, we may assume that our author learned the principle of regarding God's revelations from different angles from al-Tustarī. Another fundamental idea of al-Tustarī is that Muhammad's heart is a source of illumination to the hearts of all human beings:[5] we may conjecture here that such an idea about the central role of the Prophet in causing revelation in the human heart affected the Akbarian notion of the Perfect Man embodied

1. On the connection between Ibn al-'Arabī and al-Tustarī see pp.39f. On al-Tustarī's life, see Chap. II.

2. *Fut.*III:62; *FM.*II:40, l.17.

3. Of course Ibn al-'Arabī mentions this verse several times, but not as a part of a tripartite division.

4. Böwering, *Mystical Vision*, Chap. IV.

5. Ibid. pp.160–5.

in the personality of Muhammad, who contains all the forms of the phenomenal world.[6]

Now we shall turn to issues which are linked to al-Tustarī in Ibn al-ʿArabī's work. One of the most quoted is the prostration of the heart (*sujūd al-qalb*).[7] Ibn al-ʿArabī considers *sujūd al-qalb* an obligation that cannot be cancelled, contrary to the prostration of the face which comes to an end. As corroboration of this obligation he relates the story of al-Tustarī who, at the beginning of his Sufi career, saw his heart prostrating without stopping. He remained perplexed and began to ask Sufi shaykhs about this phenomenon to no avail, until he was informed about a shaykh in ʿAbādān who could help him. This ʿAbādānī told him that the heart prostrates forever. Consequently, al-Tustarī remained with him and served him.[8] The eternity of the prostration is explained elsewhere: prostration means submission (*khuḍūʿ*). Submission to God derives from one's knowledge of God's greatness and man's baseness. Once one gains this knowledge it does not leave him, hence the prostration, being the result of this knowledge, does not stop.[9]

Ibn al-ʿArabī connects the phenomenon of the prostration of the heart with God's revelation to the saint. When a saint experiences a divine revelation, he and his knowledge (or gnosis; *maʿrifa*) become perfect, and his heart begins to prostrate. This prostration in turn gives the saint immunity from sins and mistakes (*maḥfūẓ*), and the Devil cannot hurt him. In this regard the saint is like the prophet, although the terms used to indicate their being immune are different: *ʿiṣma* refers to the prophet, and *ḥifẓ* to the saint.[10]

6. Ibid. p.264.

7. In this context, Ibn al-ʿArabī points out that in his seclusion (*khalwa*) Abū Ṭālib al-Makkī experienced a revelation owing to his recollection of al-Tustarī. *Fut.*VI:279; *FM.*III:488, ll.12–13.

8. *Fut.*II:203; *FM.*I:515, ll.25–9.

9. *Fut.*III:152f.; *FM.*II:102, ll.12–13; *SPK*, p.407, n.18.

10. *Fut.*II:203f.; *FM.*I:515, l.29 – 516, l.1.

According to the Shaykh, not all saints achieve such a level. Most of them experience only changes of the heart from one state to another. The saint who experiences changes, but also has one stable state, that is, *sujūd al-qalb*, attains the highest magnitude. This state is also connected to the preservation of the Quran in the saint's heart. Those who gain the degree in which the Quran is firmly rooted by God in their hearts (*istiẓhār al-Qur'ān*) belong to the people of the Quran, who in turn are the people of God. That is because the Quran is God's speech (*kalām Allāh*), which is identical to His knowledge and His knowledge is equal to His essence. Ibn al-ʿArabī states that owing to this state, *sujūd al-qalb* marks the beginning of Sahl's journey in the Sufi way.[11]

Apart from the term *sujūd al-qalb*, which occurs quite frequently and in many places in *al-Futūḥāt al-Makkiyya*, some issues are mentioned only once, or no more than three times. One of these is the meaning of the word *ʿadl*, which constitutes the twenty-eighth question of al-Ḥakīm al-Tirmidhī.[12] According to al-Tustarī and others, the meaning of *ʿadl* (literally: justice) is the appropriate principle through which God created the heaven and the earth (*al-ʿadl huwa al-ḥaqq al-makhlūq bihi al-samawāt wa'l-arḍ*). Abū al-Ḥakam ʿAbd al-Salām ibn Barrajān (d.1141)[13] calls this principle *al-ḥaqq al-makhlūq bihi*, for he heard God's words: 'He did not create them but through *al-ḥaqq*' (Quran 44:29; see also Quran 15:85, 17:105 to the same effect). This principle is connected with Ibn al-ʿArabī's perception of how things manifest in the cosmos. Before the things are manifested or come into existence, they exist in God's mind as *aʿyān thābita* (fixed entities), namely, models after

11. *Fut.*III:32; *FM.*II:20, ll.19–24. The state of prostration of the heart also characterizes al-Bisṭāmī, but only before his death. Sahl's question also serves as an example of the questions that the Master (*shaykh*) should know how to answer. *Fut.*III:547; *FM.*II:365, l.19. Sahl turned to some Masters but they could not explain to him the meaning of *sujūd al-qalb*, because, as Ibn al-ʿArabī notes, they did not taste (*lam yadhūqū*) this state. *Fut.*V:126; *FM.*III:86, ll.22–8.

12. For these questions see the section on al-Tirmidhī.

13. See p.135, below.

which they are made to appear in reality. *Al-ḥaqq* means the principle appropriate for each thing, the law which establishes the time, the state and the qualities of its appearance in the cosmos.[14] According to Ibn al-ʿArabī, Ibn Barrajān devotes a lengthy discussion to *al-ḥaqq*, which includes the science of the form (*ʿilm al-ṣūra*) and many other sciences, such as the science of taste (*dhawq*) and the science of causes (*ʿilal*).[15]

However, elsewhere *al-ḥaqq al-makhlūq bihi* is identical with *al-nafas* (God's Breath), that is, the being which creates the levels and entities of the cosmos.[16] It is also called the Cloud (*al-ʿamāʾ*).[17] In the Shaykh's view this being is the closest entity to God which derives from Him.[18] As an entity *al-ḥaqq al-makhlūq bihi* indicates the *logos*, the being through which God created the cosmos.[19] It seems that neither Sahl nor Ibn Barrajān mean by the term *ʿadl* a being, but rather God's order. However, Ibn al-ʿArabī interpreted their teaching as being in harmony with his doctrine of the *logos*.

A closely related issue is the creation of primordial Matter (*habāʾ*; literally: dust), which constitutes the first existent in the world. It is interesting that Ibn al-ʿArabī mentions ʿAlī ibn Abī Ṭālib and Sahl among other people of revelation, to wit, Sufis, who point to this entity. Probably influenced by the doctrine of the Ikhwān al-Ṣafāʾ, Ibn al-ʿArabī says that the philosophers call this entity the Universal Hyle (*al-hayūlā al-kull*),[20] although in their

14. *Fut.*III:91; *FM.*II:60, ll.11–30.

15. *Fut.*V:113; *FM.*III:77, l.20 – 78, l.1. Ibn al-ʿArabī regards *al-ḥaqq al-makhlūq bihi* as a science (*ʿilm*). *Fut.*V:222; *FM.*III:150, ll.6–7.

16. *Fut.*IV:31f.; *FM.*II:391, l.34.

17. *Fut.*III:471; *FM.*II:313, l.24.

18. *Fut.*III:466; *FM.*II:310, ll.23–4. For the three last references, see *SPK*, pp.133f. For other meanings of the Cloud and the Breath, see ibid. pp.125–30.

19. *MP*, p.75. For the Ismāʿīlī origin of this notion see M. Ebstein, 'The word of God and the Divine Will: Ismāʿīlī traces in Andalusī mysticism', *Jerusalem Studies in Arabic and Islam*, 38 (2011), pp.37f.

20. *Fut.*I:184; *FM.*I:119, l.27. J. El-Moor, 'The fool for love (*Foll Per Amor*) as follower of universal religion', *JMIAS*, 36 (2004), p.110; I.R. Netton, *Muslim Neoplatonists*, p.23. L. Gardet, '*Hayūlā*', in *EI*; M.A. Palacios, *The Mystical Philosophy of Ibn Masarra and His Followers*, trans. E.H. Douglas and H.W. Yoder, pp.87f.

Epistles primordial Matter is called *al-hayūlā al-ʿūlā*, and *hayūlā al-kull* occupies the second position.[21]

The high level of a Sufi is measured, *inter alia*, by the Sufi's relationship to his predecessors, especially the Prophet or the prophets.[22] In this regard, Ibn al-ʿArabī distinguishes between two groups:

1. Those who preserve (*yaḥfaẓūna*) God's laws as transmitted by the Messenger. Among them our author counts the Prophet's Companions (*ṣaḥāba*) and their Followers (*tābiʿūn*), and scholars who engaged in the Law, such as Abū Ḥanīfa and al-Shāfiʿī.
2. Those who preserve the Prophet's states (*aḥwāl*) and the secrets of his sciences (*asrār ʿulūmihi*). The list of these scholars begins with ʿAlī ibn Abī Ṭālib and ends with al-Junayd and Sahl. Actually, Ibn al-ʿArabī makes a distinction here between formal scholars and spiritual scholars or mystics.[23]

Let us now investigate Sahl's mystical traits as they occur in Ibn al-ʿArabī's writings. Sahl is affiliated with a group of mystics called the people of intention (*al-niyyatiyūn*; a term deriving from *niyya*, intention). They concern themselves with the specific states which precede the state of intention, such as aspiration (*himma*) and volition (*irāda*). Ibn al-ʿArabī points out that Sahl was very meticulous about intention, particularly with attention to the fact that sudden thought (*hājis*) is the first of several states which eventually cause intention to arise. The Shaykh considers this notion to be correct.[24] Basing himself on Quran 35:28 ('Only the erudite among

21. Our author relates this notion also to Ibn Barrajān and it is also ascribed to Ibn Masarra. Palacios, *Mystical Philosophy*, p.127. Ebstein and Sviri rightly point out 'that in al-Andalus there existed two "Tustarī traditions": the Tustarī tradition as it was known in Ṣūfī circles in the east, and, from Ibn Masarra's time onward, a different "Andalusian Tustarī tradition" in which letter speculations, in the framework of neoplatonic esoteric teachings, were attributed to Sahl'. M. Ebstein and S. Sviri, 'The so-called *Risālat al-Ḥurūf (Epistle on Letters)* ascribed to Sahl al-Tustarī and letter mysticism in al-Andalus', *Journal Asiatique*, 299.1 (2011), p.224.

22. *Seal*, Chap. 5.

23. *Fut.*I:231; *FM.*I:151, l.16.

24. *Fut.*I:323; *FM.*I:213, ll.17–18.

God's servants fear Him'), he states that Sahl adopted this idea, which means that fear of God is caused by knowledge; only those who know God fear Him.[25]

One of the curious stories related by Ibn al-ʿArabī is Sahl's encounter with the Devil (Iblīs). Al-Tustarī reported that he once met the Devil and knew him, just as the Devil knew who he was. According to the story, a controversy arose which sometimes perplexed both of them. At the end of their polemic, whose full detail is not told, the Devil quotes Quran 7:156, which reads: 'My mercy embraces all things'. The Devil draws the conclusion that God's mercy embraces him, because the word *kull* indicates generalization, the word *shayʾ* is an indefinite noun, and he is a thing. Sahl witnessed that he remained perplexed, but not for long, because he found the response to the Devil's claim at the end of this verse, which says: 'I shall prescribe it (the mercy) for the god-fearing, for those who pay the alms, and those who truly believe in Our signs.' Believing that he had refuted the Devil's contention, by adducing the end of the verse which limits the application of God's mercy only to the people who meet certain criteria, Sahl was very satisfied. However, his happiness only lasted a short while, for the Devil smiled and said to him: 'Did you not know that limitation (*taqyīd*) characterizes you and not God?' Sahl could not find a suitable response to the Devil's last claim, and they parted.

The Greatest Master, however, refutes the Devil's stand, arguing that the latter expressed his opinion from the point of view of God's absolute favour. From this angle, God bestows favours on all things. It is true, says Ibn al-ʿArabī, that God is above any limitation; however, He can oblige Himself to do something. This point of view escapes the Devil's attention. Ibn al-ʿArabī's completion of the debate between Sahl and the Devil proves that our author does not abstain from correcting what he thinks of as shortcomings in his predecessors. Notwithstanding Sahl's position in Sufism and

25. *Fut.*II:484; *FM.*I:710, ll.12–13.

Ibn al-ʿArabī's high estimation of him, the Shaykh is committed to the truth, and as such, he cannot leave this polemic with a victory for the Devil.[26]

Elsewhere we find Ibn al-ʿArabī expressing a reservation about Sahl's mystical way. According to Ibn al-ʿArabī, the possible things are infinite in number in their state of nonexistence. Thus, possibility is an endless Treasury (*khizāna*) from which God creates in perpetuity.[27] A long chapter (369) is dedicated to the discussion of God's Treasuries of Generosity (*khazāʾin al-jūd*). In section 17 of this chapter, the author writes about 'a Treasury which contains extinction (*fanāʾ*) of what cannot exist (forever) and continuity (*baqāʾ*) of that which is eternal'.[28] On this issue, says Ibn al-ʿArabī, those who receive revelation for a short while, that is, a weak revelation, stumble. Sometimes a spark of light appears to a person concerning what he seeks and he is satisfied with this state, without being aware that he does not exhaust the issue concerning which a revelation occurs to him. The short revelation experience is not enough to judge a certain matter. Ibn al-ʿArabī counts Sahl among those people who, despite being prominent in the science of the *barzakh*,[29] failed to grasp the whole situation of the people. Being influenced by a short revelation, which was like a flash of light, Sahl thought that the people would remain as they are without change until the Resurrection. His seeing them in one and the same state was correct, but his judgement that they would stay as such was incorrect.[30]

However, with regard to the place of the stations of gnosis (*maʿrifa*) and knowledge (*ʿilm*) Ibn al-ʿArabī agrees with Sahl and others: 'Our companions have disagreed concerning the station

26. *Fut.*IV:435f., VI:248; *FM*.II:662, ll.11–26, III:466, ll.21–4.

27. *SPK*, p.96.

28. *Fut.*VI:148; *FM*.III:395, l.23.

29. In Ibn al-ʿArabī's thought there are three worlds in the cosmos: (1) The spiritual world; (2) The imaginal world, or *barzakh*, which stands between (1) and (3); and (3) The corporeal world. *SPK*, pp.14, 117–18.

30. *Fut.*VI:148; *FM*.III:395, ll.23–6.

of *ma'rifa* and the *'ārif* and the station of *'ilm* and the *'ālim*. A group maintain that the station of *ma'rifa* is lordly (*rabbānī*) and the station of *'ilm* divine (*ilāhī*), including myself and the Verifiers (*al-muḥaqqiqūn*), like Sahl al-Tustarī, Abū Yazīd, Ibn al-'Arīf and Abū Madyan.'[31]

Sahl is also mentioned in the context of the question: What is the aim of human intellect? Does the human intellect exist for the purpose of acquiring knowledge or for the purpose of combating the evil inclination? Sahl's answer to this question does not occur here;[32] however, in his epistle *al-Isfār 'an natā'ij al-asfār* Ibn al-'Arabī points out that Sahl regards the intellect as the device for fighting wickedness.[33] When the war against one's passions ends, the intellect no longer has a function.

Asked once what nourishment is, Sahl, reportedly answered: 'It is God.' Then the question was redefined: 'We intend only that by which life subsists.' And he said: 'It is God.' Ibn al-'Arabī justifies Sahl's terse answer by saying that he saw only God. When those who conversed with Sahl persisted with their questioning saying that they intended the subsistence of this body, Sahl, being aware of their misunderstanding, turned to another answer, stating: 'Leave the building to its builder; if he wills, he builds it, and if he wills, he destroys it.' Here Ibn al-'Arabī advances his explanation of Sahl's analogy. It is inappropriate for the human soul (*al-laṭīfa al-insāniyya*; literally: the subtle entity of the human being) to accompany the body. Yet God, the soul's beloved and the cause of its life, obliges it to dwell in this body. This explanation is correct, says our author, if Sahl holds the same absence of disengagement of the soul from the body as I do. However, if he holds disengagement of the soul from

31. *Fut.*III:478; *FM.*II:318, ll.30–3; *SPK*, p.149.

32. *Fut.*V:60; *FM.*III:41, ll.7–10. The Jewish mystic Baḥyā ibn Paqūda also holds that the intellect has a double function: that of gaining knowledge of God's existence, unity and attributes, and that of fighting evil. Baḥyā ibn Paqūda, *Kitāb al-Hidāya ilā farā'iḍ al-qulūb* (*The Book of Direction to the Duties of the Heart*), Chaps 1, 2, 5, Section 5.

33. *Rasā'il Ibn al-'Arabī*, Part II:27.

the body, Sahl still prefers God over any entity which accompanies one (*maṣḥūb*).[34]

Ibn al-ʿArabī relates that he met Sahl in his Vision of the Light of the Hiddenness (*tajallī nūr al-ghayb*, paragraph 74 in the *Kitāb al-Tajalliyāt*) and asked him how many lights of gnosis exist. Sahl answered that there exist two lights, the light of the intellect and the light of belief.[35] Ibn al-ʿArabī also wished to know the objects of these two kinds of knowledge, and Sahl said that the light of the intellect perceives God's transcendence expressed in Quran 42:11 ('There is none like Him'), while the light of belief perceives God's Essence without limit. To this the Shaykh responded that, notwithstanding what Sahl said regarding the perception of the intellect and belief, he asserted the existence of a veil between God and the human being, which according to Ibn al-ʿArabī signifies the limitation of God. Thereafter he reproved Sahl for speaking of God's unity, for this issue deserves silence. Sahl entered into the state of annihilation and returned from it, and found that Ibn al-ʿArabī was right regarding God's unity. Strangely enough, as is well known, Ibn al-ʿArabī himself deals with God's unity in his writings.[36] However, our author seems to say that it is not appropriate for Sahl and persons like him to speak of God's unity. Ibn al-ʿArabī continued the conversation with Sahl, asking him, 'What is my position in relation to you?' To this Sahl answered, 'You are the leader in the science of God's unity, for you know what I have not known concerning this station.' Thereupon, at the end of this paragraph, Ibn al-ʿArabī positions Sahl on the luminary side of the science of unity and associates him with Dhū al-Nūn.[37]

> The happy person is the one his Lord is pleased with, and there is none but is pleased in the eyes of his Lord, because the Lordship applies to him,

34. *Fut.*III:532; *FM.*II:355, ll.14–18.
35. Cf. *Fuṣūṣ al-ḥikam*, p.85.
36. See, for example, *Fuṣūṣ*, Chap. 10.
37. I do not understand Ibn al-ʿArabī's last words regarding Sahl's position and the connection with Dhū al-Nūn.

> and hence the Lord finds him pleasing, and as a result he is happy. For this reason Sahl said: 'The Lordship has a mystery – and it is you' (meaning that) Sahl's saying refers to every entity – (because) if it had disappeared, the Lordship would have been cancelled.[38] The words 'if it had disappeared' signify the impossibility of the impossibility (*imtinā' al-imtinā'*),[39] for the condition will not appear and hence the Lordship will not be annulled, because an entity is existent only through its lord. Since an entity is always existent, the Lordship will never be cancelled.[40]

This paragraph in the *Fuṣūṣ al-ḥikam* has no equivalent in the *Futūḥāt*; it signifies the connection between every being and the entity which governs it.

To sum up, Ibn al-'Arabī considers al-Tustarī as his master and leader. He is influenced by him on some issues, such as regarding revelation from various angles, the impact of Muhammad on revelations, the prostration of the heart, and intention. However, this agreement with al-Tustarī does not prevent him from criticizing Sahl on several points, nor continuing al-Tustarī's polemics when he feels that these have not reached a satisfying conclusion in keeping with the truth. This attitude is characteristic of Ibn al-'Arabī's treatment of the Sufis.

38. Every individual is under the control of a divine name which serves as his lord. The divine name is revealed only through the servant, here indicated by the word 'you' (*anta*) hence it is a mystery, or a hidden thing, unless it is disclosed in the servant. However, since the servant is a self-manifestation of the Lord, it cannot disappear. *SPK*, p. 55; H. Corbin, *Alone with the Alone*, pp. 121ff.

39. This conditional sentence means that, because the occurrence of the condition is impossible, the conditioned thing cannot take place. Ibn al-'Arabī immediately explains this notion.

40. *Fuṣūṣ*, pp. 90f.

Abū Saʿīd al-Kharrāz

?–899

Abū Saʿīd Aḥmad ibn ʿĪsā al-Kharrāz was affiliated with the mystical school of Baghdad and linked with some important mystics of his period, among them Sarī al-Saqaṭī, Bishr al-Ḥāfī and Dhū al-Nūn al-Miṣrī. Al-Kharrāz strove to reconcile ecstatic mysticism with orthodoxy. The doctrine of annihilation (*fanāʾ*) of one's consciousness and subsistence (*baqāʾ*) in the contemplation of Godhead was so fundamental in his thought that he stated that the mystic loses his human attributes and assimilates the attributes of God. Al-Junayd refuted this doctrine and al-Sarrāj considered it heretical.[1]

Ibn al-ʿArabī mentions al-Kharrāz only in connection with a few issues; however, he holds him in high esteem, reckoning him among the People of Blame, the most perfect of the gnostics, along with Muhammad and Abū Bakr al-Ṣiddīq, and two early Sufis, Ḥamdūn al-Qaṣṣār (d.884) and al-Bisṭāmī.[2] Al-Kharrāz first appears in *al-Futūḥāt al-Makkiyya* as holding the notion that only God knows God.[3] A group of speculative theologians (*mutakallimūn*), whom Ibn al-ʿArabī knew, attacked al-Kharrāz, al-Ghazālī and others for holding this view. They were Ashʿarite theologians who believed that God has essential attributes known to human beings.[4] As is well known, our author maintains the transcendence of God's essence and the mere knowledge of His names acting in the world.[5]

1. W. Madelung, 'Al-Kharrāz', in *EI*. Al-Hujwīrī, *Kashf al-maḥjūb*, trans. R.A. Nicholson, pp.242–6.
2. *Fut.*V:50; *FM.*III:34, ll.9–14; *SPK*, pp.314, 372.
3. *Fut.*II:443; *FM.*I:681, l.28.
4. *Fut.*I:244; *FM.*I:160, ll.4–15.
5. *Fut.*I:287; *FM.*I:189f.

However, according to al-Kharrāz there is only one characteristic of God which the human being can know, and that is God's joining of contraries (*jamʿ bayna al-ḍiddayni*), a principle to which Quran 57:3 attests ('He is the First and the Last, the Manifest and the Hidden').[6] Contrary to the speculative theologians and the philosophers, explains Ibn al-ʿArabī, who hold that this principle is relative, meaning that God is Manifest in one respect and Hidden in another, al-Kharrāz believes that this combination of contraries applies to the same respect.[7] By this principle, al-Kharrāz seems to be saying that with respect to a given phenomenon God is both Manifest and Hidden at the same time. Ibn al-ʿArabī relates that he was told in a dream (*wāqiʿa;* literally: incident)[8] that God is above incomparability (*tanzīh*) through anthropomorphism (*tashbīh*) and above anthropomorphism through incomparability. Al-Kharrāz's dictum that God is known through His joining of contraries appears to be corroboration.[9] It is worth noting that in three basic books on Sufism and in al-Kharrāz's *Kitāb al-Ṣidq* I did not find this notion ascribed to al-Kharrāz.[10] Possibly the Shaykh read another source or learned this principle from one of al-Kharrāz's sayings. Al-Kharrāz says that 'every hidden thing (*bāṭin*) which is contradicted by a manifest thing (*ẓāhir*) is untrue'.[11] Consequently, the true hidden thing coincides with the manifest thing, which may mean that there are things that are simultaneously hidden and manifest.

Elsewhere Ibn al-ʿArabī tries to explain God's joining of contraries through referring to what happens in our world. The phenomena in the world are many and created one after another, so we can say that this accident (*ʿaraḍ*) was created first and after its

6. *Fut.*IV:193, VII:369; *FM.*II:500, ll.10–21, IV:251, ll.25–6.

7. *Fut.*VII:414; *FM.*IV:282, l.31. *Fuṣūṣ al-ḥikam*, p.77.

8. Or a vision. *SPK*, p.404, n.24.

9. *Fut.*II:543, III:62f.; *FM.*I:751, l.1 – 752, l.1, II:40, l.35 – 41, l.5. *Tarjumān al-ashwāq*, p.90.

10. Al-Qushayrī, *Al-Risāla al-Qushayriyya*; Al-Sarrāj, *Kitāb al-Lumaʿ fī'l-taṣawwuf*, ed. R.A. Nicholson; and al-Sulamī's *Ṭabaqāt al-ṣūfiyya*, ed. Nūr al-Dīn Shurayba.

11. Al-Qushayrī, *Risāla*, p.47, para.222; al-Sulamī, *Ṭabaqāt*, p.231.

disappearance God created another accident, which is the second after the first. However, God is one, so it is inconceivable to ascribe being the first to Him and being the second to humanity, because God and humanity are two different entities. Consequently, His being the First is equal to His being the Last. This perception is not attained by reason and moreover is scarcely perceived.[12] Only those who are acquainted with divine knowledge which is given by revelation gain the knowledge of joining contraries. However, the Shaykh al-Akbar tries to elucidate the joining of contraries through the concept of the possible things. The possible things are identical with the fixed entities (*aʿyān thābita*), which are at the same time first and last, because of the possibility of their becoming concrete in the manifest things and at the same time their staying in the state of possibility. Hence, just as the possible thing which becomes concrete after its absence does not lose its characteristic as a possible thing, so God, the Necessary Existent, when creating the world, does not lose His attribute of being necessary by virtue of Himself. In other words, just as the possible thing is both concrete and virtual at the same time, so God is both First and Last.[13]

Another explanation of God's joining contraries, that is, His being the First and the Last, is based on the structure of the human being, which is composed of different attributes and acts that are sometimes contradictory, such as motion and repose. Al-Kharrāz, says the Shaykh, states that just as it is possible to perform the prayer of Friday (*ṣalāt al-jumʿa*) in two or more mosques in one city (*miṣr*), so it is possible for God to have different names, each possessing its own sphere (*ʿālam*) of activity. Even if all God's names are different concerning their relationship to their objects (*taʿaddadat bi'l-nisab*), they derive from one essence.[14] This perception is reminiscent

12. However, the arguments for joining contraries are rational. Revelation whose content is rational appears in Ibn al-ʿArabī's writings. *Qiyās* (analogy) is legitimate when it is revealed. B. Abrahamov, 'Ibn al-ʿArabī's theory of knowledge', *JMIAS*, 42 (2007), Part II, pp. 17f.

13. *Fut.*I:287f.; *FM.*I:189, l.14 – 190, l.1.

14. *Fut.*II:125; *FM.*I:461, l.32 – 462, l.8.

of the theologians' and philosophers' solution to the problem of the multiplicity of God's attributes *vis-á-vis* His one essence. The Baṣrian Muʿtazilite Abū al-Hudhayl al-ʿAllāf (d.*c*.844) held that God knows by virtue of His essence (*ʿālim bi-dhātihi*) and all His other attributes are related to His essence in this manner.[15] Abū al-Barakāt al-Baghdādī (d. after 1164–65), the Jewish philosopher who became a Muslim, states in his *Kitab al-Muʿtabar*[16] that 'God, may He be exalted, has names that are applied to Him because of the notions that are made known through them .... Not one among these names indicates His essence.'[17]

A specific angle of the phenomenon of joining contraries is attested in the personality of the gnostic (*ʿārif*). Basing himself on Quran 11:123 ('All things [literally: the whole matter] will be returned to Him') and Quran 11:34 ('You will be returned to Him'), Ibn al-ʿArabī explains the 'return' as bringing back to the root (*radd ilā al-aṣl*), which means in turn going back to God, their Creator. The gnostics know that their essence is God's essence (*al-ḥaqq ʿaynuhum*). As an example, our author says that, contrary to the ordinary human being, the gnostic simultaneously experiences the state of perfect joy and ease (*basṭ*) and the state of constraint and compression of the soul (*qabḍ*).[18] According to al-Kharrāz, the gnostic is similar to God and to the whole world, which joins in itself contrary accidents, such as motion and rest, composition and separation. The world and the gnostic were created in the image of God, hence, they also have the trait of joining contraries.[19] In this context, Ibn al-ʿArabī reminds us that Dhū al-Nūn indicates the same notion.[20]

15. Al-Ashʿarī, *Maqālāt al-Islāmiyyīn wa-ikhtilāf al-muṣallīn*, ed. H. Ritter, pp.165, 484f.

16. S. Pines (trans.), 'Studies in Abū'l-Barakāt al-Baghdādī's physics and metaphysics', in *The Collected Works of Shlomo Pines*, Vol. I:128.

17. Ibid. pp.307f., n.148.

18. For these two terms see *Dimensions*, pp.128f.

19. *Fut.*IV:211; *FM.*II:512, ll.12–19.

20. See pp.23f. above.

Elsewhere Ibn al-ʿArabī states that the knowledge of joining contraries constitutes the knowledge of God's Oneness (*waḥdāniyya*), for one knows that there is unity in manyness. According to our author, the prominent figure in this blessed waystation (*manzil*) is al-Kharrāz. Ibn al-ʿArabī attests that he heard this from al-Kharrāz, probably by way of a dream or a vision, and knows that it is the truth. It is not a waystation attained by reason; on the contrary, reason denies this, but only revelation affirms it.[21]

Ibn al-ʿArabī tells us that he saw al-Kharrāz in a vision and taught him that God's unity is an objective value which has no relation to personal perceptions. The discovery of this unity in the world is the aim of all people. In a tone of somewhat moderate reproval he said to al-Kharrāz: 'You preceded us in time, but we preceded you in our awareness (*bi-mā narā;* read *narā* instead of *tarā*) (of the nature of unity).' As a result, al-Kharrāz felt ashamed.[22] Once again we see that our author does not hesitate to criticize his predecessors whenever he considers such criticism appropriate.

Another aspect of joining opposites is connected with God's place. On the one hand God is depicted as sitting on the Throne (Quran 20:5), while on the other He is near to human beings (Quran 53:9). A *ḥadīth* also ascribes descent to the heaven of this world to Him. However, says Ibn al-ʿArabī, ascent and descent are equal with regard to God, which means that His essence is unknown and not limited by any limitation. And this is the core of al-Kharrāz's statement concerning God's joining of opposites.[23]

That the possible (*mumkin*) joins with the impossible (or the absurd; *muḥāl*) thing is part of the principle which applies to God alone. God's presence can make one thing be in two places at once, which means that the absurd is like the possible concerning its concrete existence.[24]

21. *Fut.*IV:351, 433; *FM.*II:605, ll.9–17, 660, ll.14–25; cf. *SPK*, pp. 59, 112, 115f.
22. *Kitāb al-Tajalliyāt*, in *Rasāʾil Ibn al-ʿArabī*, para. 65.
23. Ibid. Vol. VII, pp. 57f.
24. Ibid. p. 414.

Al-Junayd

830–910

Al-Junayd was the head of Baghdad's mystical school. His only extant works are his epistles (*Rasā'il al-Junayd*), published by Ali Hassan Abdel-Kader.[1] He deals mainly with God's unity (*tawḥīd*), which he describes as being attained only through passing away from one's consciousness (*fanā'*) and being present in God. After this process takes place, the mystic returns to his consciousness and to sobriety. The doctrines of God's unity and human sobriety (*ṣaḥw*) make up the principles of al-Junayd's system of mysticism.[2] To declare God's unity means to detach the Everlasting, His essence, attributes and acts, from all else which is produced in time (*ifrād al-qadīm 'an al-muḥdath*).[3] The mystic's *fanā'* does not mean total annihilation in God, but submissiveness to God's will. Hence when the mystic returns to his consciousness, his personality is entirely altered to such a degree that he can influence others to imitate his moral traits and mystical behaviour.[4]

Al-Junayd discourses on two systems of attaining knowledge; the first is discursive and the second intuitive. Reason leads the mystic to God's unification; however, when he loses his individuality he no longer needs his intellect, because he now feels God's unity.[5]

After this very brief exposition of al-Junayd's mystical principles I now turn to his appearance in Ibn al-'Arabī's *al-Futūḥāt al-Makkiyya* and other writings. Al-Junayd belongs to the class of saints Ibn al-'Arabī calls the prophets among the saints (*anbiyā' al-*

1. A.H. Abdel-Kader (ed. and trans.), *The Life, Personality and Writings of al-Junayd.*
2. Ibid. pp.66f.
3. Ibid. p.70.
4. Ibid. pp.88–91.
5. Ibid. pp.99–102.

awliyā'). He defines this class as those who experience a revelation in which Muhammad appears conveying to them the divine laws, which causes them to believe in these laws with certainty and behave accordingly. A prophetic tradition, 'the scholars of this community are the prophets of the Children of Israel' is interpreted by Ibn al-ʿArabī to mean that the Muslim scholars are affiliated with the rank of the prophets among the saints mentioned above. Al-Junayd, says the Shaykh, is a member of this group which 'keeps the prophetic state, the heavenly knowledge and the divine secret' (*ḥifẓ al-ḥāl al-nabawī, al-ʿilm al-ladunī, al-sirr al-ilāhī*).[6]

Ibn al-ʿArabī holds al-Junayd in high esteem, and his evaluation does not differ from the opinion of other Muslim scholars, even speculative scholars, who admire him.[7] First, Ibn al-ʿArabī calls him the master of this community (*sayyid hādhihi al-ṭā'ifa*).[8] The author's attitude toward specific geographic places which influence delicate hearts demonstrates this further. Just as there is a hierarchy of spiritual ranks (*manāzil rūḥaniyya*), there is a hierarchy of material places (*manāzil jismāniyya*). One location of significance is of course Mecca. Other places brought as further examples of such influence are the house of Abū Yazīd al-Bisṭāmī, which is called the house of the pious (*bayt al-abrār*),[9] and the *zāwiya* (literally: corner, viz. the solitary dwelling place of a shaykh)[10] of al-Junayd.[11]

Before entering into my discussion of al-Junayd's appearances by name in the *Futūḥāt*, I would like to suggest that one of Ibn al-ʿArabī's principal ideas seems to me to derive from, *inter alia*, the teachings of al-Junayd. Like al-Kharrāz, al-Junayd believes that two opposites exist in one individual; the mystic can be in God's presence rising into the state of losing his self (*fanā'*), and at the

6. *Fut.*I:229–31; *FM.*I:149–52. For the relation between prophets and saints see *Seal*, especially Chaps. 3 and 5.

7. Abdel-Kader, *al-Junayd*, p. 6.

8. *Fut.*II:371, IV:331; *FM.*I:631, ll.18–19, II:591, l.31.

9. See pp. 36f. above.

10. *Dimensions*, p. 231.

11. *Fut.*I:153f.; *FM.*I:99, ll.5–9.

same time remain in a state of sobriety (*ṣaḥw*), that is, present in society. Each of these two states depends on employing a certain aspect.[12] In Ibn al-ʿArabī's thought this system of the perception of existence is prevalent; God is both transcendent and immanent.

In paragraph 54 of the *Kitāb al-Tajalliyāt*,[13] called the Vision of Debate (*tajallī al-munāẓara*), Ibn al-ʿArabī relates that God brings some of His servants into His presence (*aḥḍarahum al-ḥaqq fīhi*), then removes them from His presence, just as He caused them to be present before. Hence, Ibn al-ʿArabī concludes, their presence is the same as their absence, meaning God's presence and absence from their point of view is one. This is the station of the creation of states (*maqām ījād al-aḥwāl*). Our author relates that he met al-Junayd when they achieved the same station. Regarding the presence–absence issue, al-Junayd said that the identification of God's presence with His absence has only one meaning. Ibn al-ʿArabī responded to al-Junayd: 'You should speak only through using aspects, because speaking in an absolute manner in the inappropriate place contradicts the realities.' By this the Shaykh seems to be saying that with respect to the realities, that is, things existing in the concrete world, God is present, because He manifests Himself in them; however, with respect to His essence, He is absent. You can hold God's presence and absence at the same time, says Ibn al-ʿArabī, only when you take into account the different aspects of His presence and absence. Although his position was paradoxical Al-Junayd refused to surrender it, but without explaining how it works, and Ibn al-ʿArabī could not persuade him to change his mind.

In paragraph 58, entitled the Vision of the Sea of Unity, Ibn al-ʿArabī likens God's unity to the depth of the sea and its shore. One can speak about the shore, because it is known, while the depth of the sea can only be experienced (*al-lujja tudhāqu*). With

12. Abdel-Kader, *al-Junayd*, pp. 66, 91.

13. This word can also be rendered as 'theophanies' or divine self-disclosures. Vision emphasizes the role of the human being who experiences God's self-manifestation in various contexts.

this statement he seems to suggest that one can define God's unity but the depth of its meaning is attained only by experience. Ibn al-ʿArabī relates that in his vision he stood on the shore of the sea and then entered its depth and remained there in the centre. Thereafter, he met al-Junayd and they kissed and embraced each other. Then both of them were drowned in the sea's depth and died, not hoping for life or resurrection. Actually, Ibn al-ʿArabī describes here a state of annihilation (*fanāʾ*) in God's essence, in which he and al-Junayd wish to stay forever without returning to society. It is quite uncharacteristic of Ibn al-ʿArabī's thought that the mystic returns from his mystical experience to live with ordinary people. However, such is the case of Sahl al-Tustarī in contrast to al-Ḥallāj's continuous intoxication.

Another point to be stressed regarding this story is the affection our author feels toward al-Junayd. He shares with him the same experience and the same hope.

In paragraph 67 Ibn al-ʿArabī adds new information to that given in paragraph 58. He points out that he and al-Junayd died in the depth of the sea of unity because they drank too much from it, beyond their capacity to withstand it. In this place they met Yūsuf ibn al-Ḥusayn, one of Dhū al-Nūn's followers, who said to them that he had been thirsty for God's unity and then had quenched his thirst. Ibn al-ʿArabī responded immediately, asking him how his knowledge of quenching his thirst matched his statement that one who seeks unity can quench his thirst only by the Real. That is because the inferior person may quench his thirst by what the superior makes him drink, hence no one quenches his thirst. As a result, relates Ibn al-ʿArabī, Yūsuf ibn al-Ḥusayn realized his station and Ibn al-ʿArabī established for him a ladder of ascension to God which is not known by every gnostic.[14] Ibn al-ʿArabī's approach to God's unity is part of his attitude toward

14. According to Ibn al-ʿArabī, each mystic has his own ladder of ascension to God. *SPK*, p.219.

knowledge in general. In his view, since the cosmos, as God's self-manifestation, is infinite, so knowledge of it is infinite: 'Hence, the seeker of knowledge is like him who drinks the water of the sea. The more he drinks, the thirstier he becomes.'[15] It is worth noting that the metaphor of drinking and quenching one's thirst appears in the context of both knowledge and God's unity.

In this vision with al-Junayd Ibn al-ʿArabī also met Ibn ʿAṭāʾ, who was executed because he was al-Ḥallāj's most faithful friend.[16] Ibn al-ʿArabī relates[17] that when Ibn ʿAṭāʾ was riding his camel someone plunged the animal into the water. Thereupon, Ibn ʿAṭāʾ said: 'May God be exalted' (*jall Allāh*), by which he meant God is the most elevated. The camel said: 'God's exaltation is greater than your saying', by which the camel, who appears more cognizant of God than Ibn ʿAṭāʾ, meant God is everywhere and not only in heaven, that is, in an elevated place. And Ibn al-ʿArabī ordered Ibn ʿAṭāʾ to repent, because his teacher was a camel. Possibly this story reflects the Shaykh's unfavourable attitude toward al-Ḥallāj and his teachings.

Ibn al-ʿArabī, it seems, misses no opportunity to teach early Sufis lessons in mystical issues. Thus, in paragraph 66 of the *Kitāb al-Tajalliyāt*, entitled the Vision of the Unity of the Lordship (*tajallī tawḥīd*[18] *al-rubūbiyya*), the Shaykh writes that he saw al-Junayd in this vision and asked him about his position regarding God's unity. Behind this question lies al-Junayd's principle that God's unity is one and cannot be divided into various aspects. However, Ibn al-ʿArabī leads al-Junayd to admit that the unity of God's Lordship comprises the position of the Lord and the position of the servant,

15. *Fut.*IV:271; *FM.*II:552f.; *SPK*, p.153.

16. *Dimensions*, p.77; *Kitāb al-Tajalliyāt*, in *Rasāʾil Ibn al-ʿArabī*, para.68.

17. This story appears, with slight differences in each version, in *Fut.*VI:280f., VII:278, VIII:215; *FM.*III:489, ll.21–2, IV:189, ll.2–4, IV:431, ll.25–8.

18. Literally *tawḥīd* means to profess or to declare God's oneness, but sometimes this word appears in the meaning of oneness, that is, the principle that God or one of His names are one.

and al-Junayd can only know both positions by not being identified with either of them.

If I understand the Shaykh al-Akbar's idea correctly, he wishes to say that from an ontological point of view there is no difference between the Lord and the servant, hence one cannot affiliate himself with either, although from an epistemological point of view a difference between the two does exist. In an analogy to this diagnosis, the Shaykh teaches al-Junayd the difference between Divinity (*ulūhiyya*), the term denoting all the relationships between God and the cosmos which are expressed through His names and attributes, and the term Lordship (*rubūbiyya*), denoting one specific kind of relationship between God and humans. As a result, our author attributes unity to both Divinity and Lordship, just as unity exists in each and every name of God. Listening to Ibn al-ʿArabī's lesson, al-Junayd was ashamed and remained silent. Ibn al-ʿArabī comforted him, saying: 'What excellent people you the predecessors were, and what excellent people we the successors were!' Al-Junayd did not feel relief, because he had transmitted this erroneous idea of God's unity to other Sufis, and how could this be corrected? Ibn al-ʿArabī responded: 'Do not be afraid, one who has left behind [a successor] like me has lost nothing. I am your successor and you are my brother.'[19] Ibn al-ʿArabī concludes this paragraph with the statement that al-Junayd knows now what he did not know before.

Ibn al-ʿArabī mentions al-Junayd at the very beginning of the introduction to the *Futūḥāt*. He elaborates on the epistemological principle of attaining knowledge through emptying the mind when engaging in seclusion and invoking God's name. In this state God bestows knowledge of Him and of divine secrets on the mystic. As corroboration for this system Ibn al-ʿArabī cites Quran verses (18:65, 2:282, 8:29, 57:28), according to which God teaches the human beings, as well as al-Junayd's and Abū Yazīd al-Bisṭāmī's

19. *Nā'ib* (successor) can also be rendered as vicegerent or deputy.

experiences. Al-Junayd was asked: 'Through what did you achieve that which you achieved (meaning apparently his vast knowledge)?' He answered: 'Through staying in this stage (*daraja*) for thirty years.'[20] Along with al-Bisṭāmī, al-Junayd serves as a model for Ibn al-ʿArabī. Elsewhere, al-Junayd is introduced as a mystic who shares the same experience as the Shaykh.[21]

In Chapter 44 of the *Futūḥāt* Ibn al-ʿArabī explains the meaning of the term *wārid* (literally: that which comes or appears) as God's sudden revelation to the mystic. This kind of revelation causes the mystic to be totally deprived of his sense perception and awareness of the exterior world. The Shaykh refers to such a person as *majnūn*, one who is curtained (*mastūr*) from his own self. The verb *janna* means essentially 'he concealed', and those who experience the *wārid* are named rational persons who are detached from their self (*ʿuqalāʾ al-majānīn*).[22] Ibn al-ʿArabī divides the people who enter this station into three ranks according to the measure of the *wārid*'s impact on the individual's self-awareness and the duration of this impact.[23]

At the end of the chapter, Ibn al-ʿArabī relates his own experience in this station, saying that once when serving as an imam (prayer leader) he was completely unaware of all the actions he performed as if he had been asleep. In this context he tells us about al-Junayd who also tasted the station of *wārid*. When al-Junayd was told about al-Shiblī's experience, he said: 'When I was in the state of my absence (*ḥāl ghaybatī*), I was seeing myself amidst the general light and the greatest revelation ... devoid of motion and separated from soul and seeing it before God bowing and prostrating, knowing that it is I who bows and prostrates, and this is like the seeing of a sleeper.'[24] Al-Junayd's experience, undoubtedly, serves

20. *Fut.*I:54; *FM.*I:31, l.8.
21. *Fut.*I:378; *FM.*I:250, ll.15–19. *Kitāb al-Tajalliyāt*, in *Rasāʾil Ibn al-ʿArabī*, para. 59.
22. *Fut.*I:375; *FM.*I:248, ll.12–15. The translation of *ʿuqalāʾ al-majānīn* as 'rational madmen' (*SPK*, p.266), does not convey the exact meaning intended by the author.
23. *Fut.*I:376; *FM.*I:248, ll.27ff.; *SPK*, pp.266f.
24. *Fut.*I:378; *FM.*I:250, ll.15–19.

here to corroborate the author's station of passing outside of consciousness.

One of the Shaykh's ideas concerns the way in which the soul's traits are established. According to him, the overflow which stems from the Godhead and penetrates every human being is uniform, and what sets up the unique human personality is the composition of one's body. As a confirmative source, he cites al-Junayd. Asked about gnosis and the gnostic (*maʿrifa*, *ʿārif*), al-Junayd said: 'The colour of the water is the colour of its vessel' (*lawn al-māʾ lawn ināʾihi*). By this dictum he means to express the idea that God's bestowal is identical concerning each individual; however, it changes according to the place in which it inheres.[25]

Elsewhere Ibn al-ʿArabī brings in this saying of al-Junayd to prove that one cannot escape the notion of duality.[26] For example, God is one, but when He manifests Himself there are two entities: God and His manifestation, although all derive from Him. Al-Junayd's saying also affirms the existence of two entities: the *ʿārif* (the vessel) and the *maʿrifa* (the water). In addition, the author uses al-Junayd's statement to convey the idea of the different forms of God's manifestations. God's revelation is one (the water), but its manifestations (the vessels) are many and various.[27]

Still another use of this saying occurs in Chapter 334 of the *Futūḥāt* in the context of the relationship between the Quran and the believers. Water represents the Quran, and the heart of the believer, the vessel. The holy text is renewed each time it is recited according to the receiver's heart, called here the throne of the heart.[28] In my view, this idea is connected with Ibn al-ʿArabī's statement concerning the interpretation of the Quran: everyone sees in the Quran what he wants to see. Since the Quran is a

25. *Fut.*I:430; *FM.*I:285, l.14. *Fuṣūṣ al-ḥikam*, pp.225f.
26. *Fut.*II:452; *FM.*I:688, ll.9–14.
27. *Fut.*IV:339; *FM.*II:597, ll.4–6.
28. *Fut.*V:189; *FM.*III:128, ll.3–5.

comprehensive book which contains all the divine realities, every existent finds in it what he wants.[29]

In Chapter 341, the Shaykh further elucidates al-Junayd's saying, placing it this time in the context of knowledge. One of Ibn al-ʿArabī's principal statements in this chapter is 'You should know that you cannot judge your object of knowledge (*maʿrūf*) except through your thinking (literally: but through you: *illā bika*), for you know nothing else.' This statement actually explains not only the existence of different views among people but also different kinds of religions; all are but manifestations of God's existence, which cannot be limited. According to Ibn al-ʿArabī, the people of God (the mystics: *ahl Allāh*) must know every sect and religion in order to witness God in every form, because God pervades existence (*sārin fī'l-wujūd*). Hence, one should not limit God's manifestations.[30]

Notwithstanding the equal position of views and religions as God's manifestations, and actually in keeping with his own ideology, Ibn al-ʿArabī frequently employs another of al-Junayd's statements to demonstrate his adherence to the tenets of Islam. Al-Junayd says: 'Our knowledge (that is, mystical knowledge) is bound (*muqayyad*) by the Book (the Quran) and the Sunna (Tradition).'[31]

First, this statement serves as corroboration for Ibn al-ʿArabī's declaration that he has not deviated from the teachings of the Quran and the Sunna. His knowledge derives from the Quran and the Sunna, which serve as two witnesses of his knowledge.[32] However, the Shaykh also says two ways lead to knowledge: the first is built on the principles of religion and the second on reason. These two different ways lead to one object of knowledge (*al-maʿlūm wāḥid wa'l-ṭarīq mukhtalif*). Ibn al-ʿArabī thus creates a

29. *Fut.*V:137; *FM.*III:94, ll.1–3. Cf. I. Almond, *Sufism and Deconstruction*, p.67.

30. *Fut.*V:239; *FM.*III:161, ll.16–17.

31. *Fut.*II:41; *FM.*I:404, l.14. Another version of this dictum reads: 'Our knowledge is built (*mushayyad*) by the Book and the Sunna.' *Fut.*II:337; *FM.*I:607, l.35.

32. *Fut.*II:336; *FM.*I:607, ll.25–6.

compromise between revelation and reason, claiming that both devices direct human beings to the same aim. This is not a new idea in Islam; we encounter similar notions in the writings of the early theologians.[33] Even divine revelation experienced by mystics results from the acts of the mystics according to the Quran and the Sunna.[34] It seems that in Ibn al-ʿArabī's view the Quran and the Sunna have three functions:

1. To be sources of knowledge.
2. To serve as the incentive to mystical experience.
3. To serve as criteria of knowledge and to judge the two other foundations of Islamic law (*uṣūl al-fiqh*), that is, the consensus (*ijmāʿ*) and the analogy (*qiyās*).

Al-Junayd said: 'Our knowledge is bound by the Quran and the Sunna, and they both are the active foundations (*aṣlāni fāʿilāni*), while the consensus and the analogy are proved to be right and their teachings are valid (*yathbutāni wa-taṣiḥḥu dalālatuhumā*) through the Quran and the Sunna, for they (the consensus and the analogy) are the passive foundations' (*aṣlāni munfaʿilāni*).[35]

Elsewhere Ibn al-ʿArabī adds to this dictum the words 'And this is the balance', meaning that the Quran and the Sunna are the balance of ideas. There are ideas not mentioned in the Quran and the Sunna, but to gauge their validity they should be weighed up against the balance of these two fundamental devices. Frequently, Ibn al-ʿArabī says, reason rejects what the saints receive through revelation; however, if a prophet or a messenger expressed these ideas, they would have been accepted. Ibn al-ʿArabī extends the

33. *Fut.*II:337; *FM.*I:607, l.24 – 608, l.2. B. Abrahamov, *Islamic Theology*, Chap. 6.

34. *Fut.*II:371; *FM.*I:631, ll.18–24.

35. *Fut.*III:243; *FM.*II:162, ll.16–17. It is worth noting that the number four plays an important role in Ibn al-ʿArabī's thought. Here, apart from the four foundations of the law, he mentions the four divine realities, that is, the four creative attributes: Life, Knowledge, Will and Power; the four traits of the bodies: heat, coldness, dryness and wetness, the four elements: fire, air, water and earth; the four temperaments: the yellow, the black, the blood and the phlegm. He seems to have been influenced in this matter by the Ikhwān al-Ṣafā', who, in turn, learned the importance of the number four from Pythagoras. *Fut.*III:243f.; *FM.*II:162, ll.17–21. I.R. Netton, *Muslim Neoplatonists*, pp. 10f.

scope of the Book and the Sunna to include all that which a prophet, among the prophets from Adam to Muhammad, states.[36] Consequently, the range of these two devices is widened, so that they include both the Jewish and Christian traditions as expressed in the Bible and the New Testament respectively. So, in truth, and opposed to the dictum's literal meaning, knowledge is not so limited, and the mystic's experiences should be accepted so long as they do not explicitly contradict the tenets of Islam. In another chapter (314), the Greatest Master states that the saint should both refrain from deviating from God's Book and not order people to know laws which abrogate his own laws.[37]

In Chapter 543, Ibn al-ʿArabī reiterates the notion of the scales of a balance representing the Book and the Sunna. This time he emphasizes that learning from the Messenger is absolute, whereas learning from God, that is, revelation, must be determined by this measuring device. He justifies this weighing process, which he derives from God, by citing Quranic verses which teach that God deceives people: for example, 'We deceived them, while they were not aware' (Quran 27:50).[38] It seems to me that, according to Ibn al-ʿArabī, not all that is revealed to people is really divine. Hence, one needs the balance in order to know whether what one regards as revelation is actually revelation.[39]

A passage that establishes the relationship between reason (*ʿaql*), religious matters (*sharīʿa*) and the truth (*ḥaqīqa*) occurs in Chapter 559. These three elements are compared to a fruit which has shell,

36. *Fut.*V:12; *FM.*III:8, ll.10–21.

37. *Fut.*V:81; *FM.*III:56, ll.1–5.

38. See also Quran 7:182, 183, 86:16, 3:54. The verse cited above deals with God's hastening the punishment of the people of Thamūd as a reaction to Thamūd's deception.

39. *Fut.*VII:274f.; *FM.*IV:186, ll.32–3. The notion that the Book and the Sunna serve as the balance of mystical experience also appears in the teachings of other Sufis. For example, Sahl al-Tustarī states: 'Every ecstatic experience (*wajd*) to which the Book and Sunna do not bear witness is false.' Al-Sarrāj, *Kitāb al-Lumaʿ fīʾl-taṣawwuf*, ed. R.A. Nicholson. Böwering cites this dictum in *The Mystical Vision of Existence in Classical Islam*, p.72.

core and oil.[40] Just as the shell of the fruit preserves its core and the core preserves the oil, so reason preserves religious matters and those in turn preserve the truth. Religion cannot subsist without reason, nor the truth without religion. It is inconceivable that one claims the truth without relying on religion. Consequently, says Ibn al-ʿArabī, al-Junayd states that 'our knowledge, that is, the truths that the people of God (*ahl Allāh*)[41] bring forth, is bound by the Book and the Sunna, which means that only those who act in keeping with God's Book and the Messenger's Sunna attain such truths'.[42] Ultimately, the Truth is the most important value; however, it cannot be achieved without religion and reason, which serve here as necessary conditions.

Ibn al-ʿArabī creates an amalgamation of revelation, tradition and mystical experience, positioning the last, which shows the truth, at the highest degree, but not ignoring the important role of the first two elements. Al-Junayd's dictum corroborates for him the necessary function of the Book and the Sunna. It is important to note that the mystical experience is not always clear to the mystic. Sometimes he experiences something which he cannot transmit to others. When asked about God's unity, al-Junayd said something that the audience could not understand. They asked him again, and his second answer was more obscure than the first. Upon asking him again to dictate to them his answer so that they could learn it, he answered that if he could arrange in words his experience for himself, he would have been able to dictate it to them (*in kuntu ujrīhi fa-anā umlīhi*). According to the Shaykh, al-Junayd was alluding to the notion that he was unable to express his experience; his experience corresponded to that which was cast

40. It may be a nut, as it appears in al-Ghazālī's *Book of Unity and Trust*. In this book al-Ghazālī compares the ranks of those who utter the *shahāda* (the witness that God is one and that Muhammad is His messenger) to the parts of a nut. Al-Ghazālī, *Iḥyāʾ ʿulūm al-dīn*, al-Maktaba al-Tijāriyya al-Kubrā, Vol. IV, pp. 245f.

41. This is a term which denotes the greatest friends of God, or the greatest mystics. *SPK*, p. 388, n. 20.

42. *Fut.* VIII:199; *FM.* IV:419, ll. 29–35.

upon him in keeping with the requirements of his present moment (*waqt*).[43] Ibn al-ʿArabī utilizes al-Junayd's sayings to repeat his idea concerning the infinite various phenomena in the world. What the Divine casts on the mystic differs due to the endless variety of every moment, says our author, and nothing repeats itself in existence.[44]

In light of the last paragraph, it is possible to understand another of al-Junayd's dictums: 'no one reaches the rank of [knowing] the Truth (or Reality – *ḥaqīqa*), until a thousand righteous people testify that one is an infidel (*zindīk*)'.[45] Ibn al-ʿArabī explains this phenomenon by saying that the common people cannot identify the great mystics (those who attain the rank of *ḥaqīqa*),[46] for they have no special sign which differentiates them from others; the elite, such as the jurists (*fuqahāʾ*) and the speculative theologians (*aṣḥāb ʿilm al-kalām*) assign to them unbelief (*qālū bi-takfīrihm*). Ibn al-ʿArabī does not indicate the reason for such accusations, and we can only assume that those learned people regard the great mystics as deviating from the orthodox dogma. Finally, philosophers, who do not adhere to the revealed laws, refer to these mystics as mad people because of their false imagination and weak intellect. Hence, only God knows them as they really are. On the question of whether the great mystics know each other, the Shaykh does not answer definitely and thus leaves the issue unresolved.

43. *Waqt* is the moment in which a certain mystical state is bestowed on the mystic. The mystic is so overwhelmed by this state and stands before God's presence without awareness of the past, present and future. Hence, he is called 'the son of the present moment' (*ibn waqtihi*). *Dimensions*, pp. 129f.

44. *Fut.*IV:92; *FM.*II:432, ll.9–12.

45. The term *zindīq* is a word borrowed from the Persian (Pahlavi), in which it denotes a person who adheres to unorthodox commentary of the Sacred Books. In early Islam it designated a Manichean and then one who deviates from the tenets of religion. B. Abrahamov, *Al-Qāsim b. Ibrāhīm on the Proof of God's Existence*, pp. 180f., n.1.

46. This dictum appears also in Chap. 30, which deals with the Poles (*qutb*, pl. *aqtāb*). For this term, see *Dimensions*, index. According to Ibn al-ʿArabī, there are various kinds of Poles; *SPK*, p. 371. Here (*Fut.*I:303; *FM.*I:199, ll.34–5), Ibn al-ʿArabī identifies those who attain the rank of the Truth as the people of knowledge, who know from God that which others do not know.

Ibn al-ʿArabī states emphatically that he wishes to be one of these mystics.[47]

In both the *Futūḥāt* and *Fuṣūṣ* the Greatest Master compares al-Junayd's teaching concerning man's heart to al-Bisṭāmī's. In al-Bisṭāmī's view, the heart of the gnostic is not aware of the particulars of the world placed in the corner of his heart, even if their number is one hundred million. Ibn al-ʿArabī notes that with this number al-Bisṭāmī intends to express the endless number of the existential phenomena, and means that the heart that contains the Eternal cannot feel things created in time (*muḥdath*). Since the gnostic's heart comprises the Real (*al-ḥaqq*), it comprises everything, for everything derives from the Real. In this context the Shaykh prefers al-Junayd's statement, because it is more complete than al-Bisṭāmī's. It reads: 'If the created in time is linked (*qurina*) to the Eternal, there remains no effect (*lam yabqā lahu athar*) belonging to it.'[48]

To my mind, Ibn al-ʿArabī is referring here to the issue of causality. When the Eternal is excluded, effects are caused by things. However, if one takes into account the Eternal in comparison to the created in time, one comes to the conclusion that all effects are caused by the Eternal, not by things. As our author articulates it: 'When one links the created in time with the Eternal, one considers the effect deriving from (or through) the Eternal (*ra'ā al-athar min al-qadīm*) and the created in time is the essence of effect (*ʿayn al-athar*).' By the last words he probably means to say that God produces all effects, hence *athar* is essentially only effect and does not serve as cause. In other words, in relation to the Eternal, all things are effects.[49] Al-Junayd's dictum also occurs in the *Fuṣūṣ* in which Ibn al-ʿArabī elaborates on God's manifestations in the human being's heart: 'Thus, when the heart embraces the Eternal

47. *Fut.*IV:331; *FM.*II:591, l.31 – 592, l.3.

48. Ibn al-ʿArabī, *Kitāb al-Bā'*, in *Majmūʿat rasā'il Ibn al-ʿArabī*, Vol. I:463; *Tarjumān al-ashwāq*, ed. and trans. R.A. Nicholson, p.90, n.19; *al-Tadbīrāt al-ilāhiyya*, p.114, l.3.

49. *Fut.*VII:11f.; *FM.*IV:8, ll.1–14.

One, how can it possibly be aware of what is contingent and created?'[50]

To sum up, Ibn al-ʿArabī admired al-Junayd and learned certain basic tenets of his doctrine from him. The principle that the Truth comes from the Divine and not from rational thinking, and that one should empty his mind of all thoughts to receive revelation, is traced back to al-Junayd, as is 'the colour of the water is the colour of its vessel', used by Ibn al-ʿArabī as a metaphor in a number of different circumstances. Also, the dictum regarding the function of the Quran and the Sunna constitutes a point of departure for our author to deal with important questions such as the relationship between reason, religion and the Truth. All in all, the Greatest Master's discussion of al-Junayd's statements proves the importance of the early Sufis in the creation of Akbarian mystical philosophy.

50. *Fuṣūṣ*, p. 120; *Bezels*, p. 148.

Al-Ḥakīm al-Tirmidhī

?820–?910

After al-Sulamī (d.1021), al-Ḥakīm al-Tirmidhī is the most prolific writer in the classical period of Islamic mysticism, although he is better defined as a theosophist rather than a mystic or a Sufi. He in fact never used the term Sufi in his writings. Despite his literary productivity, the Sufi manuals of the tenth and eleventh centuries, except for Hujwīrī, barely devote any space to him, and al-Sarrāj and Abū Ṭālib al-Makkī do not mention him at all. In al-Kalabādhī and al-Qushayrī he appears only superficially.[1] Al-Sulamī and al-Ghazālī knew of his writings. However, al-Tirmidhī's teachings gained fame primarily because Ibn al-ʿArabī wrote a commentary on his *Sīrat al-awliyāʾ*.[2] The Greatest Master calls al-Tirmidhī 'imam' (leader) and characterizes him as the possessor of perfect mystical experience (*ṣāḥib al-dhawq al-tamm*). The questions al-Tirmidhī asks, says Ibn al-ʿArabī, set out the criteria for examining those who claim sainthood. The answers to these questions are

1. Such is the case in Abū Nuʿaym al-Iṣfahānī's (d.1038) *Ḥilyat al-awliyāʾ wa-ṭabaqāt al-asfiyāʾ*, ed. ʿAbdallāh al-Minshāwī *et al.*, Vol. X, pp.212–14.

2. B. Radtke and J. O'Kane, *The Concept of Sainthood in Early Islamic Mysticism*, pp.2–6. Ibn al-ʿArabī's treatise entitled *al-Jawāb al-mustaqīm ʿamma saʾala ʿanhu al-Tirmidhī al-Ḥakīm* (*The Right Reply to the Questions of al-Tirmidhī al-Ḥakīm*) consists of his answers to al-Tirmidhī's questions. A significant portion of this book was incorporated in Chap. 73 of the *Futūḥāt*; *SPK*, p.396, n.25; *Seal*, p.32. Osman Yahia attaches the text of *al-Jawāb al-mustaqīm* in the margins of his edition of *Khatm al-awliyāʾ*. Actually, it is not a commentary, but a platform which Ibn al-ʿArabī uses to elucidate his own ideas. B. Radtke, 'The concept of Wilāya in early Sufism', in L. Lewisohn (ed.), *The Heritage of Sufism*, Vol. I, p.487.

Osman Yahia published *Sīrat al-awliyāʾ* in 1965 under the title *Khatm al-awliyāʾ*, which is a later title. A new version of the text is now available in Radtke's *Drei Schriften des Theosophen von Tirmidh*. In *Fut.*III:61–207 (*FM.*II:39–139) Ibn al-ʿArabī presents the 155 questions appearing in the *Sīra*. In al-Tirmidhī's text there are 162 questions. Radtke and O'Kane, *Concept*, p.209.

gained neither through rational speculation nor through necessary immediate perception of the intellect, but rather through various kinds of divine revelation.[3]

B. Radtke and J. O'Kane characterize al-Tirmidhi's writings thus:

> Tirmidhī's individual contribution to Islamic intellectual history was the fact that he fused these various given elements[4] with his personal 'mystical' experiences to produce an integrated overview, his own system. It is in this respect that he is an exceptional case for his day and age. In fact, he is the first and, up until the time of Ibn al-ʿArabī, the only mystic author whose writings present a broad synthesis of mystic experience, anthropology, cosmology and Islamic theology.[5]

At the beginning of Chapter 24 of the *Futūḥāt*, Ibn al-ʿArabī mentions al-Tirmidhī as presenting two important ideas:[6]

1. God is the Owner of the Kingdom (*malik al-mulk*).[7]
2. Like God, who commands humans to perform His commandments, humans order God to act for their sake, such as asking Him to forgive them.

The two are interrelated. All things, including humans, belong to God, hence He is their possessor, and also He is a king, because He has vassals. In His capacity as king, He orders His vassals to perform certain acts; however, He is also attentive to their demands, which are expressed in the Quran in the manner of a command. God's obligations toward His vassals is plainly stated in the Quran and conditioned by human acts. For example, Verse 40 in Sura 2 reads: 'If you fulfil My covenant, I shall fulfil your covenant'. Thus, from the point of view of religion, God is obliged to respond to the

3. *Fut.*III:25, 61; *FM.*II:16, ll.7–12, 39, l.33 – 40, l.4.
4. Islamic sciences and Gnostic and Neoplatonic ideas.
5. Radtke and O'Kane, *Concept*, p. 6.
6. Ibn al-ʿArabī is not sure that al-Tirmidhī was the first to express these ideas.
7. *SPK*, pp. 61, 88. From the aspect of His essence, God needs nothing and has no connection to the world, and only as a Lord He refers to the creatures. *Fut.*VI:103, IV:58, V:408, VII:93; *FM.*III:364, ll.2–4, II:410, ll.7–8, III:276, ll.26–8, IV:64, l.1; *Fuṣūṣ al-ḥikam*, p. 71.

fulfilment of humans' obligations and to their orders ('My Lord, forgive me'; *rabbī ighfir lī*. Quran 7:151). As Ibn al-ʿArabī notes, the issue of God's obligations was debated among the speculative theologians.[8]

Ibn al-ʿArabī shares with al-Tirmidhī the notion of the power of the letters of the alphabet. Being emerges out of the letters (*ẓahara al-kawn ʿan al-ḥurūf*), as Quran 16:40 attests: 'When We desire a thing, the only word We say to it is "Be!" and it is.'[9]

Ibn al-ʿArabī also follows al-Tirmidhī in recommending that every person should, after completing a certain prayer, carry out two prostrations (*sajda*) against inattentiveness, because one is not safe from being distracted while in prayer. These two prostrations compel the Devil (*shayṭān*) to draw away from the person who prays.[10]

Without doubt al-Tirmidhī exerted great influence on Ibn al-ʿArabī with regard to the issue of the Friends (or Saints) of God (*awliyāʾ Allāh*).[11] That the *awliyāʾ* are the heirs of the prophets, as the tradition tells us,[12] means not only that the prophecy of legislation and mission (*nubuwwat al-tashrīʿ wa'l-risāla*) has ended,[13] but also the duration of God's revelation which is now bestowed on the *awliyāʾ*. Friendship or Sainthood (*walāya*) is the basic characteristic of everyone who receives God's revelation, be he a messenger who is also a prophet, a prophet, God's friend or saint (*walī*).[14] Moreover, according to the Shaykh 'the *rasūl* is more perfect in his

8. *Fut.*I:277–8; *FM.*I:182f. Abū Madyan (d.1197) adopts al-Tirmidhī's notion of the Owner of Kingdom. *Fut.*I:279; *FM.*I:184, ll.2–6. For the Muʿtazilite approach to God's obligations see B. Abrahamov, *Islamic Theology*, p.136.

9. *Fut.*I:256, 289; *FM.*I:168, 190, ll.12–21; *Fuṣūṣ*, p.116.

10. *Fut.*II:159; *FM.*I:485, ll.10–12.

11. B. Radtke, 'A forerunner of Ibn al-ʿArabī: Hakīm Tirmidhī on sainthood', *JMIAS*, 8 (1989), pp.42–9. J.S. Trimingham, *The Sufi Orders in Islam*, p.134. In an appendix in which Radtke cites references of later scholars of al-Tirmidhī's *Sīrat al-awliyāʾ*, he introduces Ibn Taymiyya's view to the effect that al-Tirmidhī's text was an introduction to Ibn al-ʿArabī's going astray. B. Radtke, *Drei Schriften des Theosophen von Tirmidh*, p.76.

12. Bukhārī, *ʿIlm*, 10.

13. *Fuṣūṣ*, pp.134, 135.

14. *Seal*, p.51.

capacity as a *walī* than in his capacity as a *nabī*'.[15] Ibn al-ʿArabī also defines *walāya* as unlimited prophecy (*nubuwwa muṭlaqa*) or general prophecy (*nubuwwa ʿāmma*), which means that it has no specific mission such as legislation.[16] Actually, apart from legislation, *walāya* is prophecy. Quoting ʿAbd al-Qādir al-Jīlānī's (d.1166) saying, 'O ye assemblies of prophets, you have been given the name (*laqab* of prophets), and we have been given that which you have not been given', Ibn al-ʿArabī comments: 'We have been prohibited from employing the word "prophet", although general prophecy exists among prominent persons.'[17] This means, essentially, that had there not been a legal interdiction which forbids using the name prophet, all God's friends would have been called prophets.

As well as concurring on the role of the *awliyāʾ* subsequent to the general prophecy period, Ibn al-ʿArabī, like al-Tirmidhī, also acknowledges their role as the maintainers of world existence.[18]

It is also likely that Ibn al-ʿArabī accepted al-Tirmidhī's division of the *awliyāʾ*'s gradations as a model worth following,[19] although the Shaykh's division is more complex and detailed.[20] According to al-Tirmidhī, God's saints are divided into two main groups:[21]

15. *Fuṣūṣ*, p.135, quoted in *Seal*, p.51. It is worth noting that al-Jāḥiẓ (d.869) preceded al-Tirmidhī in expressing the idea that there is no essential difference between the messenger (*rasūl*), prophet (*nabī*) and leader (*imām*), except in gradation. The notion that prophecy characterizes the perfect man appears in Philo's writings. To this fact one should add the theories of the philosophers on the natural prophecy. M.A. Palacios, *The Mystical Philosophy of Ibn Masarra and His Followers*, pp.91f.

16. *Fut.*III:75, 136; *FM.*II:49, ll.14–29, 90, l.19 – 91, l.2.

17. *Fut.*III:136; *FM.*II:90, ll.31–2.

18. Radtke, 'Forerunner', p.4; al-Tirmidhī, *Khatm*, p.344; Radtke, *Drei Schriften*, p.44.

19. Ibid. p.18. *Fut.*III:37–61; *FM.*II:24–39. Radtke, '*Wilāya*', p.488.

20. Our aim here is not to detail the division of saints made by al-Tirmidhī; for this purpose the reader may consult M. Takeshita, *Ibn ʿArabī's Theory of the Perfect Man and its Place in the History of Islamic Thought*, pp.131–5.

21. He mentions other kinds of God's friends, but the two groups we discuss are the main types.

1. *awliyā' ḥaqq Allāh* (the friends of God's laws, who fulfil His commands and obligations, or those who do the right things).
2. *awliyā' Allāh* (God's friends).

While the saints of the first kind focus their attention and actions on ethics, with which they show their devotion to God,[22] the saints of the second kind are those whom God chooses to be His friends and they come close to God through God's help.[23] Their good behaviour derives from their proximity to God. It is interesting that Ibn al-ʿArabī himself fulfilled al-Tirmidhī's doctrine in his mystical life, which begins with revelation and not with the usual Sufi practice of passing through the staged stations and states. The Greatest Master admits, 'in my case illumination (*fatḥ*) has preceded discipline (*riyāḍa*)'.[24] Probably because of al-Tirmidhī's teachings on the ranking of God's saints, Ibn al-ʿArabī was fond of his philosophy. Furthermore, like al-Tirmidhī, who considered himself the Seal of the Sainthood (*khatm al-walāya*), Ibn al-ʿArabī regarded himself as the Seal of the Muhammadan Sainthood,[25] 'the Supreme Seal, the source of all Sainthood'.[26]

Concerning sainthood, there are other similarities between the doctrines of al-Tirmidhī and Ibn al-ʿArabī. The idea that saints' knowledge is the clearest sign of their sainthood, and of constant change in the saints' states and the revelations God gives them, characterizes the doctrines of both men. However, here too the Shaykh's treatment of these issues is more comprehensive than al-Tirmidhī's.[27]

Another notion that Ibn al-ʿArabī addresses is the antecedent prophecy of Muhammad. Because Muhammad was the most

22. Radtke, *Drei Schriften*, p.2, para.4; *Seal*, p.29; Radtke and O'Kane, *Concept*, p.43; S. Sviri, 'Ḥakīm Tirmidhī and the Malāmatī Movement in Early Sufism,' in L. Lewisohn (ed.), *The Heritage of Sufism*, Vol. I, p.610.
23. Ibid. pp.94f.
24. *Fut.*II:349; *FM*.I:616, ll.22–3. *Quest*, pp.90f.
25. Radtke, '*Wilāya*', p.493; *Bezels*, 1980, p.38.
26. *Quest*, p.81.
27. Takeshita, *Perfect Man*, p.150.

perfect human being, creation began and will end with him: 'He was a prophet when Adam was still between water and clay.'[28] Following Shiʿite ideas and al-Tustarī, al-Tirmidhī held that Muhammad was first in creation,[29] a line of thought that we may assume our author developed upon.

As already noted, Ibn al-ʿArabī states that God is both transcendent and immanent depending on the aspect involved. From a passage in al-Tirmidhī's *Kitāb Sīrat al-awliyā'* one may understand that the author rejects both notions, whether transcendence or immanence, when held separately. There are two persons who abandon God, says al-Tirmidhī: the first frees God of any attribute to the point that he finally negates Him, and the second, in refuting the first, affirms God's attributes in such a way that he likens Him to creation.[30] We can assume that such a notion may well have stimulated the Shaykh to develop his own theory.

As in other cases, Ibn al-ʿArabī does not fully agree with all the views of this theosophical predecessor. With al-Tirmidhī, we can take the issue of the majesty (*jalāl*) and beauty (*jamāl*) of God as a point of difference. Al-Tirmidhī sees a connection between God's majesty and man's awe toward God on the one hand, and on the other, God's beauty and man's feeling of intimacy with God: God's two attributes serve as causes and man's feelings as effects.[31] The Shaykh says that this view is incorrect; however, in a certain aspect it can be accepted.[32] For our purpose it is sufficient to simply mention this point, because Ibn al-ʿArabī discusses it at some length.

28. *Fuṣūṣ*, p.214.
29. Al-Tirmidhī, *Khatm*, p.39, Chap. 57; Radtke, '*Wilāya*', p.491.
30. Radtke, *Drei Schriften*, p.76, ll.6–7.
31. Ibid. p.91, para.117, and pp.93, 120.
32. *Kitāb al-Jalāl wa'l-jamāl*, in *Rasā'il Ibn al-ʿArabī*, Part I:3.

Al-Ḥusayn ibn Manṣūr al-Ḥallāj

858–922

The influence of Al-Ḥallāj[1] on Ibn al-ʿArabī is a controversial issue among scholars. A.E. Affifi claims that 'of all the Ṣūfīs who may be said to have inspired Ibn al-ʿArabī's doctrine, Ḥallāj seems to have exerted the greatest influence'. He bases his contention on the many references to al-Ḥallāj in *al-Futūḥāt al-Makkiyya*, where nine points of al-Ḥallāj's doctrine appear in one way or another. I do not share Affifi's view for two reasons, one of which is the fact that, contrary to what he says, references to al-Ḥallāj are relatively scarce in the *Futūḥāt* (only 15) in comparison to, for example, Sahl al-Tustarī (33), Abū Yazīd al-Bisṭāmī (144) and al-Junayd (34). And, in point of fact, al-Ḥallāj's name is absent from *Fuṣūṣ al-ḥikam*, which summarizes Ibn al-ʿArabī's thought.

My second reason concerns content. Here are the nine points Affifi refers to:

1. The doctrine of the One and the Many.
2. Ibn al-ʿArabī's doctrine of the *logos*.[2]
3. The nature of esoteric knowledge as deriving from the Light of Muhammad.
4. The Unity which belongs to God *per se* and the Unity as attributed to Him.
5. The phenomenal world as a veil of the Real.
6. Divine love.
7. The difference between the terms *mashīʾa* and *irāda*.

1. See L. Massignon and L. Gardet in *EI*.

2. Here Affifi only states that al-Ḥallāj 'seems to have paved the way for Ibn al-ʿArabī's Logos-doctrine'. *MP*, p.86.

8. The unknowability of God.
9. Esoteric interpretation of the Quran.[3]

I accept M. Takeshita's approach here, when he states that 'most of the similarities which Affifi mentions are not necessarily from al-Ḥallāj. For instance, the ideas of the phenomenal world as veil of the Real, or the unknowability of God, or the esoteric interpretation of the Quran can be found in many Sufi circles and in some of the theological schools.'[4] It seems to me that our discussion of al-Bisṭāmī and other Sufis strengthens Takeshita's view. Ibn al-ʿArabī's criticism of al-Ḥallāj further shows that our author rejects the latter's views. Now I shall address al-Ḥallāj's appearances in the *Futūḥāt*.

In regards to the nine points of al-Ḥallāj's doctrine mentioned by Affifi, only the first, dealing with the One and the Many, or *Lāhūt* and *Nāsūt* in al-Hallāj's terminology, appears in the *Futūḥāt* bearing the unique terms of al-Ḥallāj.[5] Ibn al-ʿArabī adopts the structure of al-Ḥallāj's cosmogony here: God's breath (*nafas*) brings about air (*hawāʾ*) and the air brings about the letters (*ḥurūf*), and these in turn bring about words (*kalimāt*). Apart from the word *kun* (Be!), which is God's word of creation, other words make impressions on beings.[6]

Ibn al-ʿArabī accepts al-Ḥallāj's distinction between the spiritual world (*al-ʿālam al-rūḥānī*) and the world of nature and bodies, which al-Ḥallāj calls the length of the world (*ṭūl al-ʿālam*) and the breadth of the world (*ʿarḍ al-ʿālam*), respectively. The Greatest Master also accepts this terminology.[7]

In like manner, Ibn al-ʿArabī agrees with al-Ḥallāj's interpretation of the phrase 'in the name of God' (*bi-smi Allāh*). This phrase, says al-Ḥallāj, relates to the human being as the word *kun* relates

3. Ibid. pp. 188f.
4. M. Takeshita, *Ibn ʿArabī's Theory of the Perfect Man and its Place in the History of Islamic Thought*, pp. 18–21.
5. *MP*, pp. 13f.
6. *Fut.*I:257; *FM*.I:168, l.21 – 169, l.7.
7. *MP*, p. 14.

to God, which means that 'in the name of God' is a phrase of creation. Al-Ḥallāj adds that the greatest human beings may use the divine word *kun*, because the tradition of the supererogatory works (*ḥadīth al-nawāfil*)[8] applies to them. In this tradition it is stated that God becomes the hearing, the seeing and the speaking of the individual. Hence, the individual can utter the word *kun*.[9]

In his discussion of *ʿishq* (exaggeration of love), Ibn al-ʿArabī brings in al-Ḥallāj as an example. When al-Ḥallāj was executed, his limbs were cut off and the flowing blood created the words *Allāh*, *Allāh* in the sand. This proves the Shaykh's point, namely, that when someone is in the state of *ʿishq*, his love permeates all the parts of his entity, his body and his spirit.[10]

Ibn al-ʿArabī also refers to al-Ḥallāj in the context of the term *nikāḥ*, which literally means marriage or sexual intercourse. It is not clear whether al-Ḥallāj is responsible for the following theory or not, because Ibn al-ʿArabī says al-Ḥallāj only points to it (*ashāra ilā*). However, since I am not aware of any other source, I tend to attribute it to al-Ḥallāj. According to this theory, God's names are applied to the possible things and make them become concrete.[11] Actually, this process involves the interrelationships between the active and the receptive elements, or the father and the mother, respectively. In the example mentioned above, the Names are the father, the possible things the mother and the concrete things the children.[12] In general, every entity, be it divine, spiritual or natural, manifest or hidden, which causes the appearance of something, is its father and the result is the child. Ibn al-ʿArabī quotes al-Ḥallāj's stanza: 'My mother gave birth to her father / this is one of my marvels.'[13]

8. For this tradition, see *SPK*, p.325.
9. *Fut.*III:187; *FM.*II:126, ll.1–10.
10. *Fut.*III:505, 542; *FM.*II:337, ll.8–9, 362, l.13.
11. *SPK*, p.86.
12. *SDG*, p.304.
13. *Fut.*VII:230; *FM.*IV:156, ll.26–8.

Stephen Hirtenstein has graciously supplied me with the findings of an unpublished work by Julian Cook entitled 'Al-Ḥallāj as a source for the poetry in Ibn 'Arabī's works'. Cook's investigation reveals that Ibn al-ʿArabī quoted from at least 18 of the 138 poems included in al-Ḥallāj's *Dīwān*. However, some of his citations are only fragments and not whole poems: these cases show the Greatest Master's ability to interweave other poets' stanzas or parts of them into his own verse, perhaps demonstrating Ibn al-ʿArabī's literary taste but not necessarily indicating any influence on his thought. I have the impression, though research on all the poems may produce different results, that Ibn al-ʿArabī cites these poems as corroboration or adornment for his ideas and to illustrate al-Ḥallāj's notions and states (for example, the poem in Chapter 331[14]), but these citations do not constitute content from which Ibn al-ʿArabī learned his ideas.

In *tajallī al-ʿilla*, the Vision of the Cause, which appears in the *Kitāb al-Tajalliyāt* (paragraph 57), Ibn al-ʿArabī asks his interlocutor al-Ḥallāj whether it is correct to name God the Cause of causes (*ʿillat al-ʿillal*).[15] Al-Ḥallāj answers that this is the view of an ignorant person, because God creates the causes and He Himself is not a cause. He cannot be a cause, for He was before creation and created from nothing, and He is now as He was before creation. Al-Ḥallāj seems to hold that causality characterizes the created things, hence it cannot be God's trait. Moreover, if He had been a cause, He would have been connected to things, and if so, He would not have been perfect. In al-Ḥallāj's view, divine perfection means absolute disconnection from created things. Ibn al-ʿArabī agreed with him on this point.

In the second section of this paragraph, Ibn al-ʿArabī speaks with al-Ḥallāj on a seemingly metaphorical level. He asks al-Ḥallāj why he left his house, allowing it to go to ruin. The house seems to

14. *Fut.*V:174; *FM.*III:117, ll.33–5.

15. For the notion that God is the First Cause or the Cause of causes, see Ibn Sīnā, *Kitāb al-Shifāʾ*, *Al-Ilāhiyyāt*, Book VIII, trans. M.E. Marmura.

symbolize the body of al-Ḥallāj. Al-Ḥallāj answers that the hands of material things overwhelmed his house and so he evacuated it, meaning that when he exited his body and moved to a state of annihilation, people began to ruin his body, but they did not succeed. Al-Ḥallāj returned to his house (body), but realizing that material things (people) had dominated it, he decided to withdraw himself from his house.

The clue to this interpretation lies in al-Ḥallāj's concluding remarks: 'People said: "Al-Ḥallāj died." However, al-Ḥallāj did not die; the house (body) was ruined, but its inhabitant (the soul) moved away.' To this Ibn al-ʿArabī responded: 'I can refute your argument.' Al-Ḥallāj then cites Quran 12:76: 'And above every knower there is the All-Knowing' (meaning God). Do not resist what I expressed, says al-Ḥallāj, because you know the truth, and this is the most I can say. The Shaykh seems to have reservations about al-Ḥallāj's statement, which implies that al-Ḥallāj is still alive on earth, although his body was destroyed. Al-Ḥallāj was not impressed by Ibn al-ʿArabī's reaction and they parted company without reaching a clear conclusion to their debate.

Although he believed that in his visions and dreams he could talk with mystics who had already died, Ibn al-ʿArabī did not accept the idea that al-Ḥallāj was still alive on earth after he had been executed. By this, if I correctly understand the paragraph, Ibn al-ʿArabī adds one more reservation about the sensual miracles of the saints, as noted above.

As seen up to now, scanty information on al-Ḥallāj's personality and mystical experience is disclosed in Ibn al-ʿArabī's opus. One point to emphasize is al-Ḥallāj's tasting (*dhawq*) of the station of the seventh Pole. In Chapter 463 of the *Futūḥāt*, Ibn al-ʿArabī states that twelve poles preserve the Muslim community; each of them follows a prophet and is attached to a Quranic *sūra*. The seventh Pole follows the footsteps of the prophet Ayyūb whose *sūra* is *al-*

Baqara (Quran 2). He is characterized by the trait of majesty or magnitude, which means that his heart contains the Real.[16]

As usual, Ibn al-ʿArabī's attitude toward the Sufis carries an element of criticism. Here it appears in the author's treatment of the evaluation of one's station (*maqām*). The Sufi can know the level of his station only after leaving it: when one is in a state of revelation or intoxication, one can assess neither one's own station nor that of another. Ibn al-ʿArabī states that we accept al-Shiblī's witnessing of both his own station and al-Ḥallāj's, because al-Ḥallāj was intoxicated (*sakrān*), while al-Shiblī was sober.[17] Al-Ḥallāj has not recovered from the state of intoxication, while al-Shiblī has returned to a state of sobriety. Al-Shiblī says, 'Al-Ḥallāj and I drank from the same cup (meaning we experienced the same illumination); however, I became sober and he remained intoxicated.' Hearing this, al-Ḥallāj responded that 'had al-Shiblī drunken that which I drank, he would have attained the same situation'.[18]

Another accusation levelled against al-Ḥallāj is his attempt to emulate the Quran (*muʿāraḍa*), an act ascribed earlier to Ibn al-Muqaffaʿ (d.*c*.760)[19] and later to the poet Abū al-ʿAlāʾ al-Maʿarrī (d.1057).[20]

To sum up, as noted above, al-Ḥallāj's doctrine left no important traces in Ibn al-ʿArabī's writings in comparison to other of his predecessors. It also seems that the Greatest Master did not hold him in high esteem. I assume that examining other writings of Ibn al-ʿArabī will not change this picture.

16. *Fut.*VII:123; *FM.*IV:83, l.27 – 84, l.3; *SDG*, p.33.

17. Ibid. p.19.

18. *Fut.*IV:263, V:174; *FM.*II:546, ll.31–3, III:117, l.31. For the debate in the Sufi school of Baghdad regarding sobriety versus intoxication see H. Mason, 'Ḥallāj and the Baghdad School of Sufism', in L. Lewisohn (ed.), *The Heritage of Sufism*, Vol. I, pp.65–81.

19. J. Wansbrough, *Quranic Studies, Sources and Methods of Scriptural Interpretation*, pp.81, 160.

20. P. Smoor, 'Abū al-ʿAlāʾ al-Maʿarrī', in *EI*; *Fut.*V:25, 58; *FM.*III:17, ll.22–4, 40, l.6).

Ibn Masarra

883–931

Muhammad ibn ʿAbdallāh ibn Masarra al-Jabalī was an Andalusian philosopher and mystic. As a pupil of his Muʿtazilite father, he received theological grounding and training in asceticism. Because he was suspected of harbouring heterodox beliefs, he left Spain for the East and probably returned in 912 when ʿAbd al-Raḥmān III ascended the throne with a more lenient policy toward the people. A circle of devoted disciples followed him in his austere life. Some sources reported that he adhered to a pseudo-Empedoclean philosophy.

According to this philosophy, which contains elements of Neoplatonism, mainly with regard to the individual soul and its return to its source, the universal soul, there are five gradations of emanation:

1. Spiritual matter.
2. Intellect.
3. Soul.
4. Universal matter.
5. Matter.[1]

In his book on Ibn Masarra and his philosophy, M.A. Palacios adds a second principal thesis of Ibn Masarra, suggesting that Andalusian Sufism grew out of Ibn Masarra's school.[2] Palacios' approach has been criticized by several scholars who claim that his theory regarding the importance of Ibn Masarra's influence is built on too few sources, while others point out the inspiration of the East on Ibn Masarra's mysticism, especially his emphasis on

1. R. Arnaldez, 'Ibn Masarra', in *EI*.
2. *The Mystical Philosophy of Ibn Masarra and His Followers*, trans. E.H. Douglas and H.W. Yoder.

asceticism. Moreover, in Ibn Masarra's extant writings the influence of pseudo-Empedoclean doctrines is not so prominent, while both the pseudo-Sahl al-Tustarī's theory of the letters[3] and traditional Sufism have a clear impact on him.[4] The idea of philosophy and mysticism living together in one person should not trouble the reader, for other Islamic scholars, such as the famous al-Ghazālī, combined both approaches in their teachings.

Claude Addas also rejects Palacios' thesis that the renaissance of Sufism in Andalusia in the fifth century AH was due to the Almeria School, which followed the Ibn Masarra movement. She does not deny Ibn Masarra's influence on later generations, but stresses the fact that post-Ibn Masarra Sufis in Andalusia also derived their knowledge from other sources, especially from eastern Sufis and their own mystical experiences.[5]

Two recent articles, written by S. Stroumsa, and Stroumsa with S. Sviri, refer to the Ibn Masarra question, this time on the basis of two works by Ibn Masarra, *Kitāb Khawāṣṣ al-ḥurūf* (*The Book of the Properties of Letters*) and *Risālat al-Iʿtibār* (*Epistle on Contemplation*).[6] According to Stroumsa, Ibn Masarra's Neoplatonism resembles the Ismāʿīlī Fatimid version of Neoplatonism, and she also detects points of similarity between Ibn Masarra's views and notions appearing in *Rasāʾil Ikhwān al-Ṣafāʾ* (*The Epistle of the Pure Brethren*).[7] Ibn Masarra's main thesis in *Risālat al-Iʿtibār* is the agreement between rational thinking and revelation.[8]

3. S. Stroumsa and S. Sviri, 'The beginnings of mystical philosophy in al-Andalus', *Jerusalem Studies in Arabic and Islam*, 36 (2009), p.210, n.39. Ebstein and Sviri proved very convincingly that the ascription of *Risālat al-Ḥurūf* to Sahl is erroneous.

4. C. Addas, 'Andalusī mysticism and the rise of Ibn ʿArabī', in S.K. Jayyusi (ed.), *The Legacy of Muslim Spain*, pp.917ff.

5. Ibid. p.919.

6. Both treatises were edited by M.K.I. Jaʿfar in *Min qaḍāya al-fikr al-Islāmī*. The second work was translated and annotated in Stroumsa and Sviri, 'Beginnings'.

7. S. Stroumsa, 'Ibn Masarra and the beginnings of mystical thought in al-Andalus', in P. Schäfer (ed.) *Mystical Approaches to God*, pp.101f.

8. Stroumsa and Sviri, 'Beginnings', p.204.

After this short preface we may now assess Ibn Masarra's place in Ibn al-ʿArabī's writings, especially in *al-Futūḥāt al-Makkiyya*, wherein he is mentioned only three times, twice in Chapter 13, called 'The knowledge of the bearers of the Throne'. Here Ibn Masarra is described as 'one of the greatest masters of the mystic way with regard to knowledge, state and revelation'.[9] According to Ibn Masarra, as recorded by our author, the Throne which is carried[10] is the divine Kingship (*mulk*): 'The *Mulk* is reduced to the following: Body, Spirit, Nourishment (*ghidhā'*), Degree (*martaba*). Adam and Isrāfīl are in charge of the Forms (*ṣuwar*); Gabriel and Muḥammad of the Spirits; Michael and Ibrāhīm of the means of subsistence (*arzāq*); Mālik and Riḍwān of the Promise and of the Threat (*Waʿd* and *Waʿīd*).'[11] Following this, Ibn al-ʿArabī details the elements mentioned above. His scheme is more complex than the doctrines ascribed to Ibn Masarra and is full of elements of angelology.[12]

In his epistle *ʿUqlat al-mustawfiz* (*The Bond of the Watchman*) Ibn al-ʿArabī has a different perception of Throne, which consists of four existents: the dust (*habā'*), the nature (*ṭabīʿa*), the body (*jism*) and the sphere (*falak*).[13] He calls this Throne the Merciful Throne (*al-ʿarsh al-raḥmānī*), while there is another kind of throne called the Merciful Throne identified by the Shaykh as the *Kursī* (seat, chair, footstool). In the context of the discussion of these names, Ibn al-ʿArabī mentions Ibn Masarra as designating the names of the eight bearers, the angels of the Throne, ascribing to each of them a unique function.[14]

9. *Fut.*I:226; *FM.*I:148, ll.2–3.

10. The bearers of the Throne are eight according to Quran 69:17.

11. Arnaldez's trans. of *Fut.*I:226; *FM.*I:148, ll.3–11, in *EI.*

12. Ibid.; Stroumsa, 'Ibn Masarra', pp. 103f.

13. *ʿUqlat al-mustawfiz*, in H.S. Nyberg, *Kleinere Schriften des Ibn al-ʿArabī*, p. 56.

14. Ibid. p. 58. This seems to be a personal view of Ibn Masarra; in three commentaries of the Quran which I examined (al-Ṭabarī, Fakhr al-Dīn al-Rāzī and Ibn Kathīr) I did not find such a notion.

Ibn Masarra is also introduced in Chapter 272, entitled 'On the knowledge of the station of the transcendence of God's unity' (*tanzīh*[15] *al-tawḥīd*). On the opening of this chapter, Ibn al-ʿArabī explains this term in two forms:

1. The word *tanzīh* (to make something free of, or exempt from) is connected with unity; that is, one makes the concept of unity free from any human definition or trait; we can say nothing about the word unity when applied to God.
2. God is made free of any description through the word *tawḥīd*; in other words, the word *tawḥīd* cannot qualify God.[16]

Ibn al-ʿArabī uses a simile to exemplify this station: a house standing on five pillars covered with a roof and enclosed by solid walls without any openings, meaning no one can enter this house. However, the people of revelation are blessed with a pillar attached to one wall outside the house. Just as the Black Stone is outside the Kaʿba, but it is attributed to God and not to the Kaʿba, so this pillar is not attributed to this house but to God. The Shaykh notes that such a device is part of each divine station which otherwise is closed, and serves as a transmitter which delivers knowledge from the stations to the people. Ibn Masarra turned our attention to this idea in his *Kitāb al-Ḥurūf* (*The Book of Letters*), Ibn al-ʿArabī says.[17] Contrary to Palacios, who claimed that the five pillars might be the five emanations of pseudo-Empedoclean philosophy,[18] R. Arnaldez rightly points out that Palacios' claim cannot be accepted, because the simile refers to the transcendent character of God's unity, and not to the five elements.[19]

Ibn al-ʿArabī also shares with Ibn Masarra, who followed Sahl al-Tustarī, the notion that the entire cosmos is a book which consists

15. *SPK*, p.69.
16. *Fut.*IV:311; *FM*.II:578, ll.30–4.
17. Ibid. IV:315ff.; *FM*.II:581, ll.25–35. On Ibn Masarra's *Kitāb al-Ḥurūf* see P. Garrido, 'The science of letters in Ibn Masarra', *JMIAS*, 47 (2010), pp.47–61. I did not find this idea in *Kitāb al-Ḥurūf*.
18. Palacios, *Mystical Philosophy*, pp.75–82.
19. *EI*.

of the letters deriving from God's speech.[20] Ibn al-ʿArabī devotes a long chapter (Chapter 2) in the *Futūḥāt* to the letters and their place in the cosmic system. In his epistle, *Kitāb al-Mīm wa'l-wāw wa'l-nūn*, he exalts the science of the letters saying that it is one of God's secrets and its knowledge is the most sublime knowledge preserved in God's treasure. Hence, knowing this science singles out the prophets and God's friends who possess pure hearts: al-Ḥakīm al-Tirmidhī calls it the science of God's friends (*ʿilm al-awliyāʾ*).[21] Elsewhere in this epistle Ibn al-ʿArabī admits that in the discussion of the secrets of this science he follows Ibn Masarra's method and that of others.[22] However, Denis Gril is of the opinion that the Shaykh's interpretation of each group of isolated letters derives from his own inspiration, and not from Ibn Masarra. Considering the possible influence of Ibn Masarra's personal exegesis on the work of Ibn al-ʿArabī, Gril, however, says that this is only a partial influence.[23] Addas points out some similarities between *Kitāb al-Ḥurūf* and Ibn al-ʿArabī's notions, for example, the notion of *habāʾ* (literally: dust) being the primordial matter of the cosmos.[24] Ibn Masarra regards the divine Throne as a symbol of the prime matter,[25] while in his *al-Tadbīrāt al-ilāhiyya* Ibn al-ʿArabī designates primal matter as the divine Throne. However, he mentions other names for this matter, among them the Evident Record (*al-imām al-mubīn*) and the Mirror of the Real (*mirʾāt al-ḥaqq*). The fact that our author does not only adhere to the designation *ʿarsh* proves that Ibn Masarra's influence on him was not exclusive.[26]

20. Garrido, 'Science', p.48.

21. *Rasāʾil Ibn al-ʿArabī*, Part 1, no.8, p.2.

22. Ibid. p.7. Garrido, 'Science', pp.57–9.

23. D. Gril, 'La science des letters', in M. Chodkiewicz (ed.), *Les Illuminations de la Mecque*, p.428; Garrido, 'Science', p.60.

24. Addas, 'Andalusī mysticism', p.919. Garrido, 'Science', pp.60ff.

25. Palacios, *Mystical Philosophy*, p.94. According to Ibn Masarra as attested in his *Kitāb al-Iʿtibār*, the Throne is the first created being along with the water. Stroumsa and Sviri, 'Beginnings', pp.224, 242.

26. *Al-Tadbīrāt al-ilāhiyya*, in Nyberg, *Schriften*, pp.121, 123, 136–8. The designation *al-imām al-mubīn* is attributed by Ibn al-ʿArabī to Ibn Barrajān, who bases himself

In summary, from the materials gathered here Ibn Masarra seems to have had little influence on Ibn al-ʿArabī. I tend to agree with Addas, who concludes that the impact of Ibn Masarra and other Andalusian Sufis on Ibn al-ʿArabī should be sought in the field of morals and ways of conduct and not in the sphere of philosophical and mystical notions.

on Quran 36:12: 'We keep an account of everything in a clear Record' (trans. Abdel Haleem). Ibid. p.125. For a translation of these pages into English, see T.B. al-Jerrahi al-Halveti, *Ibn ʿArabī*, pp.23–36.

Abū Bakr al-Shiblī

861–946

Abū Bakr al-Shiblī, a learned scholar in Law and the Hadith, was an official at the ʿAbbāsid court in Sāmarrāʾ and then a deputy governor of Damāwand. At the age of forty he converted to Sufism. He became a follower of al-Junayd until the latter's death in 910. For some time he associated with al-Ḥallāj but finally rejected his ways. Al-Shiblī's unconventional lifestyle and his strange sayings and acts caused him to be repeatedly hospitalized in a lunatic asylum in Baghdad. His sayings, poems and allusions as well as his eccentricities, ecstatic states and penances appear in Sufi manuals.[1]

Al-Shiblī's name occurs in *al-Futūḥāt al-Makkiyya* relatively few times. Ibn al-ʿArabī regards him as a gnostic[2] and a lover of God who conceals his love because of jealousy of God. Ibn al-ʿArabī immediately exploits the second point and states that God, as a reactive act, concealed His essence through His attributes from those who conceal their love of God. Strangely enough, he quotes part of a verse,[3] 'those who disbelieve' (*kafarū*), using the initial meaning of *kafara* (he concealed).[4] Al-Shiblī and his like are also presented as those who concealed the secrets which were revealed to them of their contact (*wuṣla*) with God.

Al-Shiblī's distraction or unawareness of himself during prayer time causes Ibn al-ʿArabī to relate his own experience. He says that once he was an imam (prayer leader) and performed all the rites of prayer, even though he was completely unaware of what

1. F. Sobieroj, 'Al-Shiblī', in *EI*; *Dimensions*, pp.77–80; A. Knysh, *Islamic Mysticism*, pp.64–6.

2. *Fut.*I:117; *FM.*I:74, l.24.

3. According to his following citations, Ibn al-ʿArabī is probably referring to Quran 2:6.

4. Cf. *Fuṣūṣ al-ḥikam*, p.73.

he was doing. In Ibn al-ʿArabī's words: 'In this state I was absent from myself and from others' (*ghibtu fīhi ʿannī wa-ʿan ghayrī*). He ascribed this state to a revelation he experienced in which God protected him from sin (*dhanb*),[5] contrary to what happened to al-Shiblī in his state of distraction. Al-Shiblī returned during his prayers to a state of awareness; however, Ibn al-ʿArabī does not know if al-Shiblī understood his return or not. In al-Junayd's report about al-Shiblī, the latter did not sin. Al-Junayd also speaks of his own experience stating that in his state of absence (or unawareness, *ghayba*) he was aware of his own soul which was bowing and prostrating. Al-Junayd said that he was astonished by this phenomenon, knowing that the entity that he saw was neither someone else nor himself.[6] Here the story about al-Shiblī seems to be a corroboration of the fact that great personalities lose their self-awareness during prayer, that is, they experience the state of *fanāʾ*.

A lengthy passage is dedicated to al-Shiblī's conversation with a person who was preparing to go on the pilgrimage and perform all its ceremonies. The aim of the dialogue, written in a question-and-answer format, is to show the real meaning of the pilgrimage, and a spiritual journey to God in which nearness to Him and separation from worldly affairs are necessary conditions. A few examples will illustrate al-Shiblī's aim. Al-Shiblī: 'Did you enter the holy place (*al-ḥaram*)?' Al-Shiblī's follower: 'Yes.' Al-Shiblī: 'When you entered the holy place, did you think of abstaining from all forbidden things?' The follower: 'No.' Al-Shiblī: 'You did not enter the holy place.' Al-Shiblī also expects his follower to interact with God in some of the pilgrimage rites. Al-Shiblī: 'Did you touch and kiss the Black Stone?' The follower: 'Yes.' Al-Shiblī: 'Whoever touches the Stone, touches God … and whoever touches God is protected (literally: in a state of protection, *fī*

5. By sin he probably means an error in the prayer.
6. *Fut.*I:378, II:150; *FM.*I:250, ll.13–15, I:479, ll.6–11.

maḥall al-amn). Did you feel a trace of protection?' The follower: 'No.' Al-Shiblī: 'You did not touch.' Al-Shiblī: 'Did you go out to al-Ṣafā[7] and stand there?' The follower: 'Yes.' Al-Shiblī: 'What did you do there?' The follower: 'I exclaimed seven times *Allāh akbar* (God is the great), mentioned the pilgrimage and asked God to accept (my prayer).' Al-Shiblī: 'Did you exclaim *Allāh akbar* through the angels' exclamation[8] and find the real meaning of your exclamation (*ḥaqīqat takbīrika*) in this place?' The follower: 'No.' Al-Shiblī: 'You did not exclaim *Allāh akbar*.'

At the end of this series of questions and answers, Ibn al-ʿArabī states that he introduced this story to make people know the way of the people of God (*ahl Allāh*), that is, the real mystics, regarding pilgrimage. This is al-Shiblī's conception of the Pilgrimage, and all his questions and answers derive from his experience. Experiences, says the Shaykh, may differ according to the divine providence (*ʿināyat Allāh*) towards each person.[9]

Like al-Ghazālī[10] and other mystics, Ibn al-ʿArabī states that the formal rites of Islam are also indications of higher values which the mystic must cling to and accept. As with other moderate Sufis, who did not want to alienate the orthodox circles from Sufism, the formal value of the rites remains valid and one should perform them with devotion; however, they lose their value if spiritual considerations are not involved when the rites are performed. The wish to come close to God, thinking only of God, the purging of bad traits, the reception of signs from God and getting rid of one's ignorance are included in the spiritual considerations which

7. Ṣafā and Marwa are two hillocks near Mecca and running between them as part of the pilgrimage symbolizes Hajar's searching for water. See *EI*.

8. The allusion to the angels' exclamation is lost on me.

9. *Fut.*II:437f.; *FM.*I, pp. 677–8.

10. In this context, see al-Ghazālī's *The Book on the Secrets of Pilgrimage (Kitāb Asrār al-ḥajj)* in the first volume of *Iḥyāʾ ʿulūm al-dīn*, al-Maktaba al-Tijāriyya al-Kubrā. Whereas in al-Ghazālī writings the spiritual explanation of the pilgrimage rites form a succession of events leading the mystic to his utmost aim, al-Shiblī's notions are not unified and do not form a single line of thought.

the mystic should take into account. Thus, it is clear why Ibn al-ʿArabī chose to use this long passage from al-Shiblī's legacy.

A topic the Sufis often discuss is the mystic's report of his experience in a certain station. Who is better qualified to describe his station after he has experienced it, the drunk or the sober? Ibn al-ʿArabī prefers the sober Sufi's report. As we have seen, he states that 'we accepted al-Shiblī's witness of himself and of al-Ḥallāj and we did not accept al-Ḥallāj's saying of himself and of al-Shiblī, because al-Ḥallāj was drunk and al-Shiblī was sober.'[11] Ibn al-ʿArabī's attitude *vis-à-vis* intoxication and sobriety undoubtedly reflects his negative attitude and reservations toward the ecstatic sayings.[12]

In Chapter 125 of the *Futūḥāt* Ibn al-ʿArabī treats the station of patience (or forbearance, *ṣabr*), explaining some sorts of patience, such as patience for the sake of God (*ṣabr fī Allāh*) or patience through God (*ṣabr bi-Allāh*), which means that God's patience works in the mystic. The best station, in Ibn al-ʿArabī's view, is the patience learned or taken from God (*al-ṣabr ʿan Allāh*). 'Patient' (*ṣabūr*) is one of the ninety-nine most beautiful names of God, notwithstanding its absence in the Quran.[13] Quran 33:57 ('Those who injure God and His Messenger') is a verse from which Ibn al-ʿArabī learns the name Patient, for God bears patiently the injury of His creatures. Thus, just as God bears patiently the hurt of His creatures, so the mystic should bear his difficulties.

Here al-Shiblī is placed in the picture. Ibn al-ʿArabī alludes to an anecdote which appears in its complete form in al-Sarrāj's *Kitāb al-Lumaʿ*[14] in which a person asks al-Shiblī what the hardest kind of patience is. Al-Shiblī answers this question three times (*al-ṣabr fī Allāh*, *li-Allāh*, *maʿa Allāh*), but none of his answers were

11. *Fut.*III:19; *FM.*II:12, ll.11–13. See the section on al-Ḥallāj above.

12. See the section on al-Bisṭāmī above.

13. Al-Ghazālī, *Al-Maqṣad al-asnā fī sharḥ maʿānī asmāʾ Allāh al-ḥusnā*, ed. F.A. Shehadi, pp.161f.; Fakhr al-Dīn al-Rāzī, *Sharḥ asmāʾ Allāh al-ḥusnā*, pp.353f.

14. Al-Sarrāj, *Kitāb al-Lumaʿ fīʾl-taṣawwuf*, ed. R.A. Nicholson, pp.49f.

satisfactory in the eyes of his interlocutor, who finally said that the hardest patience is *al-ṣabr ʿan Allāh*. Consequently, al-Shiblī screamed so forcefully that he almost died. The most sublime patience is the patience of the mystic who is patient, because God is patient and not for any other reason.[15] Al-Shiblī's anecdote is brought here to illustrate the importance of this kind of patience.

The proximity of human traits to God's traits is also repeated in the context of the discussion on the station of travel (*maqām al-safar*). The Sufi travels for two reasons:

1. He wants to learn about God from the phenomena of the world (*tarīq al-iʿtibār*).[16]
2. He wants to come close to God, because he feels alienated from people.

Ibn al-ʿArabī explains this alienation as the outcome of the creation of humanity, for humans were created in God's image. One of God's traits is His dissimilarity to others, based on Quran 42:11 ('There is none like Him'). Consequently, humans also feel that they are not similar to other people,[17] and so they travel to flee from people and to alienate themselves from their apparent likes. As corroboration for this idea, the Shaykh states that al-Shiblī points to this meaning. Once he spent a night in conversation with one of his fellows, who said to al-Shiblī: 'Let's worship God.' Al-Shiblī retorts: 'Worship is not carried out with others' (*bi'l-shirka*).[18] Very probably, al-Shiblī, and following him Ibn al-ʿArabī, do not mean here the formal worship, but the worship of the Sufi.

The lover's jealousy of his beloved is a station which Ibn al-ʿArabī ascribes to al-Shiblī. According to our author, this station is the worthiest (*aḥaqqu*) trait found in the lover of God. Al-

15. *Fut.*III:311f.; *FM.*II:207.

16. Cf. Ibn Masarra, *Risālat al-Iʿtibār*, in M.K.I. Jaʿfar (ed.), *Min qaḍāyā al-fikr al-islāmī*.

17. According to Takeshita, the notion of the identification of Adam's traits with God's attributes is traced back to al-Shiblī and appears later in al-Ghazālī. M. Takeshita, *Ibn ʿArabī's Theory of the Perfect Man and its Place in the History of Islamic Thought*, p.67.

18. *Fut.*III:440f.; *FM.*II:293, ll.6–25.

Shiblī was led to this station because of his exaltation of God and because of his own humility. God has two kinds of lovers: those who express presumptuousness (*idlāl*) in God's presence and those who do not express presumptuousness, because they are jealous.[19]

Another station attributed to al-Shiblī is confusion (*iṣṭilām*),[20] which is caused by God's hidden revelation to the Sufi in the image of beauty (*fī ṣūrat al-jamāl*). This revelation makes the Sufi fear God. The Sufi's fear is so strong that it encompasses him and becomes a state. However, God kept an eye on al-Shiblī and returned him to consciousness at prayer times. But when he finished praying, he returned to his previous state. Ibn al-ʿArabī describes this state as the joining of contraries, because on the one hand the Sufi feels paralysed and on the other he performs acts to flee from this state.[21]

In the Vision of the Heaviness of Unity (*tajallī thiqal al-tawḥīd*) in the *Kitāb al-Tajalliyāt*, Ibn al-ʿArabī discusses the nature of the one who unifies God.[22] First, he says that this person, who takes into account all aspects of unity, cannot be a caliph because the caliph has the heavy responsibility of governing his kingdom which includes the various personal demands of state required of him, while the unification of God requires total devotion without leaving time or ability to do anything else. It is not clear to me why the Shaykh uses the example of the caliph to illustrate the impossibility of doing anything other than submersing one's self in God's unity, as the example of an ordinary individual would have sufficed. Possibly, Ibn al-ʿArabī might have thought that even a strong personality like a caliph cannot devote himself both to his leadership functions as a caliph and to God's unity.

19. *Fut.*III:536; *FM.*II:358, ll.8–11.

20. Ibn al-ʿArabī points out that in the terminology of the Sufis it is called *walah*. *Fut.*IV:240; *FM.*II:531, l.35.

21. *Fut.*IV:240; *FM.*II:532, ll.6–10. See also *Fut.*IV:23–4; *FM.*II:386, ll.25–30.

22. Ibn al-ʿArabī, *Kitāb al-Tajalliyāt*, in *Rasāʾil Ibn al-ʿArabī*, para. 56.

Within this vision, our author spoke to al-Shiblī and stated that God's unity requires the complete and undivided concentration of the human being, while the caliph divides his time and efforts between various duties. Thereupon, al-Shiblī agreed with Ibn al-ʿArabī and asked which of the two is perfect. Ibn al-ʿArabī answered saying that the caliph's leading role in the caliphate is divided into many various tasks, while unity is one principle to which one should adhere. Asked what the sign of this analysis is, the Shaykh threw the question back to al-Shiblī who said that one who unifies God knows nothing, wills nothing, can do nothing, etc. In short, the unifier is so immersed in his unification of God that he is unaware of his surroundings and has no power to deal with anything. Actually, he is in a state of annihilation (*fanāʾ*), although the term does not appear in this paragraph.

Finally, in the *Futūḥāt*'s last chapter (560), Ibn al-ʿArabī presents al-Shiblī's testament where he expresses his ascetic viewpoint. He says that if one wants to examine the whole world, one should examine a refuse tip in this world, and if one wants to examine himself, one should take a heap of sand, from which one was created and to which one will return. And when one wants to examine what one is, one should examine that which is excreted from one's body. Al-Shiblī sums up his testament saying that one who is in this state should not be arrogant toward others who are like him.[23]

To sum up, Ibn al-ʿArabī was impressed by al-Shiblī's attitude toward the formal commandments and rites, and by his spirituality which led him to search for the inner meanings in religion. He accepts his view of some stations and his contempt for this world. And Ibn al-ʿArabī's preference for the report of the sober on his intoxication to the report of the ever-intoxicated person may be as a result of al-Shiblī's impact.

23. *Fut.*VIII:377; *FM.*IV:545, ll.22–5.

Abū Ṭālib al-Makkī

?–996

Although Ibn al-ʿArabī considers the mystic and theologian Abū Ṭālib al-Makkī one of the masters of the people of mystical experience (*min sādāt ahl al-dhawq*),[1] there are few references to him in *al-Futūḥāt al-Makkiyya*. Ibn al-ʿArabī presents al-Makkī as a mystic who shares with him the notion that the letters (*ḥurūf*) constitute a community (*umma*) who are addressed by messengers and are under obligations. Only the people of revelation (*ahl al-kashf*) among the mystics, says our author, know of this. Ibn al-ʿArabī agrees with al-Makkī that, just as the cosmos is divided into three worlds – the divine world or the world of dominion (*ʿālam al-malakūt*),[2] the world of power (*ʿālam al-jabarūt*) and the lower world, the material sensible world (*ʿālam al-mulk wa'l-shahāda*) – so the letters are also divided in the same manner.[3] Ibn al-ʿArabī points out that al-Makkī uses the term *ʿālam al-jabarūt*, or the world of imagination, whereas he himself prefers *ʿālam al-ʿaẓama*, the world of exaltedness.[4] Elsewhere, he states that there are two aspects of *jabarūt*, the first being exaltedness (*ʿaẓama*), which is the view of al-Makkī and others, and the second, imagination.[5] Apparently, Ibn al-ʿArabī's statements in one place are incomplete but elsewhere he completes them. He also mentions al-Makkī in

1. *Fut.*II:329; *FM.*I:602, l.34. S. Yazaki, *Islamic Mysticism and Abu Talib al-Makki*, pp. 105–7.
2. This term is based on Quran 6:75, 7:185, 23:88, 36:83.
3. On these terms, see L. Gardet, "ālam', in *EI*. Al-Ghazālī was influenced by al-Makkī in using these terms.
4. *Fut.*I:95; *FM.*I:58, l.14.
5. *Fut.*VII:306f.; *FM.*IV:208, ll.27–8.

the context of the connection between the letters (consonants) and the vowels, this time disagreeing with him.[6]

Another disagreement Ibn al-ʿArabī had with al-Makkī arises in his discussion of the possibility of sending two messengers to perform the same task at the same time, such as Moses and Aaron, who were sent to Pharaoh. Although a group of mystics including al-Makkī, whom Ibn al-ʿArabī identifies as 'our followers and masters', deny this possibility, the Shaykh accepts it.[7] Again, we see that Ibn al-ʿArabī does not hesitate to challenge the greatest masters of Sufism. Elsewhere, he cites al-Makkī as saying that God neither revealed Himself in one form to two persons nor in one form twice. However, according to Ibn al-ʿArabī revelations are different because religions are different: God was revealed to each religion in a different form.[8] Al-Makkī's statement may have been the source of the notion that God's self-revelation never repeats itself (*lā takrār fī'l-tajallī*).[9]

Abdāl are the hidden saints who preserve the order of the world.[10] One of them, Muʿādh ibn Ishras, had contact with ʿAbd al-Majīd ibn Salama, the preacher of Marshana al-Zaytūn, a district of Seville. ʿAbd al-Majīd told Ibn al-ʿArabī that he asked this *badal* why some people are *abdāl*. Muʿādh answered: 'They become *abdāl* through four things that al-Makkī mentioned in his *Nourishment* ..., viz., hunger, sleeplessness, silence and seclusion (*jūʿ*, *sahr*, *ṣamt*, *ʿuzla*).'[11] Here al-Makkī appears to be an important source for mapping how an individual becomes a saint at the second gradation in the hierarchy of saints. Ibn al-ʿArabī clearly

6. *Fut.*I:136; *FM.*I:87, ll.8–10. This issue involves many terms and notions and requires a separate inquiry.

7. *Fut.*I:280; *FM.*I:184, ll.11–22.

8. *Fut.*I:401f.; *FM.*I:266, ll.10–20.

9. *SPK*, pp.103f.

10. I. Goldziher and H.J. Kissling, 'Abdāl', in *EI*.

11. *Fut.*I:419, III:12f.; *FM.*I:277, ll.29–31, II:7, ll.25–6.

follows al-Makkī in his *Ḥilyat al-abdāl*, mentioning the same four traits of the mystic.[12]

One obscure notion ascribed to al-Makkī claims that the sphere revolves because of the breaths of the knower (*al-falak yadūru bi-anfās al-ʿālim*).[13] I have found no source explaining what al-Makkī means by these words. However, if I may surmise, the breaths of the knower are like God's breaths, which make the world exist and function.[14] Because humans are among God's revelations, their breaths are like God's. Elsewhere, Ibn al-ʿArabī cites al-Makkī's statement that the sphere moves because of the breaths of humanity, moreover, because of the breath of each person who breathes.[15]

The Shaykh also fully agrees with al-Makkī's notion of pure occasionalism. 'Whoever knows a little portion of God's knowledge' (literally: whoever smells the scent of God's knowledge), says Ibn al-ʿArabī, does not ask why God carried out a certain action. God is the real cause of everything. His will is the dominion[16] of His essence (*mashī'atuhu ʿarsh dhātihi*; literally: His will is the throne of His essence). According to the Greatest Master, this is the view of al-Makkī.[17]

In summary, it seems to me that al-Makkī did not exert much influence on Ibn al-ʿArabī and that the former's imprint in the *Futūḥāt* is marginal.

12. S. Hirtenstein (ed. and trans.), *The Four Pillars of Spiritual Transformation*, pp.20–4, 27–48, and 5–13 of the Arabic text.

13. *Fut.*I:492; *FM.*I:326, ll.30–1. In II:95 (*FM.*I:441, l.17), the plural form (*aflāk*) appears.

14. *SPK*, pp.19, 34, 127.

15. *Fut.*III:532; *FM.*II:355, ll.7–8.

16. In *Fut.*V:70 (*FM.*III:48, ll.15–16), Ibn al-ʿArabī understands the word *ʿarsh* as dominion (*mulk*). Through the will it is evident that the essence has dominion over all things.

17. *Fut.*III:61; *FM.*II:39, l.27. *Fuṣūṣ al-ḥikam*, p.165.

THE LATER SUFIS

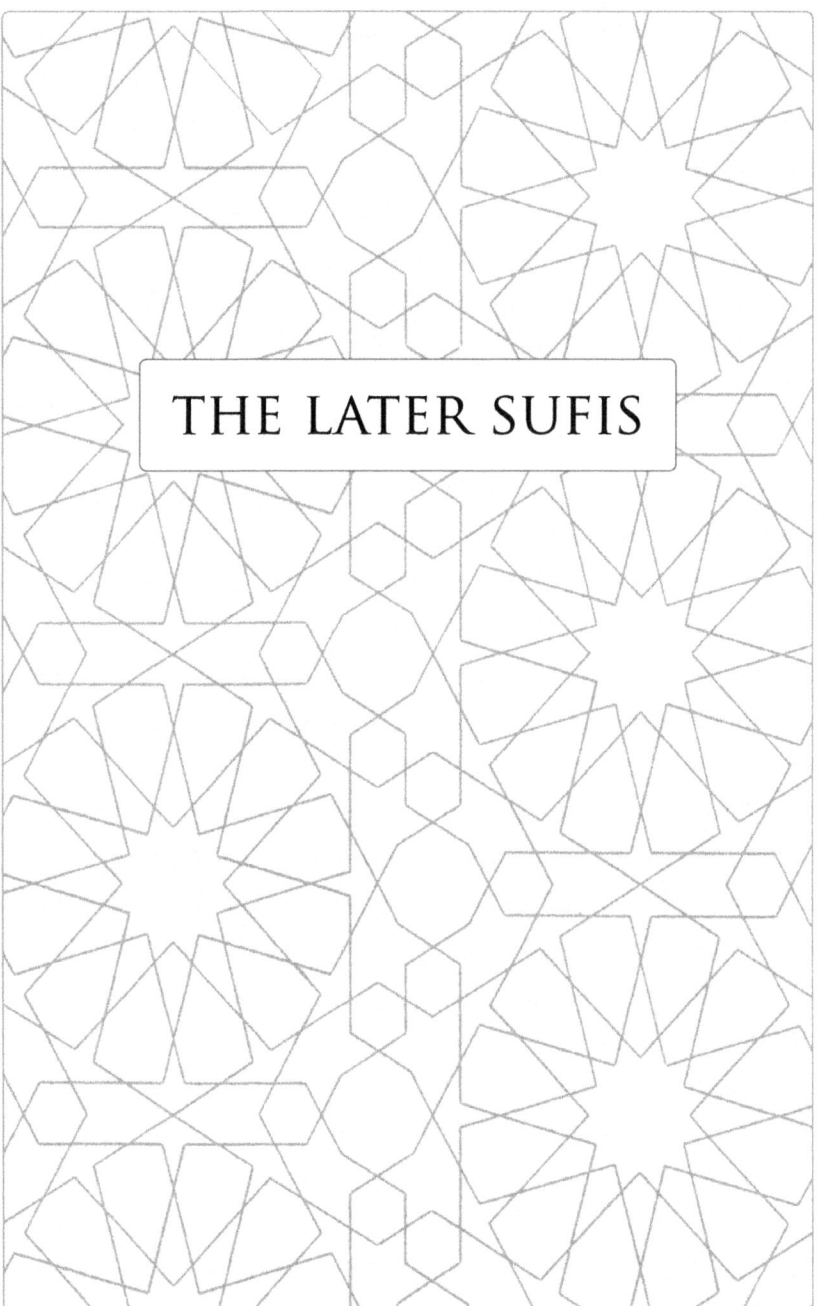

Al-Ghazālī[1]

1058–1111

In his pioneering work on Ibn al-ʿArabī, A.E. Affifi makes the following important remark concerning the sources of the Shaykh's thought:

> It is practically impossible to say that any particular philosophy or mysticism is the source of Ibn al-ʿArabī's whole system. Ibn al-ʿArabī had a foot in every camp, so to speak, and derived his material from every conceivable source. His system is eclectic in the highest degree, but we can easily find the germs from which many parts of this system seem to have developed, in the writings of older philosophers, Sufis, and scholastic theologians. He borrowed ideas from Islamic as well as non-Islamic sources, orthodox as well as heterodox.[2]

To the best of my knowledge, no one has thoroughly researched Ibn al-ʿArabī's attitude toward al-Ghazālī, although scholars comment on the former's connections with the latter. For example, in the introduction to his translation of the *Fuṣūṣ al-ḥikam* (*The Bezels of Wisdom*), R.W.J. Austin points out that Ibn al-ʿArabī 'combines the scholastic expertise of Ghazālī with the poetic imagery of Ibn al-Fāriḍ',[3] thus implying that the Greatest Master regards al-Ghazālī as a theologian. However, William Chittick says that as a rule Ibn al-ʿArabī praises al-Ghazālī as 'one of our colleagues', thus including him among the most exceptional Sufis who are the people of realities and verification (*taḥqīq*).[4] Notwithstanding, Ibn

1. An earlier version of this article was first published in Y.T. Langermann (ed.), *Avicenna and His Legacy: A Golden Age of Science and Philosophy*, by Brepols Publishers, Turnhout, Belgium, 2009.

2. *MP*, pp. 174, 184.

3. *Bezels*, p. 24.

4. Ibn al-ʿArabī distinguishes between worshippers (*ʿubbād*), ascetics (*zuhhād*), and common Sufis (*muṭlaq al-ṣūfiyya*) on the one hand, and the people of the hearts (*aṣḥāb*

al-ʿArabī criticizes al-Ghazālī for dealing with theological and philosophical questions.[5] In Gerald Elmore's view, 'the work of al-Ghazālī had a more determinate effect on the formation of the Shaykh al-Akbar's education than that of any other single author. Ibn al-ʿArabī's attitude toward the great Muḥyī l-Dīn of the fifth/eleventh century was [...] one of respectful and resolute emulation.'[6] I think that Elmore is right in his estimation of al-Ghazālī's role in the formation of Ibn al-ʿArabī's thought.

First it should be noted that Ibn al-ʿArabī's companions studied al-Ghazālī's greatest work, *Iḥyāʾ ʿulūm al-dīn*.[7] The Shaykh himself tells us that a pious person named Muḥammad ibn Khālid al-Ṣudfī al-Tilimsānī used to read the *Iḥyāʾ* before him and his companions.[8] Apart from the *Iḥyāʾ*, Ibn al-ʿArabī refers twice to al-Ghazālī's *Kitāb al-Maḍnūn bihi ʿalā ghayr ahlihi (The Book that Should be Kept from Unfit Persons)*.[9] In addition, he mentions al-Ghazālī's *Kīmīyāʾ al-saʿāda* (*The Alchemy of Happiness*), a summary of the *Iḥyāʾ*, which al-Ghazālī wrote in Persian,[10] and *al-*

---

al-qulūb), of contemplation or witnessing (*mushāhada*), and of revelation or unveiling (*mukāshafa*) on the other; the latter are the people of realities and verifications. *Fut.*I:395, V:50–1; *FM.*I:261, ll.9–13, III:34f.; *SPK*, p.392, n.34.

5. Ibid. pp.235, 392, n.34, p.405, n.1. I shall refer later to p.235 and what follows.

6. G.T. Elmore, 'Ibn al-ʿArabī's "Cinquain" (Tahmis) on a Poem by Abū Madyan', *Arabica*, 46 (1999), p.72, n.40.

7. *Fut.*VII:18; *FM.*IV:12, l.18. Al-Ghazālī's *Iḥyāʾ* was well known in Muslim Andalusia and exercised great influence on the local Sufis. A. Faure, 'Ibn al-ʿArīf' and 'Ibn Barradjān', in *EI*.

8. *Fut.*VIII:387; *FM.*IV:552, l.11. *Khātimat al-kitāb*, p.387.

9. *Fut.*VI:248, VII:156; *FM.*III:467, ll.3–6, IV:106, ll.12–14. There are two books entitled *al-Maḍnūn*, one of which is called *al-Maḍnūn al-kabīr* and the other *al-Maḍnūn al-ṣaghīr*. Both treatises are suspected of being spurious; see M. Bouyges, *Essai de Chronologie des Oeuvres de al-Ghazālī*, ed. M. Allard, pp.51–3; H.L. Yafeh, *Studies in al-Ghazālī*, pp.251–7, 280; and M. Afifi al-Akiti, 'The good, the bad, and the ugly of Falsafa', in Langermann (ed.), *Avicenna and His Legacy*. However, what is important for our discussion is the fact that Ibn al-ʿArabī considers *al-Maḍnūn* to belong to al-Ghazālī.

10. *Fut.*III:7; *FM.*II:3, l.25.

Mustaẓhirī, a book dedicated to the caliph al-Mustaẓhir, otherwise called *Kitāb Faḍā'iḥ al-bāṭiniyya* (*The Scandals of the Batinites*).[11]

Considering the great length of the *Futūḥāt al-Makkiyya*, Ibn al-ʿArabī refers to very few books other than his own, thus making the mentions of al-Ghazālī's works very significant. In spite of the importance our author ascribes to him, we shall see several points of disagreement.

To begin our survey, Ibn al-ʿArabī's *Futūḥāt* acknowledges al-Ghazālī in a positive light as a scholar who adheres to the sound position, that is, the Shaykh's position. Ibn al-ʿArabī points out that unveiling (*mukāshafa*) is connected with meanings, while witnessing (*mushāhada*)[12] relates to the essences. This is a view shared by many people of God (*ahl Allāh*),[13] among whom al-Ghazālī is reckoned.[14]

At other times al-Ghazālī is mentioned without evaluation, neither positive nor negative. Such is the case when al-Ghazālī interprets the letter *h* in *Allāh* to mean God's essence.[15] Likewise, Ibn al-ʿArabī reports without comment al-Ghazālī's statement that God's most exalted name is *huwa* (He), along with other views, such as those giving priority to *anta* (you).[16] Ibn al-ʿArabī praises early *mutakallimūn*, such as al-Ashʿarī, al-Juwaynī and al-Ghazālī, for their proof of God's unity through *dalīl al-tamānuʿ* (the proof from hypothetical mutual prevention),[17] while at the

11. *Fut.*I:504; *FM.*I:334, ll.29–30.

12. For both terms see *SPK*, pp.224–6.

13. This term is synonymous with the people of the truth (*ahl al-ḥaqq*). *SPK*, p.388, n.20, p.400, n.3. It denotes the Sufis who adhere to the correct beliefs.

14. *Fut.*IV:187; *FM.*II:496, ll.27–32.

15. *Fut.*VII:131; *FM.*IV:89, ll.13–15. Cf. VII:381; *FM.*IV:260, l.10 (*ḥadrat al-wudd*).

16. *Fut.*III:447; *FM.*II:297, ll.19–20. Al-Ghazālī is also mentioned as one of the scholars who dealt with God's names (*Fut.*IV:417; *FM.*II:649, l.30).

17. This proof states that if there were two gods the world would not be generated, because they would prevent each other from acting. The existence of a harmonious world proves that its creator is one. The Quranic basis of this proof is sura 21, verse 22, which reads: 'If there were gods in the heaven and earth except God, they would be ruined.' For some formulations of this proof in the Kalām (speculative theology) literature, see my *Al-Qāsim b. Ibrāhīm on the Proof of God's Existence*, pp.190–2, n.89.

same time accusing later *mutakallimūn* of not adhering to this proof.[18] In dealing with metaphysical matters, Ibn al-ʿArabī says that the place of nature is between the universal soul and the dust cloud (*habāʾ*),[19] which is al-Ghazālī's view, and that no other place can be ascribed to nature.[20] Concerning theodicy, Ibn al-ʿArabī agrees with al-Ghazālī's dictum that this world is the best of all possible worlds. Al-Ghazālī formulates his position thus: *laysa fīʾl-imkān abdaʿ mimmā kān*, meaning 'there is no possible world which is more wonderful than the present world (literally: than what exists).'[21] Strangely enough, Ibn al-ʿArabī cites this famous dictum incorrectly, replacing *mimmā kān* with *min hādha al-ʿālam* (than this world).[22]

In one place, Ibn al-ʿArabī even defends al-Ghazālī against the accusation that he believes in the acquisition of prophecy. Prophecy in Ibn al-ʿArabī's opinion is not acquired by man but given to man by God. When al-Ghazālī speaks of an acquirer of prophecy, says the Shaykh, he has in mind a follower of a prophet, like Hārūn who is called a prophet in Quran 19:53 because he followed Moses.[23]

We now come to the issue of al-Ghazālī's influence on Ibn al-ʿArabī. This subject can be divided into two sections: supposed influence and conspicuous influence. In the first case we assume that Ibn al-ʿArabī was influenced by al-Ghazālī, but we have no clear-cut evidence, while in the second case Ibn al-ʿArabī mentions al-Ghazālī.

18. *Fut.*III:434; *FM.*II:288, l.31 – 289, l.8.

19. *Habāʾ* is the primordial dust which corresponds to *al-hayūlā*, prime matter, of the philosophers; see *Seal*, p.68.

20. *Fut.*I:394; *FM.*I:261, l.3. I have not found this view in al-Ghazālī's writings. Very probably this notion goes back to Gnostic Hermetic tradition; see J. El-Moor, 'The Fool for Love (*Foll per amor*) as follower of universal religion', *JMIAS*, 36 (2004), pp.104–6.

21. E. Ormsby, *Theodicy in Islamic Thought*, pp.103–7.

22. *Fut.*I:393, II:257, III:155, III:517; *FM.*I:259, l.35 – 260, l.1, I:550, l.14, II:103, l.34, II:345, l.22. Cf. *Fut.*VI:98; *FM.*III:360, l.21.

23. *Fut.*III:6–7; *FM.*II:3, ll.24–5.

Al-Ghazālī's *Kitāb al-Tawḥīd wa'l-tawakkul* seems to be an important source for two of Ibn al-ʿArabī's most basic notions: the idea that God is the only real existent, and the principle of relativity. As we shall show, both issues are interrelated.

Chittick points out that Ibn al-ʿArabī followed early Sufis,[24] such as al-Ghazālī, in adhering to the first of these notions.[25] He did not, however, expand on al- Ghazālī's approach. Let us now examine his thought on this issue more closely. Al-Ghazālī divided people into a hierarchy of four levels with regard to the affirmation of God's unity (*tawḥīd*).[26] To the lowest level belong humans who only utter the words that denote *tawḥīd*, namely, 'there is no god but God', without paying attention to the meaning of the words; some even deny them. Such is the *tawḥīd* of the hypocrites. The second level is described as 'the belief of the common people' (*iʿtiqād al-ʿawwām*). They not only affirm God's unity, but also prove it through using the speculative arguments of the Kalām. In the third stratum people see many things but nevertheless consider them originating from one agent. Those who reach the fourth highest stage regard the world as only one entity; they do not see even themselves, thus passing away from their own consciousness. Sufis, says al-Ghazālī, call this stage *al-fanā' fī'l-tawḥīd* (being immersed in God's unity). In sum, the truth as it is (*al-ḥaqq kamā huwa ʿalayhi*), in al-Ghazālī's view, is the existence of only one entity. This truth is known through both revelation (*kashf* or *mukāshafa*) and reason (*nūr al-ḥaqq*).[27]

24. *Dimensions*, pp.146–8.

25. W.C. Chittick, *Imaginal Worlds*, p.16.

26. Al-Qushayrī defines *tawḥid* as the judgement that God is one (*al-ḥukm bi-anna Allāh wāḥid*): *Al-Risāla al-Qushayriyya*, p.291.

27. Al-Ghazālī, *Iḥyā' ʿulūm al-dīn*, Al-Maktaba al-Tijāriyya al-Kubrā, IV, pp.245–6. B. Abrahamov, 'Al-Ghazālī's supreme way to know God', *Studia Islamica*, 77 (1993), p.158. In this article I tried to show that al-Ghazālī preferred the intellectual way to know the truth, but now I think that al-Ghazālī intentionally merged revelation, expressed in the above-mentioned terms, with reason, expressed, as I will show, in the words *perspectives* and *considerations*.

On the question of how it is possible to perceive one entity when one observes the heavens, the earth, and other bodies, that is, how the many is one, al-Ghazālī refrains from giving a direct answer, claiming that this problem belongs to the secrets of revelation which cannot be written in books. However, he is ready to divulge a clue to this apparent contradiction between the many and the one. A thing, says al-Ghazālī, may be one from one perspective[28] and many from another. For example, a human being is many when we consider his bodily parts, but one in relation to another. Thus, a thing may be one and many at the same time. Likewise, existence is one from one point of view and many from another.[29]

Elsewhere al-Ghazālī explains the phenomenon of double existence through a Neoplatonic image:

> In existence there is none but God, may He be extolled and exalted, and His acts. If one observes God's acts as such [*min ḥaythu hiya afʿāluhu*], confining himself to this observation, or does not see them [*lam yarahā*] as heaven, earth and trees [i.e. as particulars], but as God's making [*min ḥaythu annahā ṣanʿuhu*], since his knowledge cannot reach [literally: exceed] the Godship's presence,[30] it is possible for him to say: 'I know only God and see only God.' If a person conceives [that] he sees only the sun and its light spreading out in the horizon it is right for him to say: 'I see only the sun', since the light which emanates from it [*al-fā'iḍ minhā*] is a part of its totality and is included in it. Everything in existence is a light of the lights of the eternal power [*al-qudra al-azaliyya*] and an effect of its effects. Just as the sun is the source of light [*yanbūʿ al-nūr*] which emanates on every thing that is lit, so the essence [*al-maʿnā*] which no expression can be given about and which is designated as the eternal power is the source of existence which emanates on every existent thing. Consequently, in existence there is only God, may He be extolled and exalted. Therefore it is admissible for the knower [*al-ʿārif*] to say: 'I Know only God.'[31]

28. In al-Ghazālī's language 'by means of a kind of observation and consideration' (*bi- nawʿ mushāhada wa-iʿtibār*): *Iḥyā'*, IV, 246.26.

29. Ibid. 246–7.

30. By this statement al-Ghazālī means that a human being cannot know God's essence (*dhāt*), but only His attributes and actions.

31. Al-Ghazālī, *al-Maqṣad al-asnā sharḥ asmā' Allāh al-ḥusnā*, pp. 58–9. I translated this paragraph in 'Supreme Way', pp. 159–60. What derives its existence from something

What al-Ghazālī is saying here is that logically one can distinguish between God's acts and His essence, but since the world in all its parts emanates from God, like the rays of light from the sun, the only real existent is God.

Both the notion of God as the only real existent and the notion of observing the world from different perspectives are fundamental ideas of Ibn al-ʿArabī. According to the first idea, which later became known by the term *waḥdat al-wujūd* (the unity of existence),[32] existence is one, meaning that the only real existent is God, and the phenomena observed in the cosmos are nothing but manifestations of God.[33] Elucidation of this theory is not the aim of this chapter. One aspect of it, however, is relevant to the subject: the place of God in the world. To put it in the form of questions: Can one find (*wajada*) God? And if one can, where is He? Like al-Ghazālī, who states that a thing may be one and many at the same time, Ibn al-ʿArabī puts forward the idea that existence is one and many at the same time and that God is both transcendent and immanent simultaneously.

The same solution to the conflict between the one and the many and the same example used by al-Ghazālī appear in the *Fuṣūṣ*:

> There is no real conflict implicit in the variety of forms. They are in fact twofold. All these forms are like the limbs of Zayd. It is quite clear that Zayd is a single personal reality, and that his hand does not look like his foot [...]. In other words he is multiple and single, multiple in form [*al-kathīr bi'l-ṣuwar*] and single in essence [*al-wāḥid bi'l-ʿayn*], just as man is, without doubt, one in His essence. We do not doubt that ʿAmr is not Zayd [...] nor that the various individual parts of this one essence are infinite in existence.

else has no real, but only a metaphoric, existence, says al-Ghazālī in *Mishkāt al-anwār*. Here God is called not only 'the true existent' but also 'the true light'. *Mishkāt al-anwār wa-misfāt al-asrār*, ed. ʿAbd al-ʿAzīz ʿIzz al-Dīn al-Sayrawān, p. 137. I did not find the term 'true light' in the *Futūḥat*, although the reasoning is clear: if God is true existent and He is also light, He is also true light.

32. Ibn al-ʿArabī himself never used this term, which was coined by his commentators; *SPK*, p. 79.

33. Ibid. Chap. 6.

> Thus God, although One in His Essence, is multiple in forms and individual parts.[34]

According to Ibn al-ʿArabī, existence is one; however, from one point of view it is God, and from another it is creation. The distinction between God and creation is not real but is rather an outcome of different considerations.[35]

The term *tanzīh* (literally: to deem something to be above another) denotes God's transcendence; God is above all things, that is, He cannot be compared to anything, for existence belongs only to Him. Rationalist theologians, especially the Muʿtazilites, share this opinion. However, from another perspective, there is no existence except God, for existence (*wujūd*) means to find or to be found (*wajada* or *wujida*), and man finds himself and others. Therefore, there is a common ground between God, who can be said to truly 'find', and man, who 'finds', that is, experiences, his own existence. This is the perspective of *tashbīh* (literally: likening), which in our context means the likening of God to man or declaring a kind of similarity between God and man.[36] Those who have perfect knowledge of God, that is, the gnostics (*ʿārifūn*) or the people of God (*ahl Allāh*), see existence through both perspectives, *tanzīh* and *tashbīh*.[37]

Ibn al-ʿArabī makes a similar observation in Chapter 382 of the *Futūḥat*, where he writes of the beginnings (*sābiqa*, pl. *sawābiq*) and terminations (*khātima*, pl. *khawātim*) of things. According to the Shaykh, each concrete thing in existence has a permanent archetype (*ʿayn thābita*, pl. *aʿyān thābita*) eternally subsisting in the world of the Unseen. These permanent archetypes are the essential forms of God's names and potentialities in the Divine Essence. From the point of view of external existence, the permanent

34. *Fuṣūṣ al-ḥikam*, pp. 183–4; *Bezels*, p. 232.
35. Cf. *Fuṣūṣ* (Affifi's commentary), p. 58.
36. *SDG*, p. xxi.
37. Ibid. p. xxiii.

archetypes are non-existent, although they exist, as concepts exist in one's mind.[38] Now, things that exist externally have beginnings and terminations, but, from the point of view of the Divine, they perpetually exist as *aʿyān thābita*.[39] On the other side of the coin, non-existence is the essence of the sensible thing, for the cause of its external existence lies outside the thing.[40] This notion appears also in al-Ghazālī's *al-Maḍnūn al-ṣaghīr* and *Mishkāt*: 'From the point of view of their essences, things have only non-existence' (*laysa liʾl-ashyāʾ min dhawātihā illā al-ʿadam*).[41]

In like manner, the word *jazāʾ* may be defined in two ways, depending on the perspective. In the sensible world it means compensation for the human being's deeds, that is, reward or punishment. However, in its inward perspective it means all that God gives to the existents in accordance with their natures.[42]

Yet another notion, that of Muhammad's spirit, which exists primordially before the concrete creation of the world, occurs in al-Ghazālī's *al-Maḍnūn al-ṣaghīr*. He refers to the *ḥadīth*: 'I am the first prophet with regard to creation and the last to be sent' (*anā awwal al-anbiyāʾ khalqan wa-ākhiruhum baʿthan*). Here the author differentiates between creation (*khalq*) and bringing into existence (*ījād*). He interprets *khalq* to mean *taqdīr*, that is, literally giving measure or determining, but in this particular case, it signifies God's establishing the aims and perfections of Muhammad's personality in His thought. This is like an architect preparing a building plan, a process that explains the *ḥadīth* 'I was a prophet when Adam was between water and clay' (*kuntu nabiyyan wa-ādam*

38. T. Izutsu, *Sufism and Taoism*, Chap. 12, pp.159–96. The theory of permanent archetypes is reminiscent of Plato's theory of the Ideas.

39. *Fut.*VI:313–15; *FM.*III:511–13.

40. *Fut.*VI:315, l.8; *FM.*III:512, ll.30–2.

41. Al-Ghazālī, *al-Maḍnūn al-ṣaghīr*, in the margins of 'Abd al-Karīm al-Jīlānī's *al-Insān al-kāmil fī maʿrifat al-awākhir waʾl-awāʾil*, p.94. Al-Ghazālī, *Mishkāt*, p.137. Possibly this idea goes back to Ibn Sīnā; *Al-Najāt*, ed. M. Fakhri, pp.261–3.

42. *Fuṣūṣ*, p.99.

bayna al-mā' wa'l-ṭīn),[43] which means that the idea of Muhammad existed before Muhammad was born. The idea of Muhammad is called 'the holy prophetic Muhammadan spirit' (*al-ruḥ al-qudsī al-nabawiyy al-Muḥammadī*), which corresponds to Ibn al-'Arabī's *al-ḥaqīqa al-Muḥammadiyya*, the Muhammadan reality.[44]

There is a striking similarity between Ibn al-'Arabī's theory of the diversity of entities and that of al-Ghazālī. Like al-Ghazālī,[45] our author states that things are different because of their different states of preparedness for existence. For example, partial souls differ with respect to their preparedness to receive the light of the Universal Soul. Ibn al-'Arabī uses the simile of lamps and their wicks: the measure of light and its quality depend on the cleanliness of the wicks and the purity of the oil in the lamps. What kindles the wicks is the first lamp, corresponding to the Universal Soul.[46] Al-Ghazālī points out that the relation of the souls of human beings to the souls of angels is like the relation of lamps to a great fire that kindles them.[47]

We find a similar structure in the beginning of both the *Iḥyā'* and the *Futūḥat*, that is, the first part dealing with knowledge and the second with the five essential commandments (literally: elements) of Islam (*arkān al-islām*). Moreover, we find similarities in two basic issues:

1. The attitude toward jurists (*fuqahā'*).
2. The explanation of the essential commandments.

43. Ibn al-'Arabī repeats this tradition several times. For example, *Fut.*I:207; *FM.*I:134, l.35.

44. Al-Ghazālī, *al-Maḍnūn al-ṣaghīr*, p.98.

45. Ibid. pp.89–98.

46. *Fut.*III:100–1 (the answer to al-Ḥakīm al-Tirmidhī's question no.39); *FM.*II:66f.; cf. *SDG*, p.273.

47. Al-Ghazālī, *al-Maḍnūn al-ṣaghīr*, p.98. This notion is reminiscent of Ibn Sīnā's idea in *al-Ishārāt wa'l-tanbīhāt*, ed. J. Forget, Leiden, 1892, pp.126–7, in which he states that the Active Intellect (*al-'aql al-fa''āl*) is like a fire that causes the potential intellect to be active.

Al-Ghazālī regards the jurist as a scholar who deals with outward matters concerning this world; he does not master the believer's heart. In other words, spiritual issues are not his concern.[48]

Ibn al-ʿArabī's criticism of jurists resembles that of al-Ghazālī. In his view, jurists pay no attention to the spiritual basis of religion or the aim of revelation. Moreover, they judge on the basis of their passions, not on the basis of reason. He calls them formal scholars (*ʿulamāʾ al-rusūm*),[49] who prefer this world to the world to come, and creation (meaning material values) to the truth. They are also reproached for learning from books and people instead of learning from revelation.[50]

Like al-Ghazālī, Ibn al-ʿArabī examines the five essential commandments through the prism of their secrets. Both scholars devote much space to the laws of each commandment, except the *shahāda*, and add internal meanings to each.[51]

Also in both works a discussion of the secrets of ablution (*ṭahāra*) precedes the discussion of the commandments. We cannot offer here a detailed comparison between the approaches of al-Ghazālī and the Shaykh to each of the commandments. Suffice it to say that, although both scholars deal with the laws of each commandment, Ibn al-ʿArabī devotes much more space to this subject than al-Ghazālī, who concentrates on the internal meanings of every commandment.

Both scholars also maintain a similar conception of the structure of the world. According to al-Ghazālī, all beings exist in the form of pairs except God, who is single. To support his view,

48. *Iḥyāʾ*, I, 17–19. Al-Ghazālī has an ambivalent attitude to both sciences of *fiqh* and Kalām; on the one hand he admits their value for practical purposes, but on the other he considers them inferior to the true inward values of religion. For a detailed discussion of al-Ghazālī's attitude toward jurists and speculative theologians, see Yafeh, *Studies*, pp. 373–90.

49. *Fut.*VI:59; *FM.*III:333, l.24. This term appears for the first time in al-Ghazālī's writings. Yafeh, *Studies*, pp. 105–10.

50. *Fut.*I:421–2; *FM.*I:279. J.W. Morris, 'Ibn al-ʿArabī's "Esotericism"', *Studia Islamica*, 71 (1990), pp. 49, 54, 57, 59.

51. *Fut.*II:14–558; *FM.*I:386–763. *Iḥyāʾ*, I, 145–272.

he cites Quran 51:49: 'And all things We have created by pairs'[52] (*wa-min kull shay' khalaqnā zawjayn*).[53] Ibn al-ʿArabī expresses a similar view when saying: 'God says, *By the even and the odd* (89:3). We have already explained that evenness is the reality of the servant, for oddness is appropriate for God alone in respect of His Essence.'[54]

Sometimes even Ibn al-ʿArabī's use of words is reminiscent of al-Ghazālī. For example, in al-Ghazālī's view the eminence of knowledge is determined by the eminence of the object of knowledge (*sharaf al-ʿilm bi-qadar sharaf al-maʿlūm*). Since God is the highest object of knowledge, man's knowledge of Him is the most eminent knowledge.[55] Ibn al-ʿArabī follows al-Ghazālī on this idea, even employing the same superlatives: 'The True Existent is the greatest (*aʿẓam*) existent, the most sublime (*ajall*) and the most eminent (*ashraf*), and the knowledge of Him is the most eminent, greatest and sublime knowledge.'[56] The most frequently repeated words relating to God and the knowledge of Him used by both al-Ghazālī and Ibn al-ʿArabī are eminence (*sharaf*) and most eminent (*ashraf*).[57]

Another stylistic feature that the Shaykh may have learned from al-Ghazālī is the description of the relationships of God's names to one another, as well as the relationships between His names and contingent things. These relations are expressed through human conversations, that is, the names talk to each other.[58]

Likewise, al-Ghazālī depicts the conversations between the elements that participate in the performance of human acts

52. M.M. Pickthall, *The Meaning of the Glorious Koran*.
53. *Iḥyā'*, III, 27.13–14.
54. *Fut.*II:166; *FM.*I:489, ll.32–3 (para. *waṣl fī faṣl ṣifat al-watr*); *SDG*, p.175.
55. *Iḥyā'*, IV, 308.14.
56. *Fut.*VI:100; *FM.*III:361, ll.18–19.
57. Cf. al-Qūnawī's saying: 'The eminence of knowledge differs in accordance with the eminence of the object known' (*sharaf al-ʿilm yatfāwatu bi-ḥasab sharaf al-maʿlūm*), in G. Shubert (ed.), *al-Murāsalāt bayna Ṣadr al-dīn al-Qūnawī wa-Naṣīr al-dīn al-Ṭūsī*, p.16.
58. *Fut.*I:487–8; *FM.*I:322ff.

beginning with God's attributes such as knowledge and will and ending with the human attributes of knowledge, will and so on.[59]

In sum, there is clear evidence that al-Ghazālī influenced Ibn al-ʿArabī on both cardinal and marginal issues. Notwithstanding, Ibn al-ʿArabī criticizes al-Ghazālī and accuses him of holding inappropriate views. A sign of his ambivalent attitude toward al-Ghazālī is revealed when Ibn al-ʿArabī refers to the former's Sufism. He once points out that al-Ghazālī and al-Muḥāsibī belong to the common group of the Sufis (*ʿāmmat ahl hādhā al-ṭarīq*; literally: the common people of this way) as distinguished from *ahl Allāh* (the people of God), that is, the real adherents of Sufism.[60] But elsewhere al-Ghazālī appears as 'one of the people of God, the followers of revelation or unveiling' (*aḥad min ahl Allāh aṣḥāb al-kashf*), a title most favoured by Ibn al-ʿArabī.[61]

We now turn to several issues concerning which Ibn al-ʿArabī disagrees with al-Ghazālī. The first topic is the nature of God. As is well known, the Shaykh holds to the view of the absolute transcendence of God's essence: humans cannot know God's essence, and all they know about Him are His names and attributes.[62] Ibn al-ʿArabī presents al-Ghazālī as holding two contradicting views: on the one hand he states that only God knows God, which implies the absolute transcendence of God,[63] while, on the other, in his *al-Maḍnūn bihi ʿalā ghayr ahlihi*, he discusses God's essence from a rational point of view.[64] Our author

59. *Iḥyāʾ*, IV, 248–52 (para. *ḥaqīqat al-tawḥīd alladhī huwa al-tawakkul*).

60. *Fut.*II:312; *FM.*I:590, ll.14–15.

61. *Fut.*III:6; *FM.*II:3, ll.15–16.

62. *SPK*, Chap. 4. This view coincides with the traditionalist approach based on the *ḥadīth*: 'Do not reflect on God's essence' (*lā tafakkarū fī dhāt Allāh*). B. Abrahamov, *Islamic Theology*, p. 2. Ibn al-ʿArabī cites Quran 6:103: 'All kinds of perceptions [*al-abṣar*; literally, 'glances'] do not perceive Him [*lā tudri-kuhu*]' to corroborate his claim that reason cannot perceive God's essence; *Fut.*VII:44, 55; *FM.*IV:30, ll.5–10, 38, ll.1–8.

63. *Fut.*I:244; *FM.*I:160, ll.4–15. Here some contemporary *mutakallimūn* of Ibn al-ʿArabī reprove al-Ghazālī for adhering to this view.

64. *Fut.*VI:248–9; *FM.*III:467, ll.4–6. In VII:156 (*FM.*IV:106, ll.12–14), al-Ghazālī's notion also appears in other works besides *al-Maḍnūn*.

fully recognizes this self-contradiction and says that even if it springs from al-Ghazālī's desire to disguise his true views, this should be regarded as wrongful conduct.[65] In like manner Ibn al-ʿArabī rejects al-Ghazālī's notion of the affinity (*munāsaba*) between God and human beings.[66] According to al-Ghazālī, there is external as well as internal affinity between God and man. External affinity is expressed through man's imitation of God's attributes, such as knowledge and compassion, while internal affinity is hidden. However, there are clear indications that al-Ghazālī considers knowledge as that which creates affinity between God and human beings.[67]

Another point of disagreement between Ibn al-ʿArabī and al-Ghazālī is the distinction between a saint (*waliyy*) and a prophet (*nabiyy*). In al-Ghazālī's view, a saint is inspired (*mulham*), while a prophet is one to whom an angel descends, although in some matters he too is inspired, because he joins sainthood to prophecy. The Shaykh regards this view as a mistake and a sign that adherents of such a linkage are bereft of revelation (*dhawq*; literally: 'tasting'). For him, the difference lies in the content of the message the angel delivers. That which is given to a prophet–messenger is different from that given to a saint. Sometimes the angel teaches a saint that which causes the latter to understand a prophet's sayings.[68]

Yet another controversy between Ibn al-ʿArabī and al-Ghazālī, already noted by Michel Chodkiewicz, is the question of the highest spiritual stage attainable short of prophecy. In al-Ghazālī's view, it is the stage of *ṣiddīqiyya*, a term derived from Abū Bakr's nickname al-Ṣiddīq. However, Ibn al-ʿArabī places an intermediate level between *ṣiddīqiyya* and prophecy known as 'the station

65. *Fut.*IV:28; *FM.*II:389, ll.13–15.
66. *Fut.*I:145; *FM.*I:93, ll.7–9.
67. B. Abrahamov, *Divine Love in Islamic Mysticism*, pp.56–9.
68. *Fut.*VI:35; *FM.*III:316, ll.11–15.

of proximity' (*maqām al-qurba*), which is the highest stage of the saints.[69]

Ibn al-ʿArabī's most aggressive attack on al-Ghazālī focuses on the way the mystic should follow to reach the knowledge of God and His attributes. In the *Iḥyā'* al-Ghazālī describes two paths to knowledge: inspiration (*ilhām*) and reflection (*iʿtibār, istibṣār*).

The first way, the way of the Sufis, consists of exercising asceticism, erasing blameworthy qualities and sincere turning to God alone. After such a procedure, a human is ready to receive inspiration from God. This is the way of prophets and saints. Al-Ghazālī acknowledges criticism of the Sufis' method on the part of rational thinkers (*nuẓẓār, dhawū al-iʿtibār*). These scholars do not deny the possibility of reaching knowledge through the method of inspiration, but they point out that this rarely happens for most people; it works only for prophets and saints. According to these critics, it is almost impossible for man to erase his connections with this world and to continuously evade evil motives that instigate man to do evil acts. Besides, practising the ascetic life without learning true sciences may cause the ascetic to regard false imaginations as true revelation. Thus, knowledge of true sciences should precede man's ascetic practice and serve as a criterion for examining the nature of what is revealed to the ascetic.

Al-Ghazālī seems to have accepted the critics' view, for he expresses no reservations regarding it. It seems to me that al-Ghazālī refers to the claim that ascetic practice is the only condition for the revelation of truth as being false.[70] However, it should be noted that al-Ghazālī also depicts the Sufi way of gaining knowledge as not through learning but through inspiration. He unusually inserts into the present context a personal note: 'Ascetic practice also sometimes brought me to inspiration' (*wa-anā ayḍan rubbamā intahat bī al-riyāḍa wa'l-muwāẓaba ilayhi*).[71] All in all, one

69. *Seal*, pp.57–8, 114.
70. *Iḥyā'*, III, 13–14.19. Abrahamov, *Divine Love*, pp.64–8.
71. *Iḥyā'*, III, 20.

cannot discern his real view regarding the learning of the sciences. Here, of course, arises the question of al-Ghazālī's esotericism, but that is the subject of another study.

In the light of the preceding, we shall now examine Ibn al-ʿArabī's system of attaining unveiling and his criticism of al-Ghazālī's experience and mystical system. The Shaykh uses the term *ummī* to explain his method. This term appears in the Quran six times,[72] two of which (7:157, 7:158) refer to Muhammad and denote the illiterate or one who does not know the Scriptures.[73] In Ibn al-ʿArabī's thought, *ummī* does not have the sense of one who does not know the Quran or the traditions, but rather of one whose heart is free of reflection and speculation and hence receptive to divine unveiling in the most perfect manner and without delay.[74] It is unlikely that he who deals with rational arguments should receive from divine knowledge what the *ummī* receives, because the greater part of the spiritual world lies beyond the intellect. Ibn al-ʿArabī's criticism of the theologians' and the jurists' speculation concentrates on the instability of their judgements; what is correct today may be wrong tomorrow owing to changes in circumstances in the sphere of law or in the appearance of new opponents in the

72. Quran 7:157, 158; 2:78; 3:20, 75; 62:2.

73. E. Geoffroy, 'Ummī', in *EI*, x, 863. Cf. I. Goldfeld, 'The illiterate Prophet (*Nabbī Ummī*): An inquiry into the development of a dogma in Islamic tradition', *Der Islam*, 57 (1980), pp. 58–67.

74. *Fut.*IV:409; *FM.*II:644, ll.17–27. Chittick translated the beginning of this chapter in *SPK*, pp. 235–8. In *Kitāb al-Isfār ʿan natāʾij al-asfār* (in *Rasāʾil Ibn al-ʿArabī*, Part II:7), Ibn al-ʿArabī differentiates between two kinds of travellers (*musāfirūn*), namely, people who seek metaphysical knowledge. The first group of 'travellers' are the philosophers who base themselves only on their intellect and hence deviate from the true way. The second kind are prophets and chosen saints, like the verifiers among the Sufis, who receive their knowledge through unveiling and thus attain the truth. Cf. F. Rosenthal, 'Ibn ʿArabī between "Philosophy" and "Mysticism"', *Oriens*, 3 (1988), p. 8. It is worth noting that in Ibn al-ʿArabī's opinion part of what the philosophers state is true: they express wise sayings (*ḥikam*) and advocate righteousness (ibid. p. 12).

sphere of theology. In contradistinction, the divine revelation is stable and does not change.[75]

At the core of our discussion is the example Ibn al-ʿArabī brings to illustrate his point. This example comes from al-Ghazālī himself, who relates what happened to him when he wanted to join the Sufis.[76] Al-Ghazālī tells us that he relinquished his speculation and reflection, and engaged instead in the invocation of God, hoping to receive divine knowledge that he had not had before. However, he was frustrated, for he realized that what he acquired was a juridical faculty that he had already possessed. Withdrawing to his retreat and practising what the Sufis practise many times did not change his situation – his knowledge remained impure. Al-Ghazālī admitted that although he was no longer like his fellow rationalists, whether theologians or jurists, he failed to attain the Sufis' level, concluding that 'writing upon what has been erased (*maḥw*)[77] is not the same as writing upon that which has not been erased'.[78] This means that although he negated his previous scientific knowledge, he could not attain the pure state of one who had not acquired scientific knowledge at all.

In conclusion, Ibn al-ʿArabī not only opposes the Ghazālīan idea that science is a criterion for recognizing true revelation, but also the possibility of ever reaching the pure state of unveiling once the sciences have been studied. However, how can we explain the fact that the Shaykh himself, who mastered the sciences of jurisprudence, theology and philosophy, experienced, by his own reports, unveiling? Does this fact not contradict his

75. *Fut.*IV:410; *FM.*II:645. The claim that reason leads to self-contradictory arguments and to changes in ideology was already expressed by traditionalist circles in the ninth century and repeated in the following centuries. Abrahamov, *Islamic Theology*, Chap. 3.

76. I was unable to find in al-Ghazālī's writings the source of the following story about him.

77. Meaning the scholar who leaves his previous rational knowledge.

78. Meaning one who did not occupy himself with rational knowledge; trans. *SPK*, p.237.

criticism of al-Ghazālī? Ibn al-ʿArabī himself supplies the answer. He says that God revealed to him knowledge when he was in seclusion (*khalwa*).[79] Elsewhere he enumerates three ways to attain knowledge:

1. By means of the intellect, that is, through speculation (*naẓar*) or by necessity (*ḍarūratan*).
2. Through tasting (*dhawq*), which is the knowledge of the states (*aḥwāl*).
3. Divine revelation, which is called the knowledge of secrets (*ilm al-asrār*). Whoever knows by such a device knows all the sciences.[80]

In fine, Ibn al-ʿArabī's attitude toward al-Ghazālī is ambivalent. Sometimes he heavily relies on him and sometimes he severely opposes him. This is the approach of an original thinker who both learns from others and independently develops his own ideas.

79. *Fut.*I:490; *FM.*I:325, ll.19–21.
80. *Fut.*I:54–5; *FM.*I:31.

Ibn Barrajān

?–1141

Ibn Barrajān, Abū al-Ḥakam ʿAbd al-Salām ibn ʿAbd al-Raḥmān, an Andalusian mystic and theologian, was born in North Africa and taught in Seville during the first half of the twelfth century. He was very active in the Sufi opposition to the inquisition of the Almoravid legists (*fuqahā'*). Ibn Barrajān was known as a scholar of *qirā'āt* (recitation of the Quran), Tradition and Kalām (speculative theology) and as a Sufi who practised abstinence and had the capability of divination. Ibn Barrajān belongs to the great Sufi tradition of the school of Ibn Masarra;[1] however, like other Andalusian Sufis of his time he was influenced by al-Ghazālī and hence was called 'al-Ghazālī of al-Andalus'.[2] He wrote two commentaries, the first on the Quran and the second on God's names.[3] In *al-Futūḥāt al-Makkiyya* Ibn al-ʿArabī mentions him only six times and he is absent both from *Rūḥ al-quds* and *al-Durra al-fākhira*.[4]

Ibn al-ʿArabī apparently learned much from Ibn Barrajān about numerology, although he did not agree with him in certain cases and once even criticizes him for making an error.[5] When dealing with Ibn Barrajān's divination of Ṣalāḥ al-Dīn's conquest of Jerusalem (2 October 1187), a divination based on Quran 30:4, the Shaykh counters with his own method of numerology, stating that Ibn Barrajān 'did not mention this way in his book in the context in which we mentioned it, but he mentioned it in the context of astronomy' (*ʿilm al-falak*). By doing so, says Ibn al-

1. C. Addas, 'Andalusī mysticism and the rise of Ibn ʿArabī', in S.K. Jayyusi (ed.), *The Legacy of Muslim Spain*, p.925.
2. Ibid. p.921.
3. A. Faure, 'Ibn Barrajān', in *EI*; Addas, 'Andalusī mysticism', p.925.
4. These two works were translated in *Sufis*.
5. *Fut.*VII:324; *FM.*IV:220, ll.32–4.

ʿArabī, Ibn Barrajān covered his revelation, that is, he used science instead of revelation.[6]

Two mystics, Sahl al-Tustarī and Ibn Barrajān, are responsible for the notion of the Real through whom creation takes place (*al-ḥaqq al-makhlūq bihi*). As we have seen, God's essence is unknown, but His names and attributes are known and act in the cosmos. The Real is the name of God which acts in the world. This idea is corroborated by Quran verses such as 'We did not create the heavens and the earth and that which is between them, save through the Real' (*bi'l-ḥaqq*).[7]

Elsewhere Ibn al-ʿArabī mentions Ibn Barrajān among other Sufis, such as al-Qushayrī and al-Ghazālī, as holding the view that part of the waystation of bestowing favours[8] is the science of anatomy, or the structure of the human being (*tashrīḥ*). The science of anatomy is divided into two parts:

1. Knowledge of the structure of the world as illustrated in the human being, that is, the various traits of all things.
2. Knowledge of God's names and His relationships which are also found in the human being.[9]

Ibn al-ʿArabī says that Ibn Barrajān created the term *al-imām al-mubīn* (the clear record)[10] for designating the first created entity. Usually this term is equivalent to *al-lawḥ al-maḥfuẓ* (the preserved tablet), which is the heavenly source of all the Scriptures. However, for our author *al-imām al-mubīn* represents the human being, the microcosm, in which all forms of the world exist.[11]

6. *Fut.*I:97f.; *FM.*I:60, ll.1–11. Addas, 'Andalusī Mysticism', p.925.

7. Quran 15:85; *Fut.*III:155, V:113; *FM.*II:104, l.6, III:77, ll.25–6; *SPK*, p.133. Literally *bi'l-ḥaqq* means 'in true purpose', that is, the world serves a purpose which God established, for example, to benefit people.

8. This is one of God's traits which the mystic should imitate.

9. *Fut.*IV:417; *FM.*II:649, ll.25–31; *SPK*, p.284.

10. Quran 36:12.

11. Ibn al-ʿArabī, *Al-Tadbīrāt*, pp.121, 125f. M. Takeshita, *Ibn ʿArabī's Theory of the Perfect Man and its Place in the History of Islamic Thought*, p.103, n.114.

To sum up, Ibn Barrajān appears here only as a transmitter of the ideas of earlier sages without making a unique contribution to the subject matters discussed by Ibn al-ʿArabī. However, appreciating his personality, the Shaykh mentions him along with other important Sufis and counts him among the people of God (*ahl Allāh*). Yet, as Claude Addas rightly states, his position in Ibn al-ʿArabī's eyes was lower than that of Ibn al-ʿArīf.[12]

12. Addas, 'Andalusī Mysticism', p.927.

Ibn al-ʿArīf al-Ṣanhājī

?–1141

Ibn al-ʿArīf, Abū al-ʿAbbās Aḥmad ibn Muḥammad al-Ṣanhājī was a famous Sufi, traditionist, jurist, poet and reader of the Quran. He founded a Sufi school (*ṭarīqa*) in Almeria which attracted many Sufis. Abū Bakr al-Mayūrkī and Abū al-Ḥakam ibn Barrajān, two mystics suspected by the Almoravid Sultan ʿAli ibn Yūsuf of being rebels, were possibly affiliated with Ibn al-ʿArīf's group. People regarded Ibn al-ʿArīf as a holy man.[1]

The only treatise written by Ibn al-ʿArīf known today is *Maḥāsin al-majālis* (*The Attractions of Mystical Sessions*). In this work Ibn al-ʿArīf deals with the Sufi way which is divided into stations such as knowledge, will, abstinence, endurance, fear, hope and so on. Ibn al-ʿArīf's description of the stations is conventional. Where his approach differs uniquely is in his treatment of most of the stations, apart from gnosis and love, as values appropriate only for common Sufis and not for the elite Sufis. Ibn al-ʿArīf states that it is impossible to reach God through something which is not God.[2] This is not an original contribution to Sufi thought.[3] As we have stated, al-Tirmidhī already differentiated between the *ahl ḥaqq Allāh*, who engage in stations and states, and the *ahl Allāh* who are chosen by God to be His saints without previously engaging in mystical practice.[4]

What is important in this approach is the fact that the author creates no connection between practising the stations and

1. A. Faure, 'Ibn al-ʿArīf', in *EI*; Ibn al-ʿArīf, *Maḥāsin al-Majālis*.
2. Ibid. p.15.
3. C. Addas, 'Andalusī mysticism and the rise of Ibn ʿArabī', in S.K. Jayyusi (ed.), *The Legacy of Muslim Spain*, p.926.
4. See p.89 above.

attaining the highest goal. The stations and states belong to the common Sufis. In Islamic mysticism the precedent of abandoning a certain station is not unknown,[5] and Ibn al-ʿArīf's point of view is somewhat exceptional, but he has no claim to originality.

Very probably, when Ibn al-ʿArabī formulated his theory of abandoning the stations and establishing the proximity to God as the highest mystical value, he had in mind al-Tirmidhī, Ibn al-ʿArīf and perhaps al-Anṣārī.[6] However, Ibn al-ʿArabī does not deny the value of the stations altogether with respect to the Sufi who attains revelation, but recommends abandoning the stations, because stable values, such as God as the only real existent and the unity of all the phenomena in the world, override the stations. The paradox Ibn al-ʿArabī expresses is that the perfection of the stations entails their abandonment.[7] In the attitude of the Sufis to the stations, except for al-Tirmidhī, we see a gradual development which begins with scattered notes on the abandoning of some states, continues with Ibn al-ʿArīf's theory of utilizing the states as a tool for the common Sufis, and culminates in Ibn al-ʿArabī's theory of abandoning the states. According to the translators of the *Maḥāsin*, Ibn ʿAbbād of Ronda (d.1390), the most important mystic writer in the fourteenth century, exalted this theory as the essence of all Islamic spirituality.[8]

Now we turn to the conspicuous appearance of Ibn al-ʿArīf in *al-Futūḥāt al-Makkiyya*. First, it should be emphasized that our author appreciates Ibn al-ʿArīf highly. He calls him the man of

5. See my article, 'Abandoning the station (*tark al-maqām*) as reflecting Ibn al-ʿArabī's principle of relativity', *JMIAS*, 47 (2010), pp.23–46. Also in the context of abandoning the station (*tark al-makām*), Ibn al-ʿArabī cites a verse by Ibn al-ʿArīf which supports the former's thesis: 'Many people repent, but I am the only man who repents of repentance.' *Fut.*III:214; *FM.*II:143, ll.18–19.

6. Addas, 'Andalusī Mysticism', p.926. References to al-Anṣārī (d.1088) appear in the *Futūḥāt* only twice (II:126; III:421; *FM.*I:462, l.22, II:280, l.9), the second of which draws attentions to his treatise *Manāzil al-sāʾirīn*.

7. Abrahamov, 'Abandoning', p.45.

8. Ibn al-ʿArīf, *Maḥāsin*, p.18. In his article on Ibn Abbād in *EI*: Nwiya notes that he rarely cites Ibn al-ʿArabī.

courtesy (*adīb*) in his time.[9] Elsewhere, this appellation is explained as follows:

> The man of courtesy (*al-adīb*) is he who brings together all noble character traits (*makārim al-akhlāq*) and knows the base character traits without being described by them. He brings together all the levels of the sciences, both those which are praiseworthy and those which are blameworthy, since in the eyes of every intelligent person, knowledge of a thing is always better than ignorance of it. Hence, courtesy brings together all good (*jimāʿ al-khayr*).[10]

We learn about one of Ibn al-ʿArīf's character traits in the context of an event that occurred to one of his companions named Abū ʿAbdallāh al-Ghazzāl.[11] He told Ibn al-ʿArīf that when he was on his way grass and trees talked to him and urged him to take them, because they afforded such and such benefits. Ibn al-ʿArīf responded to this story by asking al-Ghazzāl what he thought was his benefit when the trees had talked to him. Al-Ghazzāl answered that it was repentance (*tawba*). Thereupon, Ibn al-ʿArīf informed al-Ghazzāl that God had tested him, for he, Ibn al-ʿArīf, guided him only to God and not to other things. He ordered al-Ghazzāl to return to the place where the trees talked to him, and said to him that the silence of the trees would testify to his true repentance. Al-Ghazzāl returned to this place and heard nothing.[12] Here Ibn al-ʿArīf taught al-Ghazzāl that the extraordinary phenomena he experienced cannot be considered as valuable in mystical life and the thing that is most important is one's inner experience, expressed here as the station of repentance. This approach of Ibn al-ʿArīf coincides well with Ibn al-ʿArabī who, as we have seen, rejects sensual miracles and praises spiritual ones.[13]

In Chapter 3 of the *Futūḥāt*, dedicated to God's transcendence (*tanzīh*), Ibn al-ʿArabī cites Ibn al-ʿArīf's statement on this topic:

9. *Fut.*I:345; *FM.*I:228, l.6.

10. *Fut.*III:428; *FM.*II:284, l.28; *SPK*, p.175.

11. See *Sufis*, pp.101f. Al-Ghazzāl was also a companion of Abū Madyan. *Fut.* VIII:384; *FM.*IV:550, l.20.

12. *Fut.*I:345; *FM.*I:228, ll.6–13.

13. See pp.48f. above, on the subject of miracles.

'He has no relationship with mankind except through divine providence (*'ināya*), and there in no relationship of cause and effect between them but God's judgement (*wa-lā sabab illā al-ḥukm*). The only time which can be referred to Him is eternity (*wa-lā waqt illā al-azal*). What is left (for humans) is only blindness and confusion (*fa-mā baqiya fa-'aman wa-talbīs*).'[14] The Shaykh praises Ibn al-'Arīf's statement and says that this is the most perfect knowledge of God, meaning God's essence.[15] In this case Ibn al-'Arīf's statement, to my thinking, serves to affirm Ibn al-'Arabī's idea about God's transcendence and is not the source of his thought, because this idea goes back to earlier mystics.[16] However, as we shall immediately see, according to Ibn al-'Arabī, Ibn al-'Arīf's notion of God's transcendence is only part of the picture.

Elsewhere Ibn al-'Arabī rejects the view of al-Ghazālī and other masters on the affinity between God and humans.[17] Affinity does not coincide with God's transcendence, because if we affirm any kind of affinity we actually state that we can know God, even if this knowledge is not complete. The Greatest Master also does not accept the notion that totally negates God's affinity held by Ibn al-'Arīf and other colleagues of his. Ibn al-'Arabī's system of thought is to imitate God in establishing knowledge of God and other entities. This means that he is led by the teachings of the Quran. So, when God tells people that 'There is nothing like Him and He is the All-Hearing the All-Seeing' (Quran 42:11), He is actually informing them that He is both transcendent and immanent. The first part of the verse teaches us about His being unequal to anything, which means absence of affinity; however, the second part conveys the notion that there is some

14. *Maḥāsin*, p.22, l.4 of the Arabic text; I did not follow the translation. *Fut.*I:145, III:78; *FM.*I:93, ll.9–11, II:51, ll.33–4.

15. *Fut.*I:145; *FM.*I:93, ll.11–12.

16. See the sections above on al-Kharrāz, al-Tirmidhī and al-Ghazālī.

17. Al-Ghazālī expands on this idea in his discussion of the causes of love in *Kitāb al-Maḥabba*. Affinity is the fifth cause of love between humans and God. See B. Abrahamov, *Divine Love in Islamic Mysticism*, pp.56–9.

affinity between God and humans – they both hear and see, but in different degrees.[18] The immanent aspect of God is proven elsewhere when Ibn al-ʿArabī mentions Ibn al-ʿArīf's notion of God's existence everywhere based on Quran 57:4 ('He is with you wherever you are').[19]

As we have seen, Ibn al-ʿArabī accepts al-Tirmidhī's concept of *walāya* according to which *walāya* is the essence of God's revelation to humans. Sometimes ideas of the ancients pass through an intermediary, which this time seems to be Ibn al-ʿArīf, who also accepts the difference between the prophecy of legislation (*nubuwwat al-tashrīʿ*) and *walāya*. In the context of the ninety-third question of al-Tirmidhī, which deals with the term *muḥiqq*,[20] the Shaykh cites Ibn al-ʿArīf's prayer: 'O God, You have closed the door of prophecy and apostleship to us, but You have not closed the door of *walāya*. O God, when You will establish the highest level of *walāya* for the highest *walī*, make me this *walī*.' According to Ibn al-ʿArabī, Ibn al-ʿArīf is one of the *muḥiqqīn*, that is, those who ask God for that which is appropriate for them. He says that even if the human being deserves prophecy and apostleship from the human point of view, because his essence is able to receive them, Ibn al-ʿArīf did not request these. That is because he knew that God, in an act of legislation, had closed the door of prophecy to humans.[21]

18. *Fut.*III:437; *FM.*II:290, l.31. It is worth noting that this verse can be interpreted to mean that God is unequal to anything because He is All-hearing and All-seeing. Abdel Haleem's translation ('There is nothing like Him: He is the All-hearing the All-seeing') connects the first part of the verse with the second in a way in which the second explains the first. It seems that our author explains this verse according to his ideology, a phenomenon best shown in his *Fuṣūṣ al-ḥikam*. Furthermore, he interprets the first part of the verse to mean immanence, for *ka-mithlihi* means that God has an image (*mithl*) which resembles no other image. The fact that He has an image likens Him to creation. *Fuṣūṣ*, p. 70.

19. Trans. M.A.S. Abdel Haleem, *The Quran.*

20. This term applies both to God, who gives what is due to everything, and to the human being who asks sincerely from God what is due to him.

21. *Fut.*III:145f.; *FM.*II:97, ll.17–18.

On the subject of the definition of love, Ibn al-ʿArabī also accepts Ibn al-ʿArīf's approach, so it seems. In an article on Ibn al-ʿArabī's approach to love, I wrote:

> Contrary to some Sufis, including al-Ghazālī who defines love as 'the inclination of one's nature toward the object which gives pleasure', Ibn al-ʿArabī expresses the idea that love cannot be defined. In his view, no one has been able to provide an essential definition of love; those who did attempt to define love identified only its results, signs and requisites. He bases his notion of love on that of Ibn al-ʿArīf.

Ibn al-ʿArīf says that one of the features of love is jealousy, and since jealousy involves concealment, love cannot be defined.[22]

As we know, Ibn al-ʿArabī believes that the truth should be sought in the esoteric realm. In this context he cites Ibn al-ʿArīf's saying that the truth becomes pure when the exoteric sign (*rasm*)[23] disappears. Naming Ibn al-ʿArīf a leader (*imām*) in this sphere of knowledge seems evidence that Ibn al-ʿArabī learned it from him.

Although Ibn al-ʿArabī mentions Ibn al-ʿArīf many times, the latter's views are not original and the former could have learned them from earlier sources, as the instance of *walāya* teaches us. It is true, as Claude Addas points out, that of the three Andalusian Sufis, Ibn Barrajān, Ibn al-ʿArīf and Ibn Qasī, it was Ibn al-ʿArīf who had the greatest influence on Ibn al-ʿArabī.[24] However, from the point of view of novelty, Ibn al-ʿArīf remains within the confines established by the early Sufis. This, of course, does not diminish his impact on Ibn al-ʿArabī regarding Sufi practice, morals and knowledge.

22. *Fut.*III:487; *FM.*II:325, ll.9–18. Abrahamov, 'Ibn al-ʿArabī on divine love', in S. Klein-Braslavy, B. Abrahamov and J. Sadan (eds.), *Tribute to Michael*, p.8.

23. Literally *rasm* denotes an external sign. Ibn al-ʿArabī is fond of using this word in the phrase *ʿulamāʾ al-rusūm*, the exoteric scholars. *SPK*, p.388, n.22. Al-Ghazālī was the first to coin this term. H.L. Yafeh, *Studies in al-Ghazālī*, pp.105–10.

24. *Quest*, p.53.

Ibn Qasī

?–1151

Abū al-Qāsim Aḥmad ibn al-Ḥusayn Ibn Qasī was a Sufi and a politician who participated in the rebellion against the Almoravid dynasty in Spain. In his youth he pursued a life of pleasure, but then turned suddenly to the Sufi life. He was not satisfied by being only a Sufi but also wished to be a politician and an imam. He succeeded in ruling over a small part of Spain, but became entangled with the Almohads by joining the Christians of Coimbra, which resulted in his assassination.

Only one of his works *Khalʿ al-naʿlayn* (*The Removal of the Sandals*) is extant. It was commented on by Ibn al-ʿArabī.[1]

Ibn al-ʿArabī mentions Ibn Qasī in the context of two principal subjects, the world to come and the hierarchy of religious leaders.[2] One of the issues discussed in Islamic theology is the question whether God created Paradise and Hell in the beginning or He will create them on the Day of Judgement.[3] In keeping with his system of thought, which takes into consideration two or more aspects, the Shaykh holds that Paradise and Hell are both created and not created. Their basic structure is created, but the tools that will serve their inhabitants have not been created up to now and will only be created on the day people enter Paradise and Hell. In this context, Ibn al-ʿArabī points out that according to Ibn Qasī, who counts as one of the People of Revelation (*ahl al-kashf*), Hell

1. A. Faure, 'Ibn Qasī', in *EI*; *Sufis*, p.26; *Quest*, p.53.
2. Ibn al-ʿArabī first regarded Ibn Qasī as an imam. *Fut.*I:209; *FM.*I:136, l.9. However, he later considered him an impostor. Addas, 'Andalusī mysticism and the rise of Ibn ʿArabī', in S.K. Jayyusi (ed.), *The Legacy of Muslim Spain*, p.926.
3. B. Abrahamov, 'The creation and duration of Paradise and Hell in Islamic theology', *Der Islam*, 79 (2002), pp.87–102.

was created in the form of a snake. One can imagine, Ibn al-ʿArabī says, that this is the form in which Hell was created.[4]

The second issue, related to the world to come, is the question of the modality of the Resurrection, or, in other words, how people will return to life. Basing himself on Quran 7:29 ('Just as He created you the first time, so you will return [to life]'), Ibn Qasī holds that people will come back to life in the manner in which they were created the first time, meaning that Adam will be created from clay and other people by way of natural procreation.[5]

Ibn al-ʿArabī disagrees with Ibn Qasī on this question of the modality of the Resurrection. The fact that only the sinners will be punished in the world to come proves that the next world differs from the present world in which even those who do not sin may suffer. For support he cites Quran 8:25, which reads: 'Beware of discord that harms not only the wrongdoers among you: know that God is severe in His punishment.'[6] Consequently, if the Resurrection were like the first creation, the punishment would apply to the sinners as well as to the righteous. He also argues that, just as the first creation takes place without a precedent, so the next world will be created without precedent.[7] Although Ibn al-ʿArabī opposes Ibn Qasī's view concerning the Resurrection, he does not take a stand on which view is correct: the majority view of the Muslims who believe that God will return their spirits to the human beings and thus revivify them, or Ibn Qasī's view.[8] This undecidedness is characteristic of Ibn al-ʿArabī's approach to various issues.[9]

4. *Fut.*I:448; *FM.*I:297, l.25.

5. *Fut.*I:471; *FM.*I:312, ll.15–21.

6. Trans. M.A.S. Abdel Haleem, *The Quran*.

7. *Fut.*III:240f.; *FM.*II:160, ll.22–3.

8. He ends this paragraph with the words: God knows best (*wa-Allāh aʿlam*). *Fut.*V:36; *FM.*III:24, ll.26–8.

9. See, for example, the section on Dhū al-Nūn al-Miṣrī, p.25, n.24 above.

Another issue connected to the Day of Judgement is the *mīzān*, the Scale[10] which weighs people's deeds on that day. Here, also, Ibn al-ʿArabī contends with Ibn Qasī's approach. I am not sure that I fully understand the following paragraph: 'The Scale is not in the state of equality of its two sides in the heaven and earth, but in a state of equality with regard to deed and reward. For this purpose the Scale was created. In this issue of the Scale a group of the people of God, among them Ibn Qasī, made an error.'[11]

As seen above, Ibn al-ʿArabī distinguishes between prophets, messengers and God's friends (*awliyāʾ*). The unique trait common to all these religious leaders is *walāya*, closeness to God. However, Quran 17:55 states that 'We have preferred some prophets to others', which means that some prophets and messengers[12] are superior to others. According to Ibn al-ʿArabī, the majority of the Muslims believe that this hierarchical structuring of prophets and messengers can be explained by pointing to a unique aspect through which a prophet is the most excellent (*fāḍil*), whereas his fellows are inferior (*mafḍūl*)[13] to him with respect to this specific aspect. Ibn al-ʿArabī states that Ibn Qasī cites as corroboration of the idea of ranking Quran 38:47 in which Abraham, Isaac and Jacob appear as the elect and the truly good (*al-muṣṭafīn al-akhyār*). Ibn Qasī brings examples to this principle: Adam was distinguished by his knowledge of God's names, Moses by receiving the Torah (*al-tawrāt*), Muhammad by receiving comprehensive words (*jawāmiʿ al-kalim*) and ʿĪsā (Jesus) by being a spirit and blowing his spirit and making the dead live. Ibn Qasī emphasizes that all these phenomena are known through the holy texts, but the relative

10. In Ibn al-ʿArabī's terminology a scale is found in every sphere, in theory and practice. It weighs logic, grammar and so on. Also the Law is the scale of one's deeds. *SPK*, pp. 172f.

11. *Fut.*II:539f.; *FM*.I:749, ll.19–20.

12. See also Quran 2:253.

13. *Mafḍūl* can also be rendered as 'one who is known to be excelled by others'. Abrahamov, 'Al-Qāsim ibn Ibrāhīm's theory of the Imamate', *Arabica*, 34 (1987), p. 89.

distinction of each prophet is known through revelation and contemplation (*kashf, iṭṭilāʿ*).[14]

The same idea of categorizing individuals according to excellence and inferiority appears elsewhere when Ibn al-ʿArabī discusses the difference between Sufis in the context of stations and states. People are equal when they adhere to a certain station, yet with regard to other stations they are different; some have a lower and some a higher status. This is Ibn Qasī's view, with which Ibn al-ʿArabī agrees.[15]

This issue is further discussed in the context of al-Tirmidhī's twenty-ninth question on the priority of some prophets and friends of God over others. Here the Shaykh points out polemics between the Sufis, whereas formerly he spoke of the consensus of the Muslims concerning this subject. Possibly the debate only took place between Sufis, and our author has developed a unique view on this question. Anyhow, Ibn Qasī establishes the rule that each prophet or God's friend is distinguished by a unique trait which others lack. Ibn al-ʿArabī does not fully agree and adds to Ibn Qasī's view saying that essentially there is no difference between the traits which belong to such leaders, because all these traits reflect divine names and realities, and it is inconceivable that any differences should be assigned to God's names and attributes. Ibn al-ʿArabī adduces two arguments to support his claim:

1. Since the relationship of God's names to God's essence is one and the same, there cannot be differences between the names.
2. The names go back to one source, namely to God's essence. Because the essence is one, and because priority of one over another requires multiplicity, priority is unacceptable. Hence, making distinctions among prophets and God's friends means making distinctions between attributes of glory and honour.[16]

14. *Fut.*III:79; *FM.*II:52, ll.6–12 (al-Tirmidhī's question no.17).
15. *Fut.*III:387; *FM.*II:257, ll.9–16.
16. *Fut.*III:92f.; *FM.*II:60, l.34 – 61, l.7.

That Ibn al-ʿArabī criticizes the views of his predecessors is borne out once again in the question of God's attitude toward people on the Day of Judgement: does God bestow favours on humans or judge them strictly according to the rules? The Shaykh opines that people actually do not know the logic behind God's reasoning in his treatment of humans, although people know that 'God's mercy precedes His wrath',[17] and that He requites humans for their deeds. By their thinking, people may acquire some knowledge of God's ways, but this knowledge is only conjecture and not certain knowledge. Certain knowledge is attained only through revelation. Here he cites Ibn Qasī as saying that God's justice (*ʿadl*) does not pass judgement on His kindness (*faḍl*) and vice versa, meaning that each value does not cancel out the other. Ibn al-ʿArabī characterizes Ibn Qasī's comment as a general statement, and adds that he does not know if it came to Ibn Qasī via revelation or reflection. From one point of view, says the Shaykh, Ibn Qasī's saying contradicts the above-mentioned *ḥadīth*, which states that God's mercy precedes His wrath, but from another point of view it coincides with reality. That is because we see, for example, that some people are granted mercy without having been judged previously according to justice. Here reality is consistent with Ibn Qasī's view.

Again, Ibn al-ʿArabī's judgement of his predecessors is objective, directed by the principle that as long as one elaborates on a certain point according to one's reflection, it is possible to refer to one's thoughts in the same way. However, revelation overrides reflection. In the case of a contradiction between a Sufi's revelation and a prophet's revelation, the prophet's revelation is preponderant. The Sufi's revelation is true, because revelation never errs, but its interpretation is faulty, hence it must be rejected.[18] In his discussion of Ibn Qasī's ideas, Ibn al-ʿArabī presents his basic views concerning reflection and revelation.

17. For the appearance of this tradition in the *Futūḥāt*, see *SPK*, pp.130, 291.

18. *Fut.*V:10f.; *FM.*III:7, ll.12–22.

At the end of Chapter 297, Ibn al-ʿArabī mentions Ibn Qasī in relation to a unique aspect of God's names. After stating, on the basis of Quran 17:110, that each divine name contains all the other names, the Shaykh al-Akbar informs us that he is alone in treating this subject, and that he does not know if anyone else among God's friends[19] (not among the prophets) has previously encountered it or received revelation about it. He admits that Ibn Qasī deals with the divine names in his *Khalʿ al-naʿlayn*.[20] Ibn al-ʿArabī beseeches others to incorporate into his book here the name of any person who has dealt with this issue, whether from his own thought or experience, as our author did himself, or from that of others. He adds a somewhat strange note that explains his request: 'I love agreement (*muwāfaqa*) and not to be alone among my colleagues.' This is surprising because Ibn al-ʿArabī does not hesitate to disagree with other Sufis whenever he thinks that they are wrong.[21] He does not always seek compromise between his own ideas and the ideas of others. Possibly, he does love agreement, but more than agreement he loves truth. So whenever there is a contradiction between the two, he prefers truth.[22]

19. Incidentally, we learn that Ibn al-ʿArabī regards himself as a *walī*, God's friend.

20. However, in *Fut.*VI:89; *FM.*III:354, ll.15–16, he admits that Ibn Qasī holds the view that each divine name includes all the other names.

21. Addas, 'Andalusī Mysticism', pp.926f.

22. *Fut.*IV:471; *FM.*II:686, ll.25–7.

ʿAbd al-Qādir al-Jīlānī

1077–1166

There is a great difference between al-Jīlānī as a historical figure and al-Jīlānī as the eponym of the Qādiriyya order. As an historical personality he was a Ḥanbalī scholar in Baghdad specializing in the sphere of Ḥanbalī Law and serving as a preacher. In this position he reportedly wrote a Ḥanbali profession of faith (*ʿaqīda*) entitled *al-Ghunya li-ṭālibī ṭarīq al-ḥaqq* (*Sufficient Provision for Seekers of the Path of Truth*). The novelty in this treatise comes at the end where the author permits the *murīdūn* (the Sufi novices; literally: the willing) to devote themselves entirely to mystical practice without the need to work for their sustenance. However, he forbids all forms of antinomianism and public display (dancing and listening to music). Living in a mystical monastery (*ribāṭ*)[1] is also disfavoured.

Disciples of the Qādiriyya ascribed two sermons to al-Jīlānī: *al-Fatḥ al-rabbānī* (*The Divine Revelation*) and *Futūḥ al-ghayb* (*Revelation of the Hidden*). Later generations regarded al-Jīlānī as a legendary figure and a saint.[2] Scholars have so far not been able to explain the transition of al-Jīlānī's image from Ḥanbalī pietistic scholar to mystic.[3] Consideration of Ibn al-ʿArabī's attitude toward al-Jīlānī, which we are about to discuss, makes this issue more acute, since the Shaykh was active only a few decades after al-Jīlānī's death. I shall not deal with this difficult question, which requires analysis of historical texts, but consider only the figure of al-Jīlānī as seen by Ibn al-ʿArabī.

1. Its parallel term in the East is *khānqā* and in the West *zāwiya*. N. Rabbat, 'Ribāṭ', in *EI*.
2. J. Chabbi, "Abd al-Qādir al-Jīlānī', in *EI*.
3. *Dimensions*, pp.247f.; *SDG*, p.376.

Ibn al-ʿArabī holds al-Jīlānī in high esteem, because he regards him as one of the Mounted Poles (*al-aqṭāb al-rukbān*) to whom he dedicates a whole chapter (30) in his *al-Futūḥāt al-Makkiyya*. Ibn al-ʿArabī reports that, just as the Arabs who ride noble camels are called the Mounted (*al-rukbān*) and possess traits such as eloquence, heroism and generosity, so these Poles are distinguished by their noble aspirations and works. Some of them are hidden, but have the power of freely acting in the world (*taṣarruf*), while others are ordered to act freely. Abū al-Suʿūd ibn al-Shibl belongs to the first group, but his master al-Jīlānī is reckoned among the second division, one whom God orders to act freely.[4]

Although our author greatly appreciates al-Jīlānī and calls him the leader of his generation (*imām al-ʿaṣr*) and the master of his time (*sayyid waqtihi*),[5] he nevertheless criticizes him for his inclination toward presumptuousness (*idlāl*): "ʿAbd al-Qādir al-Jīlī was one of those who made unruly utterances[6] toward God's friends and the prophets through the form of a *ḥaqq* in his state. Thus he was not preserved from error in his tongue.'[7] However, Ibn al-ʿArabī says, not long before his death al-Jīlānī placed his face on the earth as a sign of humbleness and servanthood, and acknowledged his fault of presumptuousness. Contrary to al-Jīlānī's misbehaviour, God preserved his disciple Abū al-Suʿūd from *idlāl*.[8] In this context, the disciple's position is higher than his master's because, in Ibn al-ʿArabī's view, *idlāl* causes the mystic's knowledge of God to decrease.[9]

Al-Tirmidhī's Question 83 (Chapter 73) deals with the issue of prophecy and its essence. We have already discussed Ibn al-ʿArabī's

4. *Fut.*I:305, II:308, III:462; *FM.*I:201, ll.31–2, I:588, l.3, II:308, ll.7–8; *SDG*, pp.378f.

5. *Fut.*III:136, 430; *FM.*II:90, l.30, 286, l.12.

6. *Shaṭaḥāt*. As we have seen in the section on al-Bisṭāmī, Ibn al-ʿArabī does not like this phenomenon.

7. *Fut.*VI:386; *FM.*III:560, ll.17–18; *SDG*, p.303.

8. *Fut.*I:353, III:430; *FM.*I:233, ll.27–30, II:286, l.12; *SDG*, p.380.

9. Ibid. p.380.

position, which distinguishes between general prophecy (*nubuwwa ʿāmma*) and legislative prophecy (*nubuwwat al-tashrīʿ*). While the first term refers to individuals who receive revelation, the second term refers to those who receive revelation and laws from heaven. Ibn al-ʿArabī finds corroboration for this distinction in a statement expressed by al-Jīlānī as follows: 'O community of prophets, you have been given the nickname (of prophecy), whereas we have been given that which you have not been given.' The Shaykh explains the first part of this statement as a prohibition against naming all great people who receive revelation prophets, although general prophecy is distributed among them. The second part refers to al-Khiḍr, who is said in the Quran to surpass Moses in knowledge (Quran 18:65–82). Al-Khiḍr belongs to the group of God's friends who have the gift of general prophecy (*anbiyāʾ al-awliyāʾ*) and who from one point of view, for example knowledge, are most excellent (*fāḍil*), but from another, for example bringing laws, are inferior (*mafḍūl*) to other prophets.[10]

Al-Jīlānī's high status is also attested by his being classified as a friend of God – one of those who are brought close. Ibn al-ʿArabī divides these into two groups: to the first belong those who attain God without the intermediacy of the Prophet, and in the second are the people who see the Prophet's footsteps before them in their travels, so that the Prophet serves as a mediator between them and God. Al-Jīlānī and Abū al-Suʿūd are members of the first group.[11] Moreover, sometimes a Pole, like al-Jīlānī, serves as a mediator for another mystic, and sometimes a mystic might see the footprints of prophets and of more than one mediator. All depends on the spiritual status of the traveller to God. The higher his position, the fewer mediators he will see on his way. Thus, he who sees before him no footprints, like al-Jīlānī, stands above all

10. *Fut.*III:136; *FM.*II:90, ll.30–1; *SDG*, p.378.
11. *Fut.*III:74; *FM.*II:48, l.31 – 49, l.4.

others.[12] Elsewhere, al-Jīlānī, whom our author calls 'our master', is depicted as one who exceeds all people from the point of view of dominion over them.[13]

However, as we have seen, from other perspectives al-Jīlānī does not always occupy the uppermost echelons. For example, the station of *ṣidq* is defined by Ibn al-ʿArabī as firmness in religion, or the faculty of belief.[14] In this area al-Jīlānī's placement is inferior to that of his disciple Abū al-Suʿūd, because the latter possesses the station (*maqām*) of *ṣidq*, while the former possesses the state (*ḥāl*) of *ṣidq*.[15] However, Ibn al-ʿArabī admits that in his own time, there was no person who equalled al-Jīlānī in his state and Abū al-ʿSuʿūd in his station.[16]

Al-Jīlānī had another extraordinary trait – the ability to know people by smelling, which he used in regard to Ibn Qāʾid al-Awānī[17] when he wished to join the Sufis. He also possessed the faculty of governing control (*taḥakkum*).[18] For example, he swore that he would not lift his head after prostration until God sent abundant rain, and God relieved him of his vow.[19] Add to this al-Jīlānī's claim that he has knowledge by the year, month, week and day of what will happen,[20] and without any doubt one can conclude that al-Jīlānī appears in the *Futūḥāt* as an unusual personality with remarkable qualities. It is no wonder that his disciples admired him so much.[21]

12. *Fut.*I:305, III:120f., 193f.; *FM.*I:201, ll.21–7, II:80, ll.11–21, 130, ll.10–20; *SDG*, pp. 144f.

13. *Fut.*III:23; *FM.*II:14, l.20; *SDG*, p. 378.

14. I do not know why Chittick renders this term as 'truthfulness' (*SDG*, p. 381), as the author defines the term differently at the beginning of Chap. 136.

15. Ibid. p. 381.

16. *Fut.*III:335f.; *FM.*II:222, l.15 – 223, l.10; *SDG*, p. 381.

17. Ibid. p. 377.

18. *SPK*, pp. 265, 313.

19. *Fut.*IV:222f.; *FM.*II:520, ll.17–18.

20. *Fut.*IV:398; *FM.*II:637, ll.3–4.

21. *Fut.*IV:384; *FM.*II:627, ll.21–7.

It seems appropriate to sum up this section with Ibn al-ʿArabī's appreciation of al-Jīlānī as one of the Malāmiyya (the People of Blame). This is not the historical group of the Malāmiyya, but the most perfect of the gnostics in Ibn al-ʿArabī's view, the hidden pious among whom are reckoned the Prophet, Abū Bakr al-Ṣiddīq, Ḥamdūn al-Qaṣṣār, Abū Saʿīd al-Kharrāz, Abū Yazīd al-Bisṭāmī, Abū al-Suʿūd ibn al-Shibl, Muḥammad al-Awānī and others.[22] However, as previously pointed out, one cannot escape the several passages in the *Futūḥāt* in which the disciple Abū al-Suʿūd is exalted above his master.[23] The enigma of how al-Jīlānī turned into a prominent Sufi figure and an eponym of a Sufi order remains unsolved. Again, we see that our author makes no bones about the relative measure of these two figures, al-Jīlānī and Abū al-Suʿūd, ascribing to each the status he deserves.

22. *Fut.*V:50–2; *FM.*III, pp.34f.; *SPK*, pp.372–5.
23. *Fut.*I:353; *FM.*I:233, ll.27–32; *SDG*, p.377.

Abū Madyan

1126–1198

Although Ibn al-ʿArabī never met Abū Madyan, Shuʿayb ibn al-Ḥusayn,[1] and gained all his knowledge of the latter's mystical practice and ideas from Abū Madyan's disciples, he regarded him as his master (*shaykh*). That this was the case proves his spiritual connection with Abū Madyan.[2] The following notes aim at showing Ibn al-ʿArabī's knowledge of and attitude toward him. As Claude Addas rightly points out, all the historians who report on Abū Madyan refer to external aspects of his life, ignoring his spiritual rank and personality. Ibn al-ʿArabī's writings fill this gap.[3]

Abū Madyan had a special status not only *vis-à-vis* Ibn al-ʿArabī, but equally if not more so in comparison to all other mystics. Ibn al-ʿArabī mentions him along with al-Tirmidhī as one of the Poles (*quṭb*, pl. *aqṭāb*), that is, one of the four persons who are responsible for the existence of the world.[4] Abū Madyan used to say that his *sūra* is *sūrat al-mulk* (Quran 67), whose first verse reads: 'Blessed be He in Whose hand is the Kingdom (*mulk*), and He can do everything.'[5] Ibn al-ʿArabī also places him, together with al-Tustarī, al-Bisṭāmī and Ibn al-ʿArīf, among the Verifiers (*al-muḥaqqiqūn*).[6]

1. Vincent Cornell wonders why Ibn al-ʿArabī did not meet Abū Madyan in 1194, for he was not staying far from Abū Madyan's residence at that time. V.J. Cornell, *The Way of Abū Madyan*, p.16, n.35.

2. *SPK*, p.404, n.19. G. Marçais, 'Abū Madyan', in *EI*. Ibn al-ʿArabī, *Al-Tadbīrāt*, p.126.

3. C. Addas, 'Abu Madyan and Ibn 'Arabī', in S. Hirtenstein and M. Tiernan (eds.), *Muhyiddin Ibn 'Arabi*, p.169.

4. On the meaning of the term 'Pole', see *Fut.*I:279; *FM.*I:184, ll.3–11; *Quest*, pp.172, 178.

5. *Fut.*I:279; *FM.*I:184, ll.3–4. *Al-Tadbīrāt*, pp.158f.

6. *Fut.*III:478; *FM.*II:318, l.31; *SPK*, p.149. In *Tarjumān al-ashwāq* (pp.15f.) Abū Madyan and al-Bisṭāmī are mentioned as saints who renounced the powers of control (*taṣrīf*) conferred on them by God.

Generally in the Shaykh's writings the Verifiers belong to the highest echelons of God's friends. They are so called because they reach the truth (*ḥaqq*) through unveiling, following no authority (*taqlīd*).[7] We shall see later why Abū Madyan is entirely deserving of this epithet. Elsewhere, Abū Madyan is reckoned among the greatest gnostics (*'ārifūn*).[8]

Concerning Abū Madyan's status, Ibn al-'Arabī relates a strange encounter involving one of Abū Madyan's disciples, named Mūsā al-Sadrānī:

> Having arrived at Mount Qāf, which according to tradition surrounds our universe, he met the serpent who himself encircled the mountain. After the customary greetings, an astonishing dialogue started up between them: 'How is Shaykh Abū Madyan?' asks the serpent of the traveller. 'I left him in good health, but how do you know him?' 'Is there a single being, on the face of the earth', replies the astonished serpent, 'who does not know him or love him? Since God put his name on earth, there is not one amongst us who does not know him.'[9]

In Chapter 334 Ibn al-'Arabī continues to discuss the matter with Mūsā, asking him where it is written in the Quran that all the creatures should love Abū Madyan. Mūsā did not know the answer. Then Ibn al-'Arabī gives him the answer: God created humans in His image and just as all the created things and many people praise God (Quran 22:18) so humans, who are created in His image, are praised by all things but not by all people. This last idea explains why some people hated Abū Madyan and did not believe in him. In other words, the human attitude toward God, which is expressed in belief or unbelief, is identical to human attitudes toward each other.[10]

7. *SPK*, p.389, n.11.
8. *Fut.*VIII:310; *FM.*IV:498, ll.28–9.
9. *Fut.*IV:465f.; *FM.*II:682, l.33 – 683, l.7. Trans. Addas, 'Abū Madyan', p.173; Ibn al-'Arabī, *Manzil al-quṭb*, in *Rasā'il Ibn al-'Arabī*, Part II:4 (of the epistle).
10. *Fut.*V:192f.; *FM.*III:130, ll.9–29.

Abū Madyan did not leave writings for succeeding generations which would enable one to learn his mystical practice and ideas from him directly, but rather his disciples wrote about him and his conduct.[11] Many people admired him and it is incumbent on us to examine why they did so. There are two reasons. The first is his ascetic practice: he, together with Abū Yazīd al-Bisṭāmī, is considered as towering above all others regarding the practice of abstinence.[12] The second reason is provided by Ibn al-ʿArabī, who reports that Abū Madyan used to say that one of the signs of the Sufi disciple's truthfulness is his flight from people (*al-firār ʿan al-khalq*) and his existence for the sake of God, because in so doing the disciple follows the pattern of the Prophet who secluded himself from people in the cave of Ḥarāʾ in order to worship God (*taḥannuth*). Abū Madyan's statement is cited in the context of the famous prophetic saying that God's friends (*awliyāʾ*) are the heirs of the prophets. Consequently, just as prophets return from their seclusion to guide the people, so God's friends have to follow suit. The return to the people is one of the signs of the truthfulness of being with God. Abū Madyan is distinguished from Abū Yazīd in that he returned from seclusion out of free choice (*ikhtiyāran*), whereas Abū Yazīd was compelled to return.[13]

In Ibn al-ʿArabī's view, *futuwwa* (literally: chivalry) means to prefer (*īthār*) others to oneself. In the context of the relationship between God and humans, this term means to prefer God's commandments to one's passions and desires. Our author brings Abū Madyan's practice as an example of *futuwwa*. Abū Madyan understood that whatever he received was determined by God, hence whatever food reached him, whether good or bad, he would eat it. If he was starving and he received money, he would know that

11. Cornell, who published some texts which are ascribed to Abū Madyan, discusses the problem of the authenticity of his writings. Cornell, *Way*, pp. 36–8.

12. *Fut.*I:370; *FM.*I:244, ll.33–5.

13. *Fut.*I:379–81, III:35; *FM.*I:250, l.34 – 252, l.13, II:22, ll.24–5; Addas, 'Abū Madyan', p. 171.

God made him choose that which is appropriate for his health and hence for the worship of God, which is dependent on good health. In any case, what determines his conduct is the Law: even if he had received in revelation a divine order which makes lawful that which is forbidden by the Law, he would obey the Law and not the revealed order. Indeed, Abū Madyan says that if there is a contradiction between the content of the Law and the content of revelation, one should adhere to the Law, because confusion may occur in received revelation. Hence, it seems that one should prefer the clear order of the Law to the occasionally obscure character of revelation.[14]

Further to the idea that one should accept whatever God gives one, Abū Madyan's view concerning hospitality is relevant here. One of the directives (*waṣiyya*) mentioned in the last chapter of the *Futūḥāt* is receiving guests hospitably. The Law prescribes hospitality for three days, after which hospitality becomes almsgiving (*ṣadaqa*). As we have seen, Abū Madyan relied on God for his subsistence and called people not to earn (*kasb*) any means of subsistence (*asbāb*). Then, people told him that eating by earning a means of subsistence is better than eating without earning. Responding to their statement, Abū Madyan referred to the rule of hospitality mentioned above. He said: 'If the guest ate in these three days from his own means of subsistence, would it not be a shame for the host?' After they affirmed that this would be shameful, Abū Madyan said: 'The people of God leave human beings and become God's guests for three days, and a day according to God is like a thousand days according to your counting.'[15] Since we are God's guests, says Abū Madyan, we would be wrong not to enjoy His hospitality, if we did not eat what He (the host) gave us. Ibn al-ʿArabī admires Abū Madyan's discussion on this matter and his agreement with

14. *Fut.*III:352; *FM.*II:233, l.27 – 234, l.6.
15. Quran 22:47.

the Sunna, saying that God illuminated Abū Madyan's heart, thus emphasizing that hospitality is one of the parts of belief.[16]

A similar story concerning trust in God is related about Abū Madyan. Once, a merchant told Abū Madyan that if a poor person turned to him for help he was ready to help them. Then a naked poor person asked Abū Madyan to supply him with clothes. Abū Madyan's station and state in cases like this was not to rely on anyone except God in all matters concerning himself as well as those of others. Abū Madyan went with the poor man to the merchant to accept clothes from him. On the way he met a person who identified himself as a polytheist (*mushirk*). Abū Madyan immediately knew the connection between the appearance of this polytheist, a phenomenon unknown in this country, and the good deed he was trying to accomplish. He regarded the appearance of the apparent polytheist as a sign that his conduct concerning the poor man was not right, for he intended to ask help from the merchant and not directly from God, which means that he associated someone with God. Being aware of his error, he repented. Ibn al-ʿArabī notes that God sent the polytheist to Abū Madyan to call his attention to his failing.[17]

The Shaykh agrees with Abū Madyan in elevating the knowledge gained through personal mystical experience above the knowledge coming from other people. In this preference, Abū Madyan follows Abū Yazīd al-Bisṭāmī.[18] When Abū Madyan heard the formula 'Someone says on the authority of someone else' and so on, he said, 'We do not want to eat dried meat, give us fresh meat',

16. *Fut.*VIII:291f.; *FM.*IV:485, ll.24–34.

17. *Fut.*I:538; *FM.*I:356, ll.26–32. I understand the term *ifnāʾ* (annihilation), through which Ibn al-ʿArabī describes Abū Madyan's state, as the cancellation of the means of subsistence in one's mind so that one searches only for the help of God without turning to a means of subsistence. *Fut.*III:302f.; *FM.*II:204, ll.4–21. This notion coincides with Abū Madyan's view that only God acts. *Fut.*III:334; *FM.*II:222, ll.5–13. It is reminiscent of al-Ghazālī's division of the people of unity into four groups. The third group are those who see that all events and things in the world derive from God. *Iḥyāʾ*, Vol. IV, pp. 245f.

18. See *SPK*, p. 310.

meaning give us your personal experience and not the sayings of others. You should relate the speech that comes from your Lord, says Abū Madyan, because He is alive and near to you and because the divine overflow (*al-fayḍ al-ilāhī*) does not stop.[19]

One of the mystical traits of Abū Madyan is revealed in his statement: 'In everything that I see, the letter '*bā*'' is written above it.' By the letter '*bā*'' he means the word '*bī*' (through me) which precedes the verbs in the famous tradition on the supererogatory works, indicating that everything the individual does is actually done by God. God says: 'The mystic hears through Me (*bī yasmaʿu*), sees through Me (*yubṣiru bī*)' etc.[20] This elevated station of the mystic finds favour with Ibn al-ʿArabī.

Abū Madyan is affiliated with the people of God (*rijāl Allāh*) who are also named 'the world of the breaths' (*ʿālam al-anfās*).[21] This group is divided into many subgroups, such as *nuqabāʾ* (leaders).[22] Abū Madyan specifically belongs to the group of people who are disclosed through God's order, thereby obeying God's commandments without increasing or decreasing them. They not only carry out what is due to God, but also reveal to the people God's graces and his miracles. Through these acts they are unveiled, so justifying the name 'those who are disclosed through God's order'.

Abū Madyan's spiritual connection to the world is attested in the following story. Once, when he was in a state of disengagement (*tajrīd*)[23] from material things and collected nothing of the material world, he forgot a dinar in his pocket. At that time he used to seclude himself on a mountain. Every time he went to this place a

19. *Fut.*I:423; *FM.*I:280, l.28; Addas, 'Abū Madyan', p.170; *SPK*, p.249.

20. *Fut.*II:106; *FM.*I:448, ll.21–2.

21. *Fut.*III:11; *FM.*II:6, ll.20–1. As Chittick points out this term has several meanings: the spiritual realities which govern the material world, God's Breath, the world which is unveiled during God's self-disclosure, and fragrances of nearness to God. *SPK*, p.402, n.18.

22. *Seal*, pp.104, 107.

23. This term means the severance of the soul from its connection to the body. *SPK*, p.120; *SDG*, p.274.

gazelle came to him and he drank her milk. However, after a while the gazelle refused to give him her milk and drew away from him. On considering this strange situation, Abū Madyan came to the conclusion that the cause of the gazelle's behaviour was the dinar in his pocket. He threw the dinar far away so that he could not find it. The next time he went to the mountain the gazelle came near to him, and he drank her milk.[24] This story also proves that the world is a unified entity, each of whose parts may influence another.

Abū Madyan also appears in the *Futūḥāt* as a Quran exegete. For example, Ibn al-ʿArabī brings up Abū Madyan's commentary to Quran 95:5 which reads: 'When you finished [your work], exert your efforts'. Abū Madyan understands the verse as expressing the idea that when one finishes dealing with perishable things and events (*akwān*),[25] one must turn one's attention to God's unveiling or witnessing (*mushāhada*).[26]

Ibn al-ʿArabī stresses the impact that hearing the melodic reading of the Quran has on one's heart, even if one does not apprehend the meaning. In this case, the Quran's message is delivered through one's heart. If this is the Quran's function, then, says our author, everyone finds in it what he wishes. As corroboration, he cites Abū Madyan's statement to the effect that the Sufi novice (*murīd*) does not become a novice unless he already finds all that he wishes (*yurīd*) in the Quran. The Shaykh sums up this idea by saying that every discourse that does not have such a trait of generality is not Quran (*kull kalām lā yakūnu lahu hādha al-ʿumūm fa-laysa bi-qurān*).[27]

Thus, according to Ibn al-ʿArabī, the Quran possesses spiritual power which encompasses all that the novice needs, even if he does not know Arabic. The novice can find guidance in the Quran which fits his wishes. I assume that our author is suggesting here that the

24. *Fut.*II:152; *FM.*I:480, ll.17–21. Addas, 'Abū Madyan', pp.165f. For a similar story in al-Bisṭāmī, see pp.38f. above.

25. *SPK*, p.41.

26. *Fut.*II:368; *FM.*I:628, ll.24–5. Cf. *Fut.*III:393; *FM.*II:261, ll.15–23.

27. *Fut.*V:137; *FM.*III:94, ll.2–3.

novice desires the means appropriate to the novice's mystical state. Another possible interpretation is the idea of the Quran as a source of inspiration. Whenever the novice hears the Quran recited, he becomes inspired, and this inspiration causes him to find whatever he wishes to fulfil his spiritual needs.

In spite of Ibn al-ʿArabī's reverence for Abū Madyan, he does not hesitate to criticize a statement of his which he characterizes as a simple and general saying (*qawl ummī ʿāmmī*): Abū Madyan's remark that 'the secret of life flows in all existents'. Ibn al-ʿArabī asserts that Abū Madyan did not receive the charisma of expression, which is given only to a perfect Muhammadan (*al-Muḥammadī al-kāmil*), even if, in other aspects, he is the heir of another prophet, other than Muhammad.[28]

As Addas writes in her excellent article, there was 'a kind of spiritual intimacy' between the Greatest Master and Abū Madyan.[29] This spiritual intimacy very probably derived from Abū Madyan's mystical practice, his position in the hierarchy of the saints, his absolute devotion to God, his being an integral part of nature, his knowledge of hidden things and capacity to perform miracles,[30] and his search for mystical experiences to prove his views. Clearly, such a perfect personality serves as an inspiration for Ibn al-ʿArabī. Abū Madyan's influence on our author came to him through followers of Abū Madyan, such as Abū Yaʿqūb Yūsuf al-Kūmī and Abū Muḥammad al-Mawrūrī, who brought him accounts of Abū Madyan.[31]

28. *Fut.*IV:201, VII:388; *FM.*II:506, l.2, IV:264, ll.30–4. Addas, 'Abū Madyan', p.170.

29. Ibid. p.178.

30. Once Ibn al-ʿArabī felt a strong desire to see Abū Madyan. Abū Madyan being aware of this desire sent a messenger by means of instantaneous translocation to Ibn al-ʿArabī, who was far away, to assess Ibn al-ʿArabī's state of mind. *Sufis*, p.121; S. Hirtenstein (ed. and trans.), *The Four Pillars of Spiritual Transformation*, p.14.

31. S. Hirtenstein, *The Unlimited Mercifier*, pp.80f.

Abū al-ʿAbbās al-ʿUraybī[1]

?–?

As previously noted, it seems that most of the teachings Ibn al-ʿArabī inherited from his immediate masters concern Sufi practices and morals. Al-ʿUraybī, who was Ibn al-ʿArabī's first master, is the best example of this tendency.[2] He is characterized as a pious person who devoted himself entirely to the worship of God, aspiring always to be with Him. I will bring some proofs to substantiate this statement.

One of his prominent practices was the intensive invocation of God (*dhikr*). Ibn al-ʿArabī mentions him at the beginning of Chapter 298 of *al-Futūḥāt al-Makkiyya*, which deals with the waystation of the invocation of God. According to our author, al-ʿUraybī was firmly grounded in this waystation.[3]

Although Ibn al-ʿArabī generally disfavours miracles (*karāmāt*),[4] he writes admiringly of miracles that al-ʿUraybī performed. Once the people of Kutāmah asked al-ʿUraybī to beseech God to bring them rain. So he went there and prayed for them, a prayer which brought rain within an hour. As if to strengthen his reputation as a

1. The text of *al-Futūḥāt al-Makkiyya* (I:282; *FM*.I:186, l.2) alludes to al-ʿUryabī, but in *Rūḥ al-quds* (*Majmūʿat rasāʾil Ibn al-ʿArabī*, Vol. I:159; *Sufis*, p.63) the name al-ʿUryanī appears. M. Chodkiewicz spells the name al-ʿUraybī and points out that sometimes he is known in the texts as Abū Jaʿfar; *Seal*, p.77, n.8. Stephen Hirtenstein has kindly supplied me with another proof, which appears in two manuscripts, for reading ʿUraybī instead of ʿUryanī: Evkaf Muzesi, 1849, fol. 26a (Chap. 67 of *FM*), in the hand of the author; and University, A79, fol. 41a (*Rūḥ al-quds*), possibly in the hand of Badr al-Ḥabashī, but with many *samāʿ*s with the author as *musmiʿ*.

2. *Quest*, p.61. After Abū Madyan, al-ʿUraybī is cited more than any other Sufis, and also very often without alluding to his name. Ibid. p.50.

3. *Fut*.IV:471; *FM*.II:687, l.3. *Rūḥ al-quds*, in *Majmūʿa*, Vol. I:159. *Sufis*, p.63. S. Hirtenstein, *The Unlimited Mercifier*, p.174.

4. See pp.48f. above, on the subject of miracles.

miracle worker, the rain that fell in the vicinity did not reach and discomfort him.[5]

As a result of his intensive spiritual states, people forced al-ʿUraybī to leave his city. God reacted to this shameful deed of the citizens by sending a *jinni* to the house of their leader. This *jinni* exposed the numerous sins of the people in such a manner that they implored al-ʿUraybī to return to the city and to have mercy on them despite what they had done to him. He returned to the city and the *jinni* disappeared.[6]

Ibn al-ʿArabī relates the following story about his master:

> Once I enquired of him how his spiritual life had been in the early days. He told me that his family's food allowance for a year had been eight sack-loads of figs,[7] and that when he was in spiritual retreat his wife would berate him and abuse him, telling him to stir himself and do something to support his family for the year. At this he would become confused and would pray, 'O my Lord, this business is beginning to come between You and me, for she persists in scolding me. Therefore, if You would have me continue in worship, relieve me of her attentions; if not tell me so.' One day God called him inwardly, saying, 'O Muhammad, continue in your worship and rest assured that before this day is over I will bring you twenty loads of figs, enough to last you two and a half years.' He went on to tell me that before another hour had passed a man called at his house with a gift of a sack-load of figs. When this arrived, God indicated to him that this was the first of the twenty loads.[8]

These three stories are noteworthy in that in each God Himself intervened and changed the situation, in the first and third case after al-ʿUraybī's prayer, while in the second story not a word is said about al-ʿUraybī's effort to change what had been determined for him. In characterizing the miracles here, there is

5. *Rūḥ al-quds*, p.160; *Sufis*, p.64.

6. Ibid. p.68.

7. The author explains that each load weighed one hundred rotls. A rotl is equal to 2.88 kilograms.

8. *Rūḥ al-quds*, p.160; *Sufis*, pp.65f.

a disconnection between the miracle and the body of the saint; in contradistinction, a connection between the miracle and the body of the saint is expressed, for example, in walking on the water or flying through the air. Also, the miracles are the outcome of prayer, or in one case God's intervention even without prayer being performed. This proves that Ibn al-ʿArabī favours miracles which occur as a result of prayer and because of the personality for whom they are done.

That God's friends (or saints, *walī*, pl. *awliyāʾ*) assimilate the traits of the prophets is an important tenet of the Shaykh's theory of the *walāya*. A *walī* may adopt the characteristics of one prophet or of a number of prophets. Walking in the footsteps of the prophets (*ʿalā aqdām al-anbiyāʾ*) also characterizes Ibn al-ʿArabī who, according to his own testimony, walked in the footsteps of ʿĪsā (Jesus), then of Mūsā (Moses), of Hūd, and of all the prophets, ending with Muhammad. Ibn al-ʿArabī points out that at the end of his master's life, al-ʿUraybī adopted the traits of ʿĪsā, which also became the first phase of our author's Sufi way.[9] Notwithstanding the miracles performed by al-ʿUraybī, as stated above, and his knowledge of hidden things,[10] one of ʿĪsā's faculties, the power to revivify the dead, is ascribed neither to Ibn al-ʿArabī nor to al-ʿUraybī. Moreover, Ibn al-ʿArabī's pretension that he absorbed in himself the traits of all the prophets remains only a declaration, being without any proof, and borders on incredibility.

Ibn al-ʿArabī's account of al-ʿUraybī, who is considered one of the people of highest standing, shows him to be a scrupulous person not only in his acts,[11] but also in his sayings. The Shaykh relates that once he entered al-ʿUraybī's abode and found him immersed

9. *Fut.*I:338, V:309; *FM.*I:223, ll.19–29, III:207, l.27. *Seal*, pp. 17, 77, 80. Hirtenstein, *Mercifier*, p. 68.

10. *Fut.*I:282; *FM.*I:186, ll.1–11.

11. *Fut.*VII:181f.; *FM.*IV:123, ll.22–4. Here he is one of the righteous (*ṣāliḥūn*). In *Fut.*VI:354f.; *FM.*III:539, ll.26–7, he is distinguished as God's servant. Al-ʿUraybī counsels Ibn al-ʿArabī to be a pure servant to God, that is, to worship him in an absolute manner. *Fut.*VIII:287; *FM.*IV:482, ll.17–23. Hirtenstein, *Mercifier*, p. 77.

in repeating the name of God (*Allāh*) without adding any other words. He asked his master why he had not said 'There is no god but God.' Al-ʿUraybī answered: 'The breaths are in God's hands .... I am afraid that God will put me to death the moment I say "there is no god", so that I will die uttering the negation of God's existence. This has been the norm of some people of God.'[12]

One of al-ʿUraybī's followers wanted to give alms. Another Sufi who attended the meeting in al-ʿUraybī's home said to him: 'The closest relatives (*al-aqrabūn*) are most entitled to receive alms.' Immediately al-ʿUraybī reacted and corrected this formula by saying '*ilā Allāh*' (to God), that is, those who are nearest to God are most entitled to receive alms. Ibn al-ʿArabī agrees with this correction.[13] Elsewhere he adds that there is no entity closer to the human being than God (*lā aqrab min Allāh*). Whereas people sometimes come close to each other and other times their relationships are interrupted, God always remains close to human beings.[14]

Al-ʿUraybī's devotion to God and the nearness he feels to God is manifested in the following anecdote from Ibn al-ʿArabī:

> I was once in Seville with my master Abū al-ʿAbbās al-ʿUryānī and he said to me: 'My son, concern yourself with your Lord!' I left his house exhilarated, reeling under the effect of the teaching he had given me. I then went to see my master Abū ʿImrān Mūsā b. ʿImrān al-Martulī .... I greeted him and he welcomed me, and then he said: 'My son, concern yourself with your soul (*nafs*)!' So I said to him: 'Master, you have told me to concern myself with my soul, while our master Ahmad [al-ʿUraybī] told me: "Concern yourself with your Lord." What am I to do?' He replied: 'My son, each of us instructs you according to the requirements of his own spiritual state, but what the master Abū al-ʿAbbās has indicated to you is preferable, and may God grant us that!' Then I went back to al-ʿUraybī and told him what had

12. *Fut.*I:496, VII:131; *FM.*I:329, ll.2–4, IV:89, ll.13–14. Ibn al-ʿArabī first adopted al-ʿUraybī's formula of the remembrance of God (*dhikr*); however, at the end of his life he preferred to use the formula of the *shahāda* in the *dhikr*. *Quest*, p.272.

13. *Fut.*II:289f.; *FM.*I:574, ll.26–8.

14. *Fut.*VI:344; *FM.*III:532, ll.25–7.

happened. He said to me: 'My dear child, both points of view are correct: Abū ʿImrān has spoken to you about the beginning and the way to follow (*ṭarīq*), while I have drawn your attention to the final aim of the quest (the Divine Companion who is ever-present, *rafīq*), so that when you follow the way your spiritual aspiration will be raised higher than that which is other than God.'[15]

This anecdote also appears in the *Futūḥāt*[16] with some modifications, the most important of which is the need to combine these two elements in each station the Sufi performs – the adherence to God and the uninterrupted attention to one's soul.

Finally, al-ʿUraybī is not presented as a Quran exegete in Ibn al-ʿArabī's writings, and only once does our author bring forward his interpretation of a Quranic verse. This is the famous verse 'The All-Compassionate sat Himself upon the Throne' (*al-raḥman ʿalā al-ʿarsh istawā*, Quran 20:5; trans. Arberry), which has aroused theological polemics concerning the anthropomorphism in its literal meaning.[17] Al-ʿUraybī connects the verb *istawā*, which appears at the end of this verse, with verse 6, so that from the point of view of its content this verb is the first word of verse 6. Consequently, the two verses are interpreted as follows: 'The All-Compassionate is on the Throne (verse 5). Everything in the heaven and earth ... became established for His sake' (verse 6).

In sum, the first master of Ibn al-ʿArabī serves as a model for mystic behaviour and adherence to God. He was scrupulous both in his acts and speech and kept his thoughts clear of everything except God.

15. *Al-Kawkab al-durrī fī manāqib Dhī-l-Nūn al-Miṣrī* (*The Brilliant Star in the Virtues of Dhū al-Nūn al-Miṣrī*); trans. Hirtenstein, *Four Pillars*, p.3.

16. *Fut.*III:266; *FM.*II:177, ll.14–20.

17. See, for example, my *Anthropomorphism & Interpretation of the Quran in the Theology of al-Qāsim ibn Ibrāhīm*, pp.48–57.

Conclusion

We have dealt with eighteen figures, eleven of whom are earlier Sufis (i.e. pre-eleventh century), and the rest are later. The topics treated by them constitute the core of the Greatest Master's mystical philosophy and Sufi practice. What is significant in our discussion is not only the influence exerted by some Sufis on Ibn al-ʿArabī, but also his attitude toward them, which is disclosed in his criticism and rejection of their views, acceptance of their thoughts whether fully or partially, and admiration for their practices and faculties. His disputes with some of them, even in dreams, show his profound absorption in the world of his predecessors, as if he believes all of them are in some way alive and hence available for discussion with him. Thus, the views and the practices of the Sufis were for Ibn al-ʿArabī a living tradition which could be moulded by him – but also by other Sufis. As we have seen in the section on Ibn Qasī, our author invites others to add information to his book. Thus, what concerns him is the truth, which, in his view, is attained through revelation.

Generally, the material discussed shows that the earlier Sufis dealt with mystical theoretical ideas and hence affected Ibn al-ʿArabī's thought more than the later figures, whose teachings revolve mainly around Sufi practices. Some of the Shaykh's basic ideas appear in the teachings of his predecessors. We shall now summarize the data examined to draw conclusions both about Ibn al-ʿArabī's attitude toward these eighteen Sufis and the measure of their influence on him.

Two of the Shaykh's most important ideas appear in al-Kharrāz's teachings. These are God's transcendence,[1] which is expressed through the dictum that only God knows God, and God's joining

1. See the sections on al-Bisṭāmī and Ibn al-ʿArīf.

of contraries. Whereas in the teachings of the earlier Sufis God's transcendence remains a statement, in Ibn al-ʿArabī's writings it is a part of the doctrine of the One and the many. According to this doctrine, the Essence of God is unknown; only His names and attributes are known. Furthermore, God is the only real entity, in contradistinction to other entities which are but manifestations of his names and attributes. Al-Bisṭāmī stresses the seeming existence of the cosmos in general, and the human being in particular, a thesis which becomes a central theme in the doctrine of our author. God governs the cosmos and even human acts are the subject of God's will.[2]

In his *Sufi Metaphysics and Quranic Prophets*, Ron Nettler states that 'the issue of the One and the many, unity and diversity, may be seen as the bedrock of Ibn ʿArabī's Sufi metaphysics.'[3] However, behind the notion of the One and the many there is a very significant principle which underlies the whole system of Ibn al-ʿArabī's thought. Truth, in Ibn al-ʿArabī's view, derives not from one aspect, but rather from the combination of several aspects, which can be sometimes contradictory. For example, the truth is God's being, which is both transcendent and immanent, although these are two opposing elements. This notion of the joining of contraries in one entity goes back to the earlier Sufis. As we have seen, al-Bisṭāmī expresses the idea that leaving servitude to God requires distance from Him, while coming close to Him, which connotes emulation of His attributes, means nearness to Him. Thus, when God says to al-Bisṭāmī 'Leave yourself and come', He creates the paradox of being near and at the same time distant from God. The notion of joining contraries is further developed by Dhū

2. See the sections on al-Tirmidhī and Abū Madyān. Later Islamic authors, such as the historian Ibn Khaldūn (d.1406), thought of the Sufi literature of the ninth and tenth centuries in idealistic terms and contrasted it with later Sufism which was stamped in their view by monism, and hence deviation from the true religion. A. Knysh, *Ibn ʿArabī in the Later Islamic Tradition*, pp.196, 198. It seems that these authors did not know exactly the views of the early Sufis.

3. R.L. Nettler, *Sufi Metaphysics and Quranic Prophets*, p.7.

al-Nūn al-Miṣrī, who sees this phenomenon not only in God and the world to come, but also in this world. Al-Kharrāz goes even further stating that God is both Manifest and Hidden. As we have seen, similar ideas are introduced by al-Junayd and al-Tirmidhī. And for a later Sufi, Rūzbihān Baqlī (d.1209), the starting point 'is the affirmation of both transcendence and immanence of God at the same time'.[4] This principle involves not only opposite aspects, but also different aspects. Thus, the superiority of prophets can be classified in keeping with divergent aspects (as for Ibn Qasī).

In sum, our author incorporates the early foundations of the idea of observing a notion from several perspectives, and of joining contraries, whether at the same time or in different times. However, note that we cannot know definitely what or who Ibn al-ʿArabī's exact inspiration was for looking at one thing from different angles. In the section on al-Ghazālī we point out the possibility of the Ghazalian impact,[5] but earlier sources are not to be excluded. Still, we can state with certainty that this notion is not original in the Akbarian thought.

Although Ibn al-ʿArabī knew the notion of the first matter from which the world was created from the philosophers, the terms he uses in this context are important because they are not philosophical in origin. He points out that ʿAlī ibn Abī Ṭālib and al-Tustarī express this idea and use the term *habāʾ* (dust) as the primordial matter. According to the Greatest Master, the procedure responsible for the creation of the world is God's uttering the word *kun* (Be!). Al-Ḥallāj expresses this idea and adds that, since the human being assimilates God's attributes, he too can use this word for the purpose of creation. Ibn al-ʿArabī also adopts the notion that the process of production resembles marriage from al-Ḥallāj. Using

4. M. Takeshita, *Ibn ʿArabī's Theory of the Perfect Man and its Place in the History of Islamic Thought*, p.24.

5. See also al-Ghazālī, *The Niche of Lights*, annotated translation of Affifi's edition by D. Buchman, p.24 of the Arabic text.

the word *kun* as a device of creation shows the power of letters in this process. Ibn al-ʿArabī shares this view with al-Tirmidhī.

Sometimes we have the impression that his predecessors' views stimulated our author to develop a complex doctrine based on them. A case in point is the doctrine of the Perfect Human Being, which applies to the essence or spirit of Muhammad. This essence contains all the ingredients of the cosmos, both spiritual and material. In al-Tustarī's writings the heart of Muhammad serves as the source of revelation to all human beings and of the mystical union with God. Ibn al-ʿArabī possibly adopted the idea of the eternal existence of Muhammad's heart to create the doctrine of the eternal existence of the spirit of Muhammad.

One of al-Tustarī's doctrines developed later by Ibn Barrajān is the principle of *al-ʿadl* (literally: justice), which al-Tustarī defines as *al-ḥaqq al-makhlūq bihi al-samawāt wa'l-arḍ*, the principle through which God created the heavens and the earth. As we have seen, whereas al-Tustarī and Ibn Barrajān regard *al-ʿadl* as principle or order, Ibn al-ʿArabī turns this term into an entity, the *logos*, which is the first created being. Here again, our author takes a notion from an earlier mystic and changes its meaning.

In his writing, the Greatest Master uses Quranic verses and traditions skillfully; however, generally they appear as corroboration, although he tries to create the impression that his ideas come directly from the true interpretation of the Quran. He accepts al-Bisṭāmī's and Abū Madyan's conviction that knowledge gained through personal mystical unveiling is better than knowledge transmitted by people. This notion coincides with his idea that even analogy (*qiyās*) is legitimized through the revelation of the Prophet.[6]

The relationship between the content of revelation and of religion seems to be a lesson that Ibn al-ʿArabī learned from al-Junayd. Al-Junayd, the representative of moderate Sufism in

6. B. Abrahamov, 'Ibn al-ʿArabī's theory of knowledge', *JMIAS*, 42 (2007), II, pp. 17ff.

the ninth century, states that 'our knowledge is bound by the Quran and the Sunna', which literally means that every piece of knowledge gained by unveiling must be weighed up against these two sources in order to receive legitimacy. Our author adopts this dictum, indeed, to the extent that he broadens its scope to include all that the prophets have stated. Furthermore, Ibn al-ʿArabī also adds reason as a protector of religion which in turn protects truth. Truth is the most important value in Ibn al-ʿArabī's eyes, but it cannot be attained without reason and religion. Extending religious teachings to include Jewish and Christian sources, the Greatest Master increases the possibilities of true revelations.

One of the significant themes of Sufi practice is the performance of miracles, called *karāmāt* (literally: favours) in the context of God's saints. Al-Bisṭāmī refers negatively to physical miracles performed by the saints stating that they do not prove human superiority. Probably continuing al-Bisṭāmī's thread of thought, Ibn al-ʿArabī differentiates between physical and spiritual miracles and prefers the latter to the former, which he claims belong to the common people. As we have seen, the miracles al-Bisṭāmī and the Shaykh favour do not occur in the body of the saint, but through him or for his sake;[7] in this manner, they are not strictly speaking physical miracles, such as walking on water or floating on air. This posited superiority of spiritual miracles does not mean that the saints did not possess the faculty to perform physical miracles. For example, Dhū al-Nūn and al-Bisṭāmī were associated with such miracles, but as Ibn al-ʿArabī says in relation to Ibn al-ʿArīf, the highest value is ascribed to the saint's knowledge of God and his Sufi behaviour.

In some basic notions expressed by our author, the clear impact of the theosophical thinker al-Tirmidhī can be seen. The doctrine of the *walāya* was developed by Ibn al-ʿArabī based on al-Tirmidhī's ideas. As we have observed, the difference between *awliyā' ḥaqq*

7. See the case of al-ʿUraybī.

Allāh and *awliyā' Allāh* was embodied in the life of the Greatest Master. Furthermore, when Ibn al-ʿArabī gives preference to abandoning the stations,[8] because they are inferior to being close to God, he is following in the footsteps of al-Tirmidhī, who elevates those whom God chooses as His saints while placing those who undertake legal commands and Sufi practice at a lower level. As did al-Tirmidhī, Ibn al-ʿArabī regarded himself as the Seal of the Saints, and we may assume that this lofty self-estimation was one of the reasons why the Shaykh al-Akbar felt free to criticize certain Sufis. The very fact that Ibn al-ʿArabī applied himself to the task of answering al-Tirmidhī's questions proves that the former revered the latter.

Much of Ibn al-ʿArabī's writing is devoted to Sufi practice, stories, states, etc. Stations such as abstinence (*zuhd*) and scrupulousness (*waraʿ*) are associated with significant Sufis such as al-Bisṭāmī, Dhū al-Nūn and Abū Madyan. However, as noted throughout, the earlier Sufis play the more major role in the formulation of Ibn al-ʿArabī's philosophical mysticism, while the later ones served mainly as models of Sufi behaviour and ethics.

Even if the Sufis whom Ibn al-ʿArabī chose to put forward possessed flawless moral traits and outstanding Sufi behaviour, or significant mystical and philosophical ideas, he did not hesitate to criticize them whenever he felt it appropriate.[9] The most salient criterion for this criticism is the view that Sufi practice, like performing the stations, is not the highest value required of the Sufi. Hence, for example, among the Sufis al-Muḥāsibī is not reckoned worthy of the highest standing. However, even Sufis who experienced revelations are censured if their received communications are too brief to convey to them the complete knowledge they need (see the case of al-Tustarī). And of the Sufi Ibn Barrajān, who

8. See my 'Abandoning the station (*tark al-maqām*), as reflecting Ibn al-ʿArabī's principle of relativity', *JMIAS*, 47 (2010), pp. 23–46.

9. *Fut.*IV:346; *FM*.II:601, l.33 – 602, l.1.

preferred science to revelation in his divination, nothing further need be said.

Sometimes Ibn al-ʿArabī's disapproval of a Sufi's idea is expressed within a vision. This is the case with Dhū al-Nūn, when he admits that he had made an error when saying that God's characterization runs contrary to that which one imagines or thinks, which means that God is absolutely transcendent. When meeting al-Kharrāz in a vision, the Shaykh taught him that God's unity is an objective value; as a result, the former was ashamed, probably because he was not aware of this true idea. At other times, Ibn al-ʿArabī merely comments on the teachings of his predecessors, stressing the difference between his thought and theirs (see Abū Ṭālib al-Makkī). Our author also takes to task the style of the Sufi Abū Madyan, finding it insufficient, and reprimands the unruly utterances of al-Jīlānī that prove his presumptuousness.

Another characteristic of Ibn al-ʿArabī's attitude toward the Sufis is his occasional indecision in cases where he expresses a different or opposing opinion (see Ibn Qasī). Probably in such cases he had not received revelation by which he could affirm his conviction on a chosen theme. However, in other cases where our author is firmly convinced of his viewpoint, he expresses it clearly and without hesitation, as in the discussion of intoxication and sobriety ascribed to al-Ḥallāj and al-Shiblī, respectively. Sometimes the Greatest Master tries to moderate boldness discerned in a Sufi's sayings (al-Bisṭāmī). All these approaches to Sufi practice and thought show us that the Shaykh relates to the Sufis in keeping with his own principles, as clearly expressed in his writings. He also classifies the Sufis according to clear criteria, such as those who follow in the footsteps of Muhammad or other prophets and those who do not (see al-Jīlānī).[10]

10. See the classification of the people of God (*ahl Allāh*) in Chapter 25 of the *Futūḥāt*.

Ibn al-ʿArabī's notion that one should empty one's mind of all thoughts in order to receive revelation probably goes back to al-Junayd. This idea serves Ibn al-ʿArabī as a point of departure when refuting al-Ghazālī who taught, according to our author, that one should know the sciences before delving into an attempt to receive unveiling.

The spiritualization of the formal rites of Islam begins with al-Shiblī, continues with al-Ghazālī and culminates in the works of Ibn al-ʿArabī. Like his predecessors, Ibn al-ʿArabī does not reject the value of formal rites, but stresses the important role of the spiritual meanings of these rites. It is so important that the Shaykh accepts Ibn al-ʿArīf's statement that the truth resides within the esoteric realm. One cannot state with certainty the source of Ibn al-ʿArabī's chapter on the mysteries of the *Ḥajj*; however, he is obviously not the first to express the spiritual value of this commandment.

It is worth reiterating that Ibn al-ʿArabī had no qualms in adopting terms from the Sufis and integrating them into his own doctrinal framework. Such terms include, for example, the prostration of the heart (*sujūd al-qalb*) coined by al-Tustarī, and al-Tirmidhī's God as the Owner of the Kingdom. These terms play a significant role in our author's teachings.

We have dealt with two significant themes: Ibn al-ʿArabī's attitude toward the Sufis and the notions he acquired from them. His attitude toward their ideas and practices vacillates between acceptance and rejection, and he sometimes emphasizes his superior position even in dreams and visions. As for the second theme, we have seen that the Greatest Master gained much knowledge from his earlier and later predecessors. While his lessons from the earlier Sufis focused on doctrines and philosophical mysticism,[11] his knowledge of Sufi practices came mostly from the later Sufis.

Was Ibn al-ʿArabī an original thinker, notwithstanding the numerous notions he acquired from the Sufis? One should be

11. Takeshita, *Perfect Man*, p. 170.

cautious in answering this question, so we limit our reply by laying down two criteria for assessing his originality:

The measure of fundamental ideas gained from others

Some of the most fundamental ideas in Ibn al-ʿArabī's doctrine are not his. However, the idea that the cosmos is the manifestation of God and the mutual reflection of God in the human being and the human being in God,[12] and most of its ramifications, is his alone. His theory in the *Fuṣūṣ* that each prophet represents an idea prevalent in the cosmos is also unprecedented. And, uniquely, even when our author adopts a theory of an earlier thinker or school of theology, he alters it to coincide with his own theory. The Ashʿarite theory of God's continuous creation of the cosmos becomes a part of Ibn al-ʿArabī's theory of God's manifestations which are always in a process of becoming. That a certain fact can be gauged from different angles is already found in early Sufism, but the idea that all the aspects combine to create truth is Ibn al-ʿArabī's original contribution. For example, the truth about God is that He is both transcendent and immanent. Attention should also be paid to the Shaykh's sophisticated interpretation of the Quran, which is not always based on allusions, but also on rational and plain analysis of the text. When dealing with a Quranic story, the whole Quran contributes to its interpretation and supports the author's ideas.[13]

The way of dealing with the ideas that have been handed down

In most of the ideas gained from others, we observe that the Greatest Master embellishes them with a great deal of complexity and elaboration. The classification of the saints is not something novel in the period before Ibn al-ʿArabī; however, his classification is more complex and detailed than others. Early ideas are interwoven

12. *Fuṣūṣ al-ḥikam*, pp. 61f.
13. For example, see the chapter (3) on Nūḥ (Noah) in the *Fuṣūṣ*.

into our author's innovative ideas, so that what remained in an embryonic state in the first generation was developed to become a part of an all-embracing conception. The very fact that he formed a complete theory connecting God with the cosmos is a great novelty of Ibn al-ʿArabī.

It is common knowledge that all original thinkers begin by learning from others, but their originality lies in the combining of older ideas to create new ideas. My hope is that I have succeeded in proving that Ibn al-ʿArabī was indeed an original thinker, in terms of his own ideas, his interweaving of the ideas of others into his own system, and the unique way in which he did so.

Bibliography

Abdel Haleem, M.A.S. (trans.), *The Quran*, Oxford, 2010.

Abdel-Kader, A.H., *The Life, Personality and Writings of al-Junayd*, London, 1976.

Abrahamov, B., 'Al-Qāsim ibn Ibrāhīm's theory of the Imamate', *Arabica*, 34 (1987), pp. 80–105.

— 'Al-Ghazali's theory of causality', *Studia Islamica*, 67 (1988), pp. 75–98.

— *Al-Qāsim B. Ibrāhīm on the Proof of God's Existence: Kitāb al-Dalīl al-Kabīr*, Leiden, 1990.

— 'Al-Ghazālī's supreme way to know God', *Studia Islamica*, 77 (1993), pp. 141–68.

— *Anthropomorphism and Interpretation of the Quran in the Theology of al-Qāsim ibn Ibrāhīm: Kitāb al-mustarshid*, Leiden, 1996.

— *Islamic Theology: Traditionalism and Rationalism*, Edinburgh, 1998.

— 'The creation and duration of Paradise and Hell in Islamic theology', *Der Islam*, 79 (2002), pp. 87–102.

— *Divine Love in Islamic Mysticism: The Teachings of al-Ghazālī and al-Dabbāgh*, London, 2003.

— 'Ibn al-ʿArabī's theory of knowledge', *JMIAS*, 41 (2007), pp. 1–29; 42 (2007), pp. 1–22.

— 'Ibn al-ʿArabī's attitude toward al-Ghazālī', in Y.T. Langermann (ed.), *Avicenna and His Legacy: A Golden Age of Science and Philosophy*, Turnhout, Belgium, 2009, pp. 101–15.

— 'Ibn al-ʿArabī on divine love', in S. Klein-Braslavy, B. Abrahamov and J. Sadan (eds.), *Tribute to Michael: Studies in Jewish and Muslim Thought Presented to Professor Michael Schwarz*, Tel Aviv, 2009.

— 'Abandoning the Station (*tark al-maqām*), as reflecting Ibn al-ʿArabī's principle of relativity', *JMIAS*, 47 (2010), pp. 23–46.

— 'Ibn al-ʿArabī and Abū Yazīd al-Bisṭāmī', *al-Qanṭara*, 32.2 (2011), pp. 369–85.

Addas, C., 'Andalusī mysticism and the rise of Ibn ʿArabī', in S.K. Jayyusi (ed.), *The Legacy of Muslim Spain*, Leiden, 1992, pp. 909–33.

— 'Abu Madyan and Ibn ʿArabī', in S. Hirtenstein and M. Tiernan (eds.) *Muhyiddin Ibn ʿArabi: A Commemorative Volume*, Shaftesbury, Dorset, 1993, pp. 163–89.

— *Quest for the Red Sulphur: The Life of Ibn 'Arabī*, trans. P. Kingsley, London, 2000.

Affifi, A.E., *The Mystical Philosophy of Muhyid Dīn-Ibnul 'Arabī*, Cambridge, 1939.

al-Akiti, M. Afifi, 'The good, the bad, and the ugly of Falsafa: Al-Ghazâlî's Madnûn, Tahâfut, and Maqâsid, with particular attention to their Falsafî treatments of God's knowledge of temporal events', in Y.T. Langermann (ed.), *Avicenna and His Legacy: A Golden Age of Science and Philosophy*, Turnhout, Belgium, 2009, pp. 51–100.

Almond, I., *Sufism and Deconstruction: A Comparative Study of Derrida and Ibn 'Arabi*, London and New York, 2004.

al-Ash'arī, *Maqālāt al-Islāmiyyīn wa-ikhtilāf al-muṣallīn*, ed. H. Ritter, Wiesbaden, 1963.

Austin, R.W.J. (trans.), *Sufis of Andalusia: the Ruḥ al-quds and al-Durrat al-fākhirah of Ibn 'Arabī*, London, 1971.

— *The Bezels of Wisdom*, New York, 1980.

al-Baghdādī, Abū al-Barakāt, *Kitāb al-Mu'tabar*, Hyderabad, 1939.

Bashier, S., 'The standpoint of Plato and Ibn 'Arabī on skepticism', *JMIAS*, 30 (2001), pp. 19–34.

— 'An excursion into mysticism: Plato and Ibn 'Arabī on the knowledge of the relationship between the sensible forms and the intelligible forms', *American Catholic Philosophical Quarterly*, 77 (2003), pp. 499–533.

Ben-Shammai, H., 'On a polemical element in Saadya's theory of prophecy' (in Hebrew) in *Jerusalem Studies in Jewish Thought*, Vol. VII, Jerusalem, 1988, pp. 127–46.

Bouyges, M., *Essai de chronologie des oeuvres de al-Ghazālī*, ed. M. Allard, Beirut, 1959.

Böwering, G., *The Mystical Vision of Existence in Classical Islam: The Quranic Hermeneutics of the Ṣūfī Sahl al-Tustarī (d.283/896)*, Berlin and New York, 1980.

Chittick, W.C., *The Sufi Path of Knowledge: Ibn al-'Arabi's Metaphysics of Imagination*, Albany, NY, 1989.

— *Imaginal Worlds: Ibn al-'Arabī and the Problem of Religious Diversity*, Albany, NY, 1994.

— *The Self-Disclosure of God: Principles of Ibn al-'Arabī's Cosmology*, Albany, NY, 1998.

Chodkiewicz, M. (ed.), *Les Illuminations de la Mecque*, Paris, 1988.

— *Seal of the Saints: Prophethood and Sainthood in the Doctrine of Ibn 'Arabī*, trans. L. Sherrard, Cambridge, 1993.

— 'The *Futūḥāt Makkiyya* and its commentators: some unresolved enigmas', in L. Lewisohn (ed.), *The Heritage of Sufism: Classical Persian Sufism from its Origins to Rumi (700–1300)*, Oxford, Vol. I, 1999, pp. 219–32.

Clark, J., and Hirtenstein, S., 'Establishing Ibn 'Arabī's Heritage', *JMIAS*, 52 (2012), pp. 1–32.

Corbin, H., *Alone with the Alone: Creative Imagination in the Sufism of Ibn 'Arabī*, Princeton, 1997.

Cornell, V.J., *The Way of Abū Madyan: Doctrinal and Poetic Works of Abū Madyan Shu'ayb ibn al-Ḥusayn al-Anṣārī*, Cambridge, 1996.

Ebstein, M., 'The word of God and the Divine Will: Ismā'īlī traces in Andalusī mysticism', *Jerusalem Studies in Arabic and Islam*, 38 (2011), pp. 1–67.

Ebstein, M., and Sviri, S., 'The so-called *Risālat al-Ḥurūf* (*Epistle on Letters*) ascribed to Sahl al-Tustarī and letter mysticism in Al-Andalus', *Journal Asiatique*, 299.1 (2011), pp. 213–70.

El-Moor, J., 'The fool for love (*Foll Per Amor*) as follower of universal religion', *JMIAS*, 36 (2004), pp. 85–125.

Elmore, G.T., 'Ibn al-'Arabī's "Cinquain" (Tahmis) on a poem by Abū Madyan', *Arabica*, 46 (1999), pp. 63–96.

— *Islamic Sainthood in the Fullness of Time: Ibn al-'Arabī's Book of the Fabulous Gryphon*, Leiden, 1999.

Encyclopaedia of Islam, P. Bearman *et al.* (eds.), Brill Online Edition (comprised of the 2nd and 3rd edns), Leiden, 2007.

Ernst, C.W., *Words of Ecstasy in Sufism*, Albany, NY, 1985.

— 'The man without attributes: Ibn 'Arabī's interpretation of Abu Yazid al-Bistami', *JMIAS*, 13 (1993), pp. 1–18.

Ess, J. van, *Die Gedankenwelt des Ḥārith al-Muḥāsibī*, Bonn, 1961.

Frank, R.M., 'Several fundamental assumptions of the Baṣra school of the Mu'tazila', *Studia Islamica*, 33 (1971), pp. 5–18.

Garrido, P., 'The science of letters in Ibn Masarra: unified word, unified world', *JMIAS*, 47 (2010), pp. 47–61.

al-Ghazālī, *al-Maqṣad al-asnā sharḥ asmā' Allāh al-ḥusnā*, Cairo, 1968.

— *Al-maqṣad al-asnā fī sharḥ ma'ānī asmā' Allāh al-ḥusnā*, ed. F.A. Shehadi, Beirut, 1986.

— *Mishkāt al-anwār wa-misfāt al-asrār*, ed. 'Abd al-'Azīz 'Izz al-Dīn al-Sayrawān, Beirut, 1986.

— *The Niche of Lights: Mishkāt al-anwār*, annotated translation of Affifi's edition by D. Buchman, Provo, UT, 1998.

— *Iḥyā' 'ulūm al-dīn*, al-Maktaba al-Tijāriyya al-Kubrā, 4 vols., Cairo, n.d.

Goldfeld, I., 'The illiterate Prophet (nabbi ummi): an inquiry into the development of a dogma in Islamic tradition', *Der Islam*, 57 (1980), pp. 58–67.

Gril, D., 'La science des letters', in M. Chodkiewicz (ed.), *Les illuminations de la Mecque*, Paris, 1988, pp. 423–6.

Hirtenstein, S., *The Unlimited Mercifier: The Spiritual Life and Thought of Ibn ʿArabī*, Oxford, 1999.

— (ed. and trans.), *The Four Pillars of Spiritual Transformation (Ḥilyat al-abdāl)*, Oxford, 2008.

— and Tiernan, M. (eds.), *Muhyiddin Ibn ʿArabi: A Commemorative Volume*, Shaftesbury, Dorset, 1993.

al-Hujwīrī, *Kashf al-maḥjūb*, trans. R.A. Nicholson, Wiltshire, 2000.

Ibn al-ʿArabī, *Al-Tadbīrāt al-ilāhiyya fī iṣlāḥ al-mamlaka al-insāniyya*, in H.S. Nyberg (ed.), *Kleinere Schriften des Ibn al-ʿArabī*, Leiden, 1919, pp. 103–240.

— *Fuṣūṣ al-ḥikam*, ed. Abū al-ʿalāʾ ʿAffifi, Cairo, 1946.

— *Rasāʾil Ibn al-ʿArabī*, Hyderabad, 1948.

— *Tarjumān al-ashwāq*, ed. and annotated trans. R.A. Nicholson, London, 1978.

— *Al-Futūḥāt al-Makkiyya*, Dār al-Kutub al-Ilmiyya, Beirut, 1999.

— *Majmūʿat rasāʾil Ibn al-ʿArabī*, 3 vols., Beirut, 2000.

— *Rūḥ al-quds*, in *Majmūʿat rasāʾil Ibn al-ʿArabī*, Beirut, 2000, Vol. I, pp. 113–230.

— *Al-Kawkab al-durrī fī manāqib Dhī al-Nūn al-Miṣrī*, in Saʿīd ʿAbd al-Fattāḥ (ed.), *Rasāʾil Ibn ʿArabī*, Vol. III, Beirut, 2002.

— *Futūḥāt al-Makkiyya*, Dar Sadir, Beirut n.d. (rep. of the Egyptian edition of AH 1329).

Ibn al-ʿArīf, *Maḥāsin al-Majālis: The Attractions of Mystical Sessions*, trans. W. Elliott and A.K. Abdulla, Avebury, 1980.

Ibn Paqūda, Baḥyā, *Kitāb al-Hidāya ilā farāʾiḍ al-qulūb* (*The Book of Direction to the Duties of the Heart*), trans. M. Mansoor, Oxford, 2004.

Ibn Sīnā, *al-Ishārāt waʾl-tanbīhāt*, ed. J. Forget, Leiden, 1892.

— *Al-Najāt*, ed. M. Fakhri, Beirut, 1985.

— *Kitāb al-Shifāʾ*, *Al-Ilāhiyyāt*, trans. M.E. Marmura, Provo, UT, 2005.

al-Iṣfahānīʾ, Abū Nuʿaym, *Ḥilyat al-awliyāʾ wa-ṭabaqāt al-aṣfiyāʾ*, ed. ʿAbdallāh al-Minshāwī *et al.*, Egypt, 2007.

Izutsu, T., *Sufism and Taoism: A Comparative Study of Key Philosophical Concepts*, Berkeley, 1983.

Jaʿfar, M.K.I., *Min qaḍāyā al-fikr al-islāmī*, Cairo, 1978.

al-Jerrahi al-Halveti, T.B., *Ibn ʿArabī: Divine Governance of the Human Kingdom*, Louisville, KY, 1997.

al-Jīlānī, ʿAbd al-Karīm, *al-Insān al-kāmil fī maʿrifat al-awākhir wa'l-awā'il*, Cairo, 1963.

al-Kharrāz, Abū Saʿīd, *Kitāb al-Ṣidq*, ed. and trans. A.J. Arberry, Oxford, 1937.

Kinberg, L., 'What is meant by *zuhd*?' *Studia Islamica*, 61 (1985), pp.42–4.

Knysh, A., *Ibn ʿArabī in the Later Islamic Tradition: The Making of a Polemical Image in Medieval Islam*, New York, 1999.

— *Islamic Mysticism: A Short History*, Leiden, 2000.

Lewisohn, L. (ed.), *The Heritage of Sufism.* Vol. I: *Classical Persian Sufism from its Origins to Rumi (700–1300)*, Oxford, 1999. Vol. II: *The Legacy of Medieval Persian Sufism (1150–1500)*, Oxford, 1999.

Mason, H., 'Ḥallāj and the Baghdad School of Sufism', in L. Lewisohn (ed.), *The Heritage of Sufism: Classical Persian Sufism from its Origins to Rumi (700–1300)*, Vol. I, Oxford, 1999, pp.65–81.

Morris, J.W., 'Ibn al-ʿArabī's "Esotericism": the problem of spiritual authority', *Studia Islamica*, 71 (1990), pp.37–64.

— 'How to study the *Futūḥāt*: Ibn Arabī's own advice', in S. Hirtenstein and M. Tiernan (eds.), *Muhyiddin Ibn ʿArabi: A Commemorative Volume*, Shaftesbury, Dorset, 1993, pp.73–89.

al-Muḥāsibī, *Kitāb al-Riʿāya li-ḥuqūq Allāh*, ed. ʿAbd al-Qādir Aḥmad ʿAṭā', Cairo, 1970.

— *Kitāb al-Tawahhum*, ed. A.J. Arberry, Cairo 1937; trans. A. Roman, Paris, 1978.

— *Kitāb Māʿiyyat al-ʿaql wa-maʿnāhu wa-ikhtilāf al-nās fīhi*, ed. Ḥusayn al-Quwwatilī, Beirut, 1982.

Nettler, R.L., *Sufi Metaphysics and Quranic Prophets: Ibn ʿArabī's Thought and Method in the Fuṣūṣ al-Ḥikam*, Cambridge, 2003.

Netton, I.R., *Muslim Neoplatonists: An Introduction to the Thought of the Brethren of Purity (Ikhwān al-Ṣafā')*, London, 1980.

Nyberg, H.S., *Kleinere Schriften des Ibn al-ʿArabī*, Leiden, 1919.

Ormsby, E., *Theodicy in Islamic Thought: The Dispute over Al-Ghazali's 'Best of all Possible Worlds'*, Princeton, 1984.

Palacios, M.A., *The Mystical Philosophy of Ibn Masarra and His Followers*, trans. E.H. Douglas and H.W. Yoder, Leiden, 1978 (first published Madrid, 1914).

Pickthall, M. M., *The Meaning of the Glorious Koran*, New York, 1953.

Pines, S., *Studies in Abū'l-Barakāt al-Baghdādī's Physics and Metaphysics*, in *The Collected Works of Shlomo Pines*, Vol. I, Jerusalem, 1979.

— *Studies in Islamic Atomism*, trans. M. Schwarz and ed. T. Langermann, Jerusalem, 1997.
al-Qūnawī, Ṣadr al-Dīn, *al-Murāsalāt bayna Ṣadr al-Dīn al-Qūnawī wa-Naṣīr al-Dīn al-Ṭūsī*, ed. G. Shubert, Beirut, 1995.
al-Qushayrī, *Al-Risāla al-Qushayriyya*, Beirut, 2000.
Radtke, B. 'A forerunner of Ibn al-ʿArabī: Hakīm Tirmidhī on sainthood', *JMIAS*, 8 (1989), pp.42–9.
— *Drei Schriften des Theosophen von Tirmidh*, Beirut, 1992.
— 'The concept of Wilāya in early Sufism', in L. Lewisohn (ed.), *The Heritage of Sufism: The Legacy of Medieval Persian Sufism (1150–1500)*, Vol. II, Oxford, 1999, pp.483–96.
— and O'Kane, J., *The concept of Sainthood in Early Islamic Mysticism: Two Works by al-Ḥakīm al-Tirmidhī*, Richmond, Surrey, 1996.
Rasāʾil Ikhwān al-Ṣafāʾ, Beirut, 1957 (rep. of Khayr al-Dīn al-Ziriklī's edn., Cairo, 1928).
Rosenthal, F., 'Ibn ʿArabī between "Philosophy" and "Mysticism"', *Oriens*, 3 (1988), pp.1–35.
al-Sarrāj, *Kitāb al-Lumaʿ fī'l-taṣawwuf*, ed. R.A. Nicholson, London, 1963 (first published 1914).
Schimmel, A., *Mystical Dimensions of Islam*, Chapel Hill, NC, 1975.
Sells, M.A. (ed.), *Early Islamic mysticism: Sufi, Quran, Miraj, Poetic and Theological Writings*, New York, 1996.
Smith, M., *An Early Mystic of Baghdad*, London, 1935.
Stroumsa, S., 'Ibn Masarra and the beginnings of mystical thought in al-Andalus', in P. Schäfer (ed.), *Mystical Approaches to God: Judaism, Christianity, and Islam*, Munich, 2006, pp.97–112.
— and Sviri, S., 'The beginnings of mystical philosophy in al-Andalus: Ibn Masarra and his *Epistle on Contemplation*', *Jerusalem Studies in Arabic and Islam*, 36 (2009), pp.201–53.
al-Sulamī, *Ṭabaqāt al-Ṣūfiyya*, ed. Nūr al-Dīn Shurayba, Cairo, 1986.
Sviri, S., 'Ḥakīm Tirmidhī and the Malāmatī movement in early Sufism', in L. Lewisohn (ed.), *The Heritage of Sufism: Classical Persian Sufism from its Origins to Rumi (700–1300)*, Vol. I, Oxford, 1999, pp.583–613.
Takeshita, M., *Ibn ʿArabī's Theory of the Perfect Man and its Place in the History of Islamic Thought*, Tokyo, 1987.
al-Tirmidhī, *Kitāb Khatm al-awliyāʾ*, ed. Osman Yahia, Beirut, 1965. (This is an edition of *Kitāb Sīrat al-awliyāʾ*. *Kitāb Khatm al-walāya* or *al-awliyāʾ* is a later title of *Kitāb Sīrat al-awliyāʾ*. See B. Radtke and J. O'Kane, *The concept of Sainthood in Early Islamic Mysticism: Two Works by al-Ḥakīm al-Tirmidhī*, Richmond, Surrey, 1996, p.10. See also B. Radtke's edition

and translation of this text in *Drei Schriften des Theosophen von Tirmidh*, Beirut, 1992.)

Trimingham, J.S., *The Sufi Orders in Islam*, Oxford, 1971.

Twinch, C., 'Created for compassion: Ibn 'Arabī's work on Dhū-l-Nūn the Egyptian', *JMIAS*, 47 (2010), pp. 109–29.

Wansbrough, J., *Quranic studies, Sources and Methods of Scriptural Interpretation*, Oxford, 1977.

Yafeh, H.L., *Studies in al-Ghazālī*, Jerusalem, 1975.

Yahia, O., *Mu'allafāt Ibn 'Arabī ta'rīkhuhā wa-taṣnīfuhā*, Cairo, 2001.

Yazaki, S., *Islamic Mysticism and Abu Talib al-Makki: The Role of the Heart*, London and New York, 2013.

Index

The 18 Sufis discussed in the book are not indexed in their own chapters

Abdel Haleem, M.A.S. 143, 146n
Abdel-Kader, ʿAlī Ḥassan 69, 70n, 71n
Abrahamov, B. 7n, 14n, 22n, 33n, 51n, 65n, 78n, 81n, 87n, 121n, 129n, 130n, 131n, 133n, 140n, 142n, 144n, 145n, 147n, 174n
Abū Bakr al-Ṣiddīq 22, 63, 130, 155
Abū Madyan, Shuʿayb 16, 46, 60, 87n, 118n, 141n, 165n, 172n, 174, 176, 177
Abū al-Suʿūd ibn al-Shibl 152–5
al-ʿAdawiyya, Rābiʿa 9n
Addas, C. 1n, 10n, 98, 101, 102, 135n, 136n, 137, 139n, 140n, 144, 145n, 150n, 157, 158n, 159n, 162n, 163n, 164
ʿadl (justice) 55, 56, 149, 174
Affifi, A.E. 1n, 8, 10, 35, 91–2, 117, 124n, 173n
ahl Allāh (people of God) 77, 80, 105, 119, 124, 129, 137, 139, 177n
al-Akhmīmī, Ibrāhīm 32
al-Akiti, M. Afifi 118n
ʿālam al-ʿaẓama (world of exaltedness) 111
ʿālam al-jabarūt (world of imagination) 111
ʿālam al-malakūt (world of dominion, divine world) 111
ʿālam al-mulk wa'l-shahāda (material world) 111
ʿalāmāt (signs) 20
al-ʿAllāf, Abū al-Hudhayl 66
Almond, J. 77n
al-ʿamāʾ (the Cloud) 56
al-Anṣārī al-Harawī 140
ʿaqīda (belief, creed) 151
ʿaraḍ (accident) 64
Arberry, A.J. 13, 169
ʿārif (pl. *ʿārifūn*, gnostic) 28, 39, 45, 60, 66, 76, 122n, 124, 158
Arnaldez, R. 13n, 97n
ʿarsh (Throne) 22–3
al-Ashʿarī, Abū al-Ḥasan 66n, 119
Ashʿarite 2, 63, 179
Austin, R.W.J. 117
aʿyān thābita (fixed entities) 55, 65, 125

badal (pl. *abdāl*, the substitutes) 112–13
al-Baghdādī, Abū al-Barakāt 66
baqāʾ (subsistence) 3,59, 63
Baqlī, Ruzbihān 173
barzakh (intermediate world) 59
Bashier, S. 10n
basṭ (expansion, ease) 66
Bayrak, Tosun, al-Jerrahi al-Halveti 102
Ben Shammai, H. 10n
Bishr al-Ḥāfī 63
al-Bisṭāmī, Abū Yazīd 1n, 3, 5, 16, 21, 29, 53, 55n, 63, 70, 74, 75, 82, 91, 92, 106n, 152n, 155, 157, 159, 161, 163n, 171n, 172, 174, 175, 176, 177
Bouyges, M. 118
Böwering, G. 53, 79n

Chabbi, J. 151
Chittick, W.C. 1, 23n, 35, 38, 117, 121, 132n, 154n, 162n
Chodkiewicz, M. 8, 101n, 130, 165n
Clark, J. 1n
Cook, J. 94
Corbin, H. 62n
Cornell, V. 157, 159n

dhawq (taste) 56, 85, 95, 111, 130, 134
dhikr (recollection) 4, 165, 168n
Dhū al-Nūn al-Miṣrī 3, 63, 169
al-dunyā (this world) 13, 37

Ebstein, M. 4n, 56n, 57n, 98n
Elmore, G.T. 48n, 118
El-Moor, J. 56n, 120n

Ernst, C.W. 1n, 35, 43n, 46, 47n, 51n

fāḍil (excellent, ranked higher) 147, 153
fanā' (annihilation) 3, 59,63, 69, 70, 72, 104, 109, 121
faqīh (pl. *fuqahā'*, jurist) 81, 126, 135
faqr (poverty) 32
fatḥ (illumination, opening) 89
Faure, A. 118, 135, 139, 145n
fayḍ (overflow) 162
Frank, R.M. 24n
futuwwa (chivalry) 15

Gardet, L. 56n, 111n
Garrido, P. 100n, 101
Geoffroy, E. 132n
al-Ghazālī 2n, 4, 7, 9, 16, 33, 51n, 63, 80n, 85, 98, 105, 106n, 107n, 111n, 135, 136, 142, 144, 161n, 173, 178
al-Ghazzāl, Abū 'Abdallāh 141
Goldfeld, I. 132n
Gril, D. 100n, 101

ḥāl (pl. *aḥwāl*, states) 19, 35n, 57, 71, 134
al-Ḥallāj, al-Ḥusayn 5, 6, 36, 72, 73, 103, 106, 173, 177
ḥaqīqa (truth, reality) 10n, 38, 79, 81, 105, 126, 129n
ḥaqq (the Real) 56, 66, 82, 89, 101, 119n, 121, 136, 139, 151, 152, 158, 174, 175
ḥasad (envy) 13
al-Ḥasan al-Baṣrī 7
ḥashr (congregation) 23
hawā (passion) 13, 32
hawā' (air) 48, 92
hayūlā (primordial matter) 56, 57, 120n
Hell 145–6
himma (spiritual intention) 57
Hirtenstein, S. 1n, 46n, 94, 113n, 157n, 164n, 165n, 167n, 169n

Iblīs (Satan) 13, 58
Ibn 'Abbād of Ronda 140
Ibn 'Aṭā' 73
Ibn Barrajān 7, 55, 56, 57n, 101n, 139, 144, 174, 176
Ibn al-Fāriḍ 117
Ibn Khaldūn 172n
Ibn Masarra 4, 56n, 57n, 58n, 88n, 107n, 135
Ibn al-Muqaffa' 96
Ibn Paqūda, Baḥyā 60n
Ibn Qasī 144, 173, 177
Ibn Rushd 10n
Ibn Sālim 4
Ibn Sīnā 10n, 94n, 125n, 126n
idlāl (presumptuousness) 108, 152
Ikhwān al-ṣafā' (the Brethren of Purity) 10n, 56, 78n, 98
'ilm (knowledge) 3, 45–6, 56, 59–60, 70, 81, 87n, 101, 128, 135
irāda (will) 50, 57
'Īsā (Jesus) 21, 48, 147
al-Iṣfahānī, Abū Nu'aym 85
ishāra (pl. *ishārāt*, allusion) 6
'ishq (exaggeration of love) 93
'iṣma (immunity from sin) 41, 54
Israfīl 40, 41, 99
iṣṭilām (confusion) 108
Izutsu, T. 8n, 125n

jalāl (majesty) 3, 90
jamāl (beauty) 3, 90, 108
jawhar (particle, atom) 25
al-Jerrahi al-Halveti, T.B. 102
al-Jīlānī, 'Abd al-Karīm 125n
al-Jīlānī, 'Abd al-Qādir 7, 88, 177
al-Junayd, Abū al-Qāsim 5, 6, 36, 37, 57, 63, 91, 103, 104, 173, 174, 178

al-Kalābādhī, Abū Bakr Muḥammad 6, 85
karāmāt (miracles) 20, 30, 47, 165, 175
kashf (or *mukāshafa*, revelation, unveiling) 37, 111, 118n, 119, 121, 145, 148
khalwa (seclusion, retreat) 54n, 134
kharq al-'āda (the breaking of habit, miracle) 29n
al-Kharrāz, Abū Sa'īd 4, 70, 142n, 155, 171, 173, 177
khawf (fear) 32
kibr (arrogance) 13
Kinberg, L. 38

Knysh, A. 3n, 4n, 5n, 6n, 7n, 103n, 172n
al-Kūmī, Abū Ya'qūb Yūsuf 164

lāhūt (divine realm) 92
logos (Reality of Realities, first created being) 56, 91, 174

al-Ma'arrī, Abū al-'Alā' 96
Madelung, W. 63n
mafḍūl (inferior) 147, 153
al-Makkī, Abū Ṭālib 4, 6, 7, 54n, 85, 119, 177
malāmiyya (People of Blame) 16, 40, 155
manzil (pl. *manāzil*, spiritual abode) 8, 36, 42, 70, 140n
maqām (pl. *maqāmāt*, spiritual station) 14n, 19, 37, 46, 71, 96, 107, 131, 140n, 154, 176n
ma'rifa (gnosis) 3, 19, 45, 46, 54, 59–60, 76, 125n
Mason, H. 96n
Massignon, L. 91n
al-Mawrūrī, 'Abdallāh ibn al-Ustādh 30, 164
mawṭin (pl. *mawāṭin*, sphere, abode) 23n
al-Mayūrkī, Abū Bakr 139
mi'rāj (ascension) 3
al-Miṣrī *see* Dhū al-Nun
mīzān (balance, scale) 147
Morris, J.W. 46, 127n
mu'āraḍa (imitation, emulation) 96
muḥaqqiqūn (Verifiers) 45, 60, 157
muḥāsabat al-nafs (minute analysis of acts of the soul) 40
al-Muḥāsibī, al-Ḥārith 3, 5, 129, 176
muḥdath (temporal, created in time) 69, 82
mujāhada (spiritual struggle) 15
mukāshafa see kashf
mumkin (the possible) 67
murīd (aspirant) 8, 35n, 37, 50, 151, 163
Mūsā (Moses) 27, 49, 167
mushāhada (witnessing) 118n, 119, 163
mutakallimūn (speculative theologians) 63, 119–20, 129n

nafs (self) 13, 40, 168
nafas (breath) 56, 92
nāsūt (human realm) 92
nawāfil (supererogatory works) 93
Neoplatonism 9, 10, 97–8
Nettler, R. 172
Netton, I.R. 56, 78n
Nicholson, R.A. 63n, 64n, 79n, 82n 106n
nubuwwa (prophecy) 87–8, 143, 153
Nwiya, P. 140n
Nyberg, H.S. 99n, 101n

O'Kane, J. 85, 86n, 89n
Ormsby, E. 120n

Palacios, M.A. 56n, 57n, 88n, 97n, 98, 100, 101n
Paradise 22, 23, 30, 145
Pharaoh 111
Pickthall, M.M. 128n
Pines, S. 25n, 66n
Plato 10n, 38n, 125n

qabḍ (constraint, compression) 66
Qādiriyya 151
al-Qaṣṣār, Ḥamdūn 63, 155
qiyās (analogy) 65n, 78, 174
al-Qūnawī, Ṣadr al-Dīn 128n
al-Qushayrī, Abū al-Qāsim 64, 85, 121n, 136
quṭb (pl. *aqṭāb*, Pole) 37, 81n, 157, 158n

Radtke, B. 5n, 85n, 86, 87n, 88n, 89n, 90n
rajā' (hope) 32
rasm (exoteric sign) 144
riyā' (hypocrisy) 13
riyāḍa (discipline) 89, 131
Rosenthal, F. 132n
rubūbiyya (lordship) 73–4
rukbān (the mounted) 152

ṣabr (patience) 32, 106
al-Sabtī, Abū al-'Abbās 9n
al-Sadrānī, Mūsā 158
Sahl al-Tustarī 4, 41–2, 45, 72, 79n, 90, 91, 98, 100, 136, 157, 173, 174, 176, 178

ṣaḥw (sobriety) 69, 71
Ṣalāḥ al-Dīn 135
ṣalāt al-kusūf (prayer of eclipse) 23
Sālimiyya 4
samāʿ (listening) 33n
samāʿ (audition certificate) 165n
al-Saqaṭī, Sarī 63
al-Sarrāj, Abū Naṣr 6, 35, 36n, 63, 64n, 79n, 85, 106
ṣawm (fasting) 44
Schimmel, A. 4, 5
Sells, M.A. 36n
shaṭḥ (pl. *shaṭaḥāt*, ecstatic expression) 3, 43, 46–7, 151, 152
shayṭān *see* Iblīs
al-Shiblī, Abū Bakr 6, 75, 96, 177, 178
shukr (thankfulness) 32
sirr (mystery, secret) 26
Smith, M. 13
Smoor, P. 96n
Sobieroj, F. 103
Stroumsa, S. 98
ṣuḥba (companionship) 15
sujūd al-qalb (prostration of the heart) 54–5, 178
al-Sulamī, Abū ʿAbd al-Raḥmān 64n, 85
Sviri, S. 4, 57n, 89n, 101

taḥakkum (governing control) 154
taḥqīq (verification) 117
tajrīd (disengagement) 38, 162
Takeshita, M. 9n, 10, 88n, 89n, 92, 107, 136n, 173n, 178n
tanzīh (incomparability) 64, 100, 141
taqwā (piety) 13
tark al-maqām (abandoning the station) 14, 140, 176
taṣarruf (the power to act freely in the world) 152
tashbīh (similarity, anthropomorphism) 64, 124
tawakkul (trust) 4, 121, 129
tawba (repentance) 4, 13, 141
tawḥīd (unity, affirmation of unity) 69, 73, 100, 108, 121, 129
Tiernan, M. 46n, 157n
al-Tirmidhī, al-Ḥakīm 4, 5, 15, 55, 101, 126n, 139, 140, 142n, 143, 148, 152, 157, 172n, 173, 174, 175, 176, 178
Trimingham, J.S. 87n
Twinch, C. 19n, 21n

ʿubūdiyya (servitude) 45
ʿujb (self-conceit) 13
ʿulamāʾ al-rusūm (exoteric scholars) 144n; *see also rasm*
ummī ('unlettered', fully receptive) 27, 132
al-ʿUraybī, Abū al-ʿAbbās 175n

waḥdāniyya (Divine Unity) 67
waḥdat al-wujūd (unity of existence) 123
wajd (ecstatic experience) 20, 79n
walāya (sainthood) 4, 87–9, 143, 144, 147, 167, 175
walī (pl. *awliyāʾ*, saint, friend) 5, 48n, 85, 87–8, 90, 130, 143, 150n, 101, 153, 167
Wansbrough, J. 96n
waraʿ (abstinence, scrupulousness) 16, 20, 38, 176
wārid (sudden revelation) 75
waṣiyya (directive) 160
wujūd (existence) 77, 123–4

Yafeh, H.L. 118n, 127n, 144n
Yahia, O. 1n, 35n, 85
Yefet ibn Eli 10n
Yūsuf ibn al-Ḥusayn 31, 72

zandaqa (heresy) 30
zindīq (infidel, heretic) 81
zuhd 15, 37–8, 176